Boned
Every Which Way

A Collection of Skeletal Literature
2016

BONED
EVERY WHICH WAY

A Collection of Skeletal Literature
2016

Edited by
Nate Ragolia

SPACEBOY BOOKS

Denver, Colorado

Published in the United States by:

Spaceboy Books LLC
1627 Vine Street
Denver, CO 80206

www.readspaceboy.com

Content from BONED: bonedstories.wordpress.com

First printed June 2017

ISBN-10:
0-9987120-4-3

ISBN-13:
978-0-9987120-4-8

Profits from sales of this book will benefit the Bone Marrow Foundation
(www.bonemarrow.org)

To each contributing author who showed just how creative we could be with a simple idea about skeletons and bones.

To each reader who proved that there's a hunger for original, weird, spooky, and magical writings.

To Jenny for talking me down whenever I feared missing a Tuesday posting deadline.

TABLE OF CONTENTS

JUST ONE MORE – NATE RAGOLIA

I hate days like this, Clyde thinks, grimacing against the damp, bitter wind that whips between the buildings. He gathers the lapels of his sport coat in his right hand and clenches, as if it will make any difference.

Clyde turns the corner at 15th and California. A sign sneers at him: SIDEWALK CLOSED—Pedestrians Cross Over.

"Fuck." His breath pours from him like a soul. *I'll just take the alley. Ice sheets be damned.*

Clyde turns toward the dripping, trash-strewn alley. He turns up his collar, takes a deep breath, and holds it. He isn't interested in smelling what remains of last night's four-star dining experience.

Plumes of hot steam exhale around Clyde from the neighboring hotel's laundry and gym. Clyde enjoys the sensation, but worries that it will ruin his carefully composed hair, and thereby, the morning's meeting. Clyde does not notice that he can no longer see the alley walls. He does not notice that the sky above has disappeared. The strange loss of light doesn't occur to him. He only thinks: *It's fucking dark in this alley. It's a good thing it's daytime.*

The boney fingers gripping his sleeve feel like a simple snag at first. Clyde swings his arm, frustrated, trying to free it from whatever dumpster's edge or errant vent encumbers him.

It does him no good.

Cold and knotted, the skeletal hand wraps around his throat. Clyde gasps and struggles, turning fiercely to face his attacker.

If he could scream, he would, but the last air in him blasts from his nose in two powerful streams. The skeleton's empty eye sockets express no sympathy. Its lipless mouth expresses no snarling hatred. Its hand just clamps tighter.

Clyde hears his windpipe crackle, and feels the bony fingers close tighter.

Steamy darkness collapses around him.

Color dissolves. Light evaporates.

"I'm sorry," hisses the last voice Clyde hears.

* * *

The body collapses in a heap onto the dingy alley floor. With care, Mark extends the legs out straight, and the arms at the body's side. He stands above the still warm corpse, lowers himself over the vacantly staring face, and reaches out with one boney hand into its gaping mouth.

Deftly, Mark grips the base of the skull, gives it a gentle twist, and pulls. The body's skeleton and viscera slip out through the mouth in a single mass, which Mark lowers carefully into a neighboring dumpster.

Mark looks down at the empty suit of skin on the ground. "I'm sorry," he hisses again. "You can't understand, but I'm sorry."

Feet first. Mark inserts one boney foot—then the other—into the skin. He shimmies down, slipping both legs into their appropriate dermal proxies, then his hips, rib cage and boney arms. Were anyone around to see it, they might liken the scene to a live rat burrowing into a dead snake.

Finally, Mark ducks his skull into the skin's mouth, as if raising the hood on a sweatshirt. He pulls at the cheeks and ears and neck. He wriggles and jiggles his arms and legs, getting the fit right. Then Mark reaches into the skin's jacket pocket, extracts a cell phone, and holds it out at arm's length.

CLICK.

Mark spies the tiny screen. "Good as new," he says through the foreign mouth.

* * *

Mark finds it surprising difficult to deal with the skin's shoes. First, he succumbs to an icy slip while he exits the alley. Then he rolls an ankle so horrendously that it draws a young woman toward him to ask "Are you sure you're okay?" Mark gets up, dusts himself off, and finally begins to walk as he used to.

He turns the familiar corner at 19th and Market, and a smile comes across his stolen lips.

It's still here, Mark thinks. *She's still here.*

Mark's borrowed fingers touch the glass door, grip the handle, and pull it open. A bell rings above on the door. A bouquet of tropical scents flood into his costume nostrils. The woman behind the counter lifts her gaze from an iPad.

"Welcome to Blooming Flowers and Gifts! Is there something I can help you with today?"

"Christine," Mark says. "It's me."

"It's who?" she asks, perplexed. "I don't believe we've met, sir."

"Oh, you don't recognize me," Mark says, contorting his surrogate visage into a smile. "But one night, years ago, I won you a stuffed sloth and you named him 'Nigel.'"

Surprise splashes across her face.

"How do you know about that?" she asks.

"I know because I was there," Mark replies.

"You were not there," she insists.

"After you got 'Nigel' we sat in my car and listened to *Rumours* on the radio in my dad's Dart."

Surprise turns to shock.

"We spent that entire summer together," he continues. "And all of Senior year. And we would have gone to State together. We were supposed to have so many things."

"Mark?" Christine probes. "But the fire..."

"I know," Mark says, head bowed. "It has haunted me ever since."

"This is insane," Christine says. "It is. I know. But it's *real*."

She pushes back toward the refrigerator of flowers behind her, nearly falling into the glass doors. She breathes deep, shakes her head, and then paces behind the counter. Christine crosses her arms, uncrosses them, recrosses them, as if unsure what's to be done with her own body.

"This can't be happening," she says, still pacing.

"But it is, darling."

"Why now? After thirty years? What do you want?" she demands. Her face is red. Her hands are balled into fists.

"I just want one last kiss," Mark states. "I'm sorry that the face—the lips—aren't right. I had to steal the first available suit."

"Suit? What do you mean suit?"

"I needed something to walk around in other than what the fire left me," Mark says. "The soft parts burned up quickly."

Christine's eyes widen. "You mean skin? You stole a man's skin? Was he alive?"

"If you can call his pattern of pouting disappointment a life."

"You're a murderer," Christine says.

"No. I'm a romantic," Mark replies. "I couldn't leave this plane without kissing you one last time. And I couldn't kiss you unless I had lips. And lips by themselves on a skeleton would look pretty silly, you must admit."

Christine stares past him, through him. "Mark is dead, and if he weren't he wouldn't do this. I don't know who you are, but this sick fucking joke ends right now."

"There's no joke," he says softly. "I am Mark. We met on the last day of Spring semester 1983. You were wearing a pink miniskirt and a baggy Vassar sweater. You were reading *Tropic of Cancer*."

"It is you..."

"What's left of me."

"Mark..."

4

"I love you, Christine," Mark pleads. "Please, just one more kiss."

Christine looks at him again. "I can't believe this."

"No one else would have gone to all this trouble. No one else could ever love you the way I did. The way I *do*."

"But you killed a man. What about him?" she demands.

"Many more than he have been slain in the name of Love."

Christine furrows her brow. A fire burns in her eyes.

"If there was any other way, I would have done it," Mark says. "I've searched for another way for years, but I couldn't bear to miss you any longer."

"I've missed you too," she whispers.

She walks around the back of the counter to the front, carefully avoiding stalks of cat's tail, and ornate, potted orchids. She stands before Mark-in-Clyde.

"One kiss and then I'll move on," he says.

Christine doesn't say a word. She moves in close, and their lips meet. The kiss is soft, gentle, slow. Mark feels it permeate him. It is in his bones. After a moment, he pulls away, but Christine's arms hold him tightly. He takes her hands in his borrowed palms and peels them off of him. Mark steps back, recreating the space between them. They stare at each other, once more separate.

Christine frowns. Her eyes well with tears, calling to him; pleading.

"Goodbye, Christine."

"Goodbye, Mark." Her last words to him drown in the clatter of the door-mounted bell.

* * *

Mark wanders back toward the alley, back to where he borrowed his skin. As if by regurgitation, his bones slip and slink back out through the rapidly desiccating mouth.

With dry, bleached fingers he lofts the skin into the dumpster to join its former contents. Mark looks down over the deconstructed mass and wishes he could shed a tear.

"Thank you," he hisses.

A breeze rushes down the alleyway, whipping the steam into a frenzy. Mark looks down at his skeletal hands and feet. Like motes in a sunbeam they break down, flutter, and sail away.

Soon his cursed architecture is fully consumed.

Dust to dust.

03   80

Nate Ragolia is the author of There You Feel Free; a novella. Creator of the Illiterate Badger and Lark & Robin web comics, and occasional chatterer on music, film, &c.

INARTICULATED – MICHAEL J. O'CONNOR

Glenn Haynes was 50 years-old, and still feeling pretty strong. He was certain that 70 year-old men felt the same way.

Fear is a great motivator for positive thinking.

As he came out of the bathroom, Glenn walked past his two sons' rooms. It was 10:30 a.m., and they were still asleep. He remembered what it was like being a teenager, how tired he felt, and he let them be. He went down to the kitchen, where his wife was making coffee and keeping her hands busy. She always did that, sometimes simply rearranging things on the counter, not making any sort of real change to it.

Treading water, killing time.

They said good morning and he sat down at the table to read the paper, a ritual he had inherited from his father. He opened up the paper and glanced through it. He wasn't sure why. He would be on the internet all day at work. There was nothing to see here that he couldn't read all about later. He was a payroll clerk for a farm equipment company, and in this town, like in a lot of farming towns, there wasn't much business to be had. He turned to the last page, the obituaries, to start the grim ritual of looking for his contemporaries... as older people do.

He instantly recognized a picture on that back page. Jim Canton, his science teacher in the 7th grade, had passed away. As soon as he saw the name he was 12 years old again, watching Mr. Canton do science experiments and blow things up. He loved the man, and remembered that his imagination had never been so wide open than when he was in his class. Mr. Canton kept a reticulated Rhesus monkey skeleton on his desk, and Glenn thought it was the most fascinating thing in the world. He had forgotten all about it until this very moment.

The next day, there was an estate sale for Mr. Canton, and Glenn wondered if there was a small chance the monkey skeleton would be there. He had been feeling decent lately, but it had been a long time since he had felt young. The skeleton could be an excellent reminder not to get too old too fast, if it wasn't already too late.

* * *

He drove up the dirt road to Mr. Canton's house. Mr. Canton had lived on a large farm plot, barren for years, and even dustier now from the drought. Outside, there was all manner of furniture, bird cages, and other oddities, shined up and priced to move. Glenn was the first customer of the day, and felt that if the skeleton was there, he would be certain to get it. After he parked and walked up the driveway, it didn't take long for him to find it. It was sitting under a glass dome and looking just like it did in the 7th grade. The man working the sale walked up and was oddly friendly.

"Hi there! How are you? Good to see you!"

Glenn just nodded and smiled. He figured he had enough time to look around a little bit.

Look around, look all around.

As he was eyeing some old cigar boxes, he turned to see another man admiring the skeleton—*his skeleton*—and his heart sank. He knew the man, and he knew him well. His name was Peter Karbowski, and he and Glenn were the only friend the other one had from ages five to sixteen. Peter looked at Glenn and immediately recognized him.

The two men approached one another and shook hands warmly. They proceeded with "How've ya been?" and "What do ya do now?" but it was all pleasantries. When they were in high school, the life-long friends had a fight after too many Coors Lights at Amy Hickey's bonfire party. That same year, Peter changed schools and they never saw each other again.

Glenn heard that Peter had moved to Sacramento and become some kind of big time lawyer or executive. When Mr. Karbowski died, Glenn went to the funeral, but he didn't see Peter there. He assumed that Peter never wanted to come back to the dusty township, but apparently he had seen Mr. Canton's obituary, remembered the skeleton, and was struck with the same youthful feeling.

It was awkward.

Peter smiled, pawing at the skeleton.

"I actually came here for that," Glenn stuttered, "and I'm afraid I was here first."

"I should have known!" Peter's voice raised immediately, as if he had been expecting this argument all along and had escalated it in his mind already.

"Should have known what, Peter? I was here first!"

Peter grabbed the glass dome, and hugged it close to him.

"No, you don't get it! You always get your way, and you don't care about anyone else!"

"What the hell are you talking about? I haven't seen you in 35 years, what do you know about me!?"

Peter's lip quivered which Glenn found pathetic in a man his age, and Peter hugged the skeleton tighter.

"I know," he whispered, "I know."

Fear is a great motivator for negative thinking.

Glenn became enraged and tried grabbing the skeleton from Peter, who resisted. Soon, the two middle aged men—in clothes their wives dressed them in—were wrestling, rolling around on the ground and knocking over tables and paintings, making an awful, embarrassing scene. They were finally broken up by the man running the estate sale, and when the literal dust settled, the glass dome was shattered on the ground, and the monkey skeleton was smashed to pieces.

The man running the sale held the two apart and yelled, "Stop it! Stop it! This is ridiculous! You guys were friends! A man we loved has died and this is how you act!?"

Glenn and Peter's faces puckered up, and Peter asked "How do you know we used to be friends?"

The man's eyes widened and he began to tug at his hair. "Are you...!? Are you serious!?" He began poking himself in the chest, "Jimmy! Jimmy Canton? Mr. Canton's son!?"

Glenn and Peter exchanged confused glances.

"We went to kindergarten *together*! We went to high school *together*!"

For the life of him, Glenn couldn't remember the guy, and it seemed Peter didn't either. He let them go, exasperated, and began clearing up the mess. Peter and Glenn helped, wordlessly resetting tables and putting the items back on them. Soon, they had everything the way it was before.

Glenn and Peter split the cost of the skeleton and gave the money to an infuriated Jimmy Canton who snatched the cash out of their hands.

Do a good turn daily.

They walked together down the driveway, still silent. When they got to the parking lot, they faced each other.

Glenn said it first, and he meant it.

"I'm sorry."

Peter looked up and said, "I'm sorry, too."

With that, they nodded at each other, got into their cars, and drove away.

* * *

When Glenn pulled into the driveway of his house, no one was home. His wife and two teenage boys were gone. It was probably for the best, since his Dockers and golf shirt were covered in dirt and he had a skinned elbow. He walked into the house and into the living room.

On his mantle he had a couple of old clocks, a shark's tooth, and a few other odds and ends to display. He reached into his pocket, pulled out the lower jaw bone of a Rhesus monkey, and placed it on the mantle. He knew that his old friend would probably be doing the same, and he smiled at the mischief they had made.

CR ED

Michael J. O'Connor is a WRITER / MUSICIAN / WHATEVER

THE CONTRACT – JARED HORNEY

"This is terrible." said Clive, seriously irritated at Stephen's lack of initiative.

Stephen glared at Clive from behind his drumset. Clive felt like it was all Stephen ever did these days, aside from play wildly off-beat and not make it through two verses before speeding up gradually.

"Well" said Stephen, and Clive could hear the incoming criticism weighing down the words before they even escaped his stupid, stupid, skull.

"*Well*, I don't see *you* taking any steps to branch out our sound. Are we a cover band or are we going to practice some of *my* songs?"

His songs. He'd been trying his hand at writing songs and they were terrible. All of them.

Fiona, the bassist and trombonist, coughed politely, which was a goddamned miracle considering that she didn't have any lungs. None of them did. "Guys" she said, "can't we just hammer out the covers we've got for now, and maybe we can work on Stephen's songs afterward?"

Clive set down his trombone and leaned on it, trying hard to convey a weary patience. "I think that's fine. That's fine, right, Larry?"

Larry was fiddling with the rotary valve on his trombone and didn't even look up. "Yep."

Stephen clapped his bony hands together enthusiastically. "Awesome, guys. Awesome. OK, so we can start out with, what, Stevie Wonder's track and then maybe bounce over to 'Skeletons In The Closet' and then maybe, uhh, 'Skeleton On Display'? And then -"

"Nah" objected Larry verbosely. "None of us can sing like that dude for that one, and man" he sighed, setting his trombone down, "man, it's just so fuckin' *sad*, you know? Like that's not why I got into music, guys."

Stephen idly hit his hi-hat with a femur. "None of us are doing this to be sad, Larry, we're doing it to be *artists*."

"I'm sad" said Larry.

Fiona spit on the rehearsal space floor. "Let's be real. We're a trombone cover band so I don't know too much about us becoming some sort of groundbreaking superband. Seriously."

"Well" said Stephen yet again, a little too loudly. "Well, that's why I wanted us to start performing original material, guys! Christ, I'm really *trying* here to make something worthwhile but none of you seem to want to really get on board about it! I'm *trying* to make a *statement!*"

No one said anything. Outside, the world turned onward in a trajectory that presumably had nothing to do with an all-skeleton trombone cover band called The Skele-tones on the verge of breaking up.

"*I'm* trying", added Stephen quietly.

The ambient hum of the bass amplifier buzzed in the background, waiting for notes that would never come, not anymore, not after today.

"OK" said Clive. "OK, so I don't think I want to do this anymore. We're all here together, playing terrible cover songs for eternity. Oh my god, what if this is *hell*?"

Fiona maintained steady eye-socket contact with Stephen and said "If we take on another Third Eye Blind cover I'm pretty sure that description would be accurate."

"Fuck you" spat Stephen, who had a bizarrely strong affinity towards that particular band for reasons that Clive could never quite identify and which always disgusted him, regardless.

"All I know is that this is clearly some form of afterlife and we're just going to keep pressing on" said Stephen, now standing up behind his drum kit.

"Maybe you are. I want out. We're bad musicians and we write bad songs and we're bad at what we do. All of us, each in our own ways" said Clive, now far beyond caring about any manner of civility.

"Hey" objected Fiona.

"It's true, Fiona. You're not too good at trombone" said Larry.

"You're not too good at not being a skeleton" Fiona said, confused immediately at what she initially thought would be a more cutting insult.

"What?" said Larry.

Abruptly, the guitar amp burst into a shower of sparks, with a remaining electrical buzz quickly fading out from the dying circuit board.

"God *dammit!*" shouted Clive. "This keeps happening! Our gear keeps shorting out, Stephen hasn't been able to stay on the the 2s and 4s since we got here, my trombone had a *pile of spiders* in it the other night, and really, nothing seems to go right! Like, even more so than before!"

There was a knock on the studio door. All four skeletons looked at one another, as if facial expressions were even an option for any of them. Without pause, the door swung open and a skeleton wearing a three-piece suit and an absurdly oversized top hat regarded all of them with hollow sockets. No one said anything.

"Hello" said the skeleton. "Hello to each of you. I have a letter here for, ah, let's see." He reached into his suit pocket and pulled out a pair of thin reading glasses, holding them up to his skull while reading a slip of paper. Clive paused to consider why any skeleton would need glasses in the first place before discarding the thought immediately out of fear that he would lose his mind.

"...ah, the Skele-tones? Is that everyone here?"

Clive nodded. "Yep. That's us. Sorry. We can keep it down if you need us to. You probably do need us to because we're not very good at all."

"On the contrary, my employer finds your brand of trombone-themed covers to be quite... inspired. He'd like to make all of you an offer."

"Go ahead" said Stephen, leaning over his snare now with interest.

"My employer has stated that he would like to offer a recording contract to The Skele-tones and, if accepted, he would be happy to restore each of you to a proper living form. Above ground and all that."

Larry looked excitedly at Clive, Fiona, and Stephen. "Guys. Guys! Yeah!"

"Sounds fair." said Stephen. "What's the catch?"

"No catch, sir. Simply sign this contract after reading all terms and conditions and you'll be on your way."

"I'm sorry" objected Clive, "but I can't understand how I can read anything without proper eyeballs, sir. I don't understand any of this. The only thing I understand is that there's never been any song in the history of musicianship that has required a 'trombone breakdown' in the bridge of a song. Oh my god, I want to quit."

The suited skeleton laughed, the sound dusty and rattling. "You can't quit, though. You absolutely can't."

Clive was cautious. "And why's that?"

"Because" chortled the skeleton wearing a suit. "The only reason any of you are still animated at all is due to the wishes of my employer. This could change at any moment, but all of you showed potential in the world of the living."

Clive burst out laughing. "Absolutely no fucking way *anyone* thought that. We played a venue once where the place was actively labelled as condemned and shut down by the city. *While we were playing.* We never even got paid! Seriously?"

"Yes. Quite seriously. You may review the contract terms here," he said, laying a small, gray envelope on the now-fried guitar cabinet.

He tipped his hat with a bony hand in a macabre version of a living gentleman and slid out of the doorway, closing it behind him. He had left a mild scent of ash, of something distantly burning.

"That was sort of intense, ya'll" said Larry helpfully.

"It was. It's also an offer. Wait, did he say anything about money?"

Clive strode towards the envelope. "Let's take a look."

He slid his bony digit underneath the envelope's red wax seal, which was pressed with what looked like a capital letter "L". Opening it, there seemed to Clive to be a small, translucent cloud of black smoke that briefly curled out of it before dissipating into the air. He looked back. No one else seemed to have seen it. Unfolding the weathered paper, the others gathered around him as he scanned the text.

Clive sighed, which was tremendously difficult to achieve without an active pair of lungs.

"It says *'You all complained so much about a lack of a record contract when you were alive, so I've decided to offer you one right now. Simply sign below for full rights to your songs as well as a free return to the world of the living. Love, The Devil.'*"

Clive paused and then his shoulderblades slumped in defeat.

"And at the bottom, in small print, it says *"Must sign in blood."*"

Larry's jaw fell open. Clive noted even in the midst of his own total demoralization that Larry apparently had always had impeccable teeth with no visible fillings.

Fiona stared. "Wh... we're skeletons! We don't *have* any blood!"

Clive sighed again. "And... and at the very end, in smaller text, it says 'fuck ya'll'."

Stephen distantly recalled all of the times that he had shouted at his bandmates to go to hell in the past and now felt a tinge of regret.

❦ ❧

Jared Horney is a writer, dog lover, music aficionado and all-around handsome fella.

FRAGMENTED – DEAN MOSES

The summer of 2043 was notable for its brisk winds punctuating its long days, especially on the season's last day. On this particular date, a coarse breeze forced its way through rotting wood and chipped paint, allowing it to stroke a sleeping woman's face.

Annabel awoke. Panting heavily she pawed at her nose, for she could not smell the seasonal scents carried in by the draft. She ran her hands over her head to find a bald cranium. Her appendages felt numb—lifeless, like an amputee's false limbs. The rocking chair in which she was sitting let out a long, whining creek as she stumbled from it. The blanket draping her upper body unraveled, creating an oversized scarf that trailed behind the woman on her journey to the bathroom. The door swung open, a scream followed.

What the fuck? She thought. *God, help me.*

The bathroom mirror showed a harrowing image—*a skeleton*. A paper-thin layer of skin remained, but the ruined flesh did nothing to hide the jagged bones it clung to. The reflection's dark eyes had almost completely receded into its sockets, with said skin creating a film over them, leaving only two tiny, dead ovals. Annabel winced, revealing five blackened teeth enduring amongst a decaying pallet.

The woman backed out of the bathroom, and with that the hairless creature she looked upon diminished from view.

Did I die in my sleep? While the question rattled around her gaunt skull like a loose bone fragment, an alarming realization dawned upon the skeleton: She could not remember anything—about the night prior, or the one before that. Her boney head felt clouded, as if her mind were a burnt film reel. Blurred faces, places, and actions could be seen but the damage made the narrative impossible to follow.

Her dead ovals wandered, passing over everything in sight, searching for a clue as to why she was in this ghastly situation. The all-encompassing studio apartment intimidated Annabel. The wind whistled at the fractured windows. The rocking chair rocked. The windows bore the sun's rays as spotlights directed at patches of threadbare carpet.

She forced her skeletal frame through the light and into the small kitchen area. She pushed aside a stool and pulled out steel drawers and ripped open cabinets, emptying their contents onto the linoleum below: Wooden spoons, silverware, plates, cups, corkscrew, spatula, whisk, wire mesh colander, ketchup packets, cheese grater, containers of vitamin pills, and a half-emptied box of fiber cereal.

Turning to the refrigerator: ice cube trays, an unopened carton of orange juice, almond milk, broccoli, carrots, beets, cabbage, apple sauce, prunes, and frozen fruit packets flowed freely. Over the course of a few minutes Annabel had emptied the kitchen's innards, its entrails were left piled.

"The food's fresh," she heard her raspy voice say, but that's not all she heard.

A series of short, strident thumps emitted from behind her. Turning, she focused on the apartment's entrance door. The door jolted forward, sprinkling a cloud of dust into the air. It jerked again, harder, faster. Annabel attempted to conjure up imaginings of what could lay beyond the door, yet she could not think of anything more terrifying than what she had already seen in that bathroom mirror.

The doorknob rattled, rotating vigorously. The female skeleton stepped backwards, foot slipping on the hanging blanket—she fell, crumbling to the carpet in the sun's spotlight. She felt pain course through her emaciated arm.

The door opened, a shadowy figure emerged—moving swiftly over the runner. Annabel wanted to flee, but the tumble had left her unable to move.

"The *fucking* door was stuck again. This place is falling apart, I wish we could move," a voice said from somewhere within the darkness.

The shadow strode into the light, revealing a man holding two plastic bags—a man with a familiar face.

"*What* are you doing down there?" the man asked, dropping the bags, cans of food rolling from the plastic.

"Who are you?" Annabel asked.

17

The man rolled his eyes. *"Every day* with this shit. I can't step outside for ten minutes, can I?"

The man wrapped his arms around the woman's slender frame, gently lifting her onto the rocking chair. "That's better," he said.

"Who are you?" she asked again.

"It's me, Davy... your *grandson*," he said in a tired tone.

Confusion ravaged Annabel's mind. "M-my grandson, huh?"

A steady stream of memories trickled into the woman's mind: A faint image of her smiling mother, the distinct roar of her father, the feeling of a wedding day's kiss, the birth of a golden haired baby, the wagging tail of a beloved dog, the loving kiss of a grandson, and the distorted picture of a gravestone. Focusing on the grave, she cut away at the fog that obscured it until she could see the inscribed name—Marie.

"Marie," Annabel repeated, this time aloud.

"I have said this a thousand times and I will say it again: You do this crap every day. It has been over forty years, *forty years* goddammit, since cancer killed my mother! I wish one day could go by without you reminding me. You better not do this shit when the news crews are here," Davy said, red-faced.

"News crews?"

"You don't remember that either? The news is coming tomorrow—for your birthday. Hopefully we get some good donations this year, otherwise your medical bills are going to be hard to pay."

Annabel's head hurt. More memories, this time they felt like cold water splashing her face. She remembered Davy—she remembered her grandson. She was no living skeleton; she was just old. Davy enveloped his grandmother in her favorite blanket and before long she had fallen back to sleep.

Davy glanced into the kitchen, seeing the mess on the ground he sighed.

* * *

Annabel awoke—strangers with cameras and microphones surrounded her, their shimmering eyes fixed in her direction.

"Happy 145th birthday, Miss Green!" a voice said.

"How does it feel to be the oldest human being alive?" another voice asked.

Annabel remained silent, ovals flitting between each face.

"Come on, Grandma," Davy said, his voice amplified for the cameras, hand resting on the woman's shoulder, "the world wants to wish you a happy birthday. Say something."

As the crowd encircled her in anticipation, like a pack of hungry wolves preparing for a kill, she caught sight of her reflection in a camera lens. "My face, what happened to my face? I am skeleton!" Annabel wailed.

The reporters fell silent, the cameramen lowered their cameras, and a reporter dropped her microphone.

Davy clutched Annabel's withered hand, but she pulled away—"I am a skeleton!" she cried again, reaching out to all the expressionless faces in the room. A laugh broke the air from amongst the crowd. The journalist in question did little to hide his mirth. One by one the blank visage of the news transformed into unbridled smiles, and, just like that, thunderous laughter took hold of the room.

Davy took his grandmother's hand once more, but even he could not keep a smirk from creeping over his face, or a harsh snicker from spitting out of his mouth. The only person with a straight face was an old woman, wondering why the room was laughing at a skeleton.

ଔ ଓ

Dean Moses is the author of A Stalled Ox, *entertainment contributor for the* Spring Creek Sun, *wordsmith extraordinaire, and hungry vegan.*

EPITAPH – DANIEL VALOT

The scene takes place in the vast dwelling of the Chartiers, in Saint-Germain en Laye, near Paris. Dinner is over. Sitting in armchairs in the salon, snifters of armagnac in hand, the guests are happily chatting on various light topics. Armagnac is delicious, yes... but pear schnaps also holds undeniable merit. "The government, this week..."—"No, no, no, my dear, we agreed: No politics on Saturday nights!" Suddenly, Richard Chanteclair, one of the guests, asks the congregation: "Say, you all knew Philippe Simon, didn't you?"

"Yes, of course," reply the men, in a neutral voice.

"Oh yes!" answer the women, crestfallen. "We miss him so!"

Some of the ladies have tears in their eyes. "Yes," says the hostess, "Philippe was a regular at our *soirées*. Then, a bit over two years ago, he was taken away by a dreadful disease. He was a charming gentleman. We miss him a great deal. Why this question, Richard dear?"

"I learned, last week, a surprising bit of news about him."

"What news?" ask the guests.

"I will tell you, of course, but first I'd like you to tell me more about this Philippe Simon, since, on my end, having joined this circle of friends only three years ago, I have seen very little of him. In fact, our paths crossed only once or twice."

"Well, I'll be glad to tell you," declares gracious Mrs. Gladys McFarlane. "You said, dear *Madame Cha'tier*, that he was *un homme cha'mant*. In fact, he was more than that! He wasn't just *un homme cha'mant*, he was *un grand cha'meur!*"

"That is so true," confirms Esther Bragance, a beautiful blonde. "I knew him well. He could not see a woman crossing his path without immediately attempting to seduce her. His goal was not at all to 'conquer', as people say, but he loved to flatter women, to court them somewhat, make them smile and giggle, and finally see a spark of complicity in their eye. Age didn't matter. I saw him deploy treasures of imagination to amuse little girls as well as grandmothers. Every time he managed to make them smile, he became the happiest man on earth."

"It must have been hell for his wife?" asks another of the guests.

"Certainly, at first," answers Esther. "Early on, Sophie would become furious. But she quickly understood that although he liked to parade around women, he nonetheless had no desire to cheat on her. He was very much in love with her, and not the fickle kind. But he couldn't help wanting to please every woman he met. Still, all this melodrama, for poor Sophie, was a tedious bore."

The lady of the house, Amandine Chartier, interrupts: "Dear Sophie has not been attending our Saturday *soirées* since she became a widow, but we see still her from time to time. But now pray tell, Richard: What is this news you learned just last week, regarding poor Philippe Simon?"

"I went for a walk through the Père-Lachaise, to pay my respects to an old friend. At a crossing in the path, I noticed a gravestone bearing the name of dear Philippe, the former heartthrob. Il was adorned with an incredible epitaph..."

"What did it read?" asks the crowd.

"You would never guess. It wasn't 'Our beloved father' or 'My dear husband.' No, it was much more original than that, and completely in accordance with what you've told me about the guy. I imagine that his skeleton, even if it now rests six feet under, must chuckle to itself just thinking about it..."

"Be nice," says the host, "and cut the suspense. What does the epitaph say?"

"Bonjour, Mademoiselle."

CR ⁊

Daniel Valot is the author of several books and short stories, including Sur Le Plus Haut Trône du Monde, et autres contes (2012). He is a Frenchman living in Switzerland.

YE SHALL NOT SURELY DIE – PAM JONES

Rex Henry Burr and Emmett Anhalt were about to become immortal.

Fame had come to them, at fifty-two and twenty-one, respectively, though they knew as well as anyone that fame dwindled. Fame went out. Fame died, even if you hadn't.

It was something they realized when the little memorials popped up, the flowers, the teddy bears, the candles, the scriptures and poems marking where the girls were last seen. *LaRue Martin, 16, was last seen on Route 2828 in Bandera; Darlene Bohannon, 20, was found on Highway 152; Renata Ansky, 15, told her mother that she would be hitchhiking home along Route 965 near Fredericksburg...*and so on.

One afternoon on the road, Rex Henry caught a radio broadcast from LaRue Martin's high school. He'd whacked Emmett in the arm. "Wake up," Rex Henry snapped, "they're doing a memorial service."

Emmett yawned hugely and sat forward.

They'd got the tail end of it. The Bandera High School choir sang

"Nearer, My God, to Thee". At the close, the principal declared, "Her star will forever shine."

"Well," Emmett had breathed that day. "That hymn was a nice touch."

"It was."

They'd gone into the post office that day. Rex Henry noted that he needed stamps. "They got those wildlife conservation ones out. If we don't get them now, we never will."

They parked.

Emmett put a hand on Rex Henry's wrist. "Hold on."

"Now what?"

The radio buzzed, "I Fall in Love Too Easily".

"I love this song," Emmett explained.

Rex Henry rearranged his arm so that the young man could take his hand; he understood. "I like it, too."

Hands laced, they sat and listened until the last of Chet Baker faded into the airwaves.

Emmett swallowed a few times, then sighed. "All right," he said, "I'm ready."

Of course, the poster was the first thing they saw, behind the clerk's grill. *Have you seen these men? Rex Henry "Royal" Burr and Emmett "Little Eminent" Anhalt were last seen driving a gray 1949 Chevrolet Coupe...*

Royal Burr let the clerk look at him for a good, long while through the grill. Little Eminent stood behind, rocking on his toes.

Then, with his face against the grill, Royal Burr said, clipped, polite, "One book of stamps, please, ma'am."

The clerk picked up the phone, scattering tiny scenes of preserved American wildlife.

* * *

The judge read the verdict. "For the murder of Renata Ansky, I sentence you to be electrocuted until you are dead. For the murder of Darlene Elise Bohannon, I sentence you to be electrocuted until you are dead. For the murder of LaRue Camille Martin, I sentence you to be electrocuted until you are dead."

* * *

Emmett wondered if the police had found their treasures, hidden in the linings of the Chevy's seats. Teeth, mostly, though he favored toes. Neither he nor Rex Henry could quite explain why they kept these tokens, not to the law or to each other.

Something Rex Henry had said a while ago, before they went into the post office, rattled in Emmett's head as the months counted down. He'd said, "I used to be a Catholic."

"Were you?" Emmet asked.

"When I was, oh, twelve or so, my dad took me on a retreat up north. This place we were at, in the chapel, there was a glass case, just a little out of sight. It was only at this place for a short while, and we were real lucky to get to see it. What do you think was in it?"

"What?"

"An arm. The whole hand to about here—" Rex Henry tapped his elbow.

"Whose was it?"

"Saint...Edgar. Elgar. I don't recall. This place had other stuff, too. Some hair. A finger."

It began to make sense.

Emmett had said then, "I used to collect baseball cards. I had a whole album. I guess it's kind of like that." He'd made a line of the little toes, tucking them one by one into the headrest of the passenger's seat. They might have stayed there forever, and no one would have known whom they belonged to. The relics of Saint LaRue, Saint Darlene, Saint Renata.

* * *

The warden asked what their plans were. "For afterward. Have you any relatives who've made burial arrangements?"

Rex Henry told him No.

Emmett told him No.

"It's just been me and the boy," Rex Henry said.

It was a sadder fact than death.

The warden gave them their options. One of them stuck out.

* * *

The state anatomical board was thrilled. Both Rex Henry and Emmett received letters, signed by four chairmen. "Thank you for your donation", the letters read. People were buying tickets to see Royal Burr and Little Eminent, students, mostly, from the University and from State. Their skeletons were to be preserved and kept at the Baylor University College of Medicine. The warden brought them this news the month before their debut, and Rex Henry seemed disappointed.

24

"We're not some science project," he growled.

Emmett was a bit more optimistic. "Well, college kids wouldn't be as squeamish. Because they can think of us as a science project."

"We're more than that."

"I know."

Though Rex Henry no longer believed, he liked to quote the Psalms. "*I shall not die, but live and declare.*" He didn't finish the verse.

Emmett did not really believe, either. He didn't think anyone ever truly did. It didn't stop him from tattooing a verse along his right wrist. "*Ye shall not surely die.*" He couldn't recall where the verse was from, or who had said it.

He wondered what would happen to the tattoo, afterward.

He kept talking, "Lots of people will come to see us. All kinds of people. We just have to be patient."

Rex Henry grunted. "Well. I don't think that's going to be our burden. Patience."

Emmett went on, "You know, being a science project, whatever you want to call it, that's where it starts."

Rex Henry looked at his hands, squeezing them. In spite of himself, he was perking up.

"Kids write up papers about us," Emmett murmured, "and then people read those papers. And then those kids go on and tell their friends about us. And those friends tell their friends, *I saw those guys, Royal Burr and Little Eminent,* and on and on. It's like that saint you told me about. It's just exactly like that." His voice trembled with the thrill of it. He didn't know when he'd taken such excitement, more so than with the girls they'd picked up. Then he bleated, "It's like the girls. I think I get it now. Like, I really get it. Everything we did. All of it. I get it."

It was not impulse.

It was not lust.

It was not wrath, or boredom, or desperation.

People remembered the saints because they had their tokens.

LaRue Martin would never fade into the ether of year after year.

Ye shall not surely die.

Ye shall be as gods.

Emmett Anhalt opened his eyes and when he did, he saw that Rex Henry Burr was crying. He mumbled heavily, all vowels, as though he were underwater.

"What's that?" Emmett asked.

"I say—" Rex Henry sniffed, and looked at his partner with great elation, such as Emmett had never seen in the older man's face. "I say—I can't wait. I can't hardly wait. They're all going to come and see us. And they'll talk about us forever?"

Emmett nodded, confirming, "Forever."

Outside, Rex Henry and Emmett were all the newspapers, the magazines, the folks in line at the post office could talk about.

* * *

In his office, the warden got off the phone with the appeals court. Unsurprisingly, no stay had been issued and they could proceed. He sighed and noted by his wristwatch that it was a quarter to six.

"It'd be better if we'd hang them."

"Hm?" He hadn't realized he'd said it aloud until his secretary appeared beside his desk. "Is it more humane? Compared to Old Sparky?"

"I wasn't thinking about that—" The warden caught sight of the newspaper lapping open across the coffee table across his office. The headline read, *Baylor campus overflowing as students await donated bodies of Royal Burr and Little Eminent.* "If we did less of this—" he waved at the paper—"—we wouldn't have any Royal Burrs in this world."

His secretary raised an eyebrow. "You think so?"

"Well, sure. They got what they really wanted. And we gave it to them. It's a screwy kind of martyrdom—not that all martyrdom isn't screwy. But–" The warden paused and flexed his wrist. Five to six.

"Anyway. It's time they made their debut. Their devotees will be thrilled." He slid into his jacket and made a slow march from his office, as though it were his own demise he were rowing toward.

His secretary blushed and turned back to her typewriter; she didn't mention that her husband was in line at Baylor that moment to buy tickets.

CR 80

Pam Jones lives and writes in Austin, Texas. She studied creative writing at Hampshire College, and is the author of the novella, The Biggest Little Bird.

Twitter: @PanimalJones
Instagram: @PanimalJones

THE SECOND SEVEN DAYS FOUND ON A METEOR FRAGMENT – BRIAN DICKSON

Day 1–

Will try carving on rock. Too many items to remember for the next six days. Here we go. See, this thing called the firmament blanketed the space around me whenever I shifted in the universe. Then, this larger shroud spread over the firmament, full of bright, flaming things–all from my dead cells. Who knew I was that hot? So hot my left over cells drifted together to form this floating blue, green, round mass in front of me. More later. My Lovely Thing, or *it* has disappeared again. All is good.

Day 2–

It lost a jaw attempting to mount a giant sloth, clamored to a tree with its arms outstretched, but fell apart, then gathered itself for sleep in a cute pyramid. Sloth just staggered away. Need second *it* to help the other one repair itself. You know? Checked on the pile. The first *it* glued itself together with mud. Maybe there isn't a need for another one. All is good.

Day 3–

Oops. Mud dried and *it* fell apart again. My ribs hurt from blowing up *its* backside. Parts flew everywhere. Perhaps that doesn't work. Destroyed fruit trees while for looking them. Sloth with blank look. Almost obliterated the sloth. Remade fruit trees. All is good.

Day 4–

Borrowed rib from muddied one to create second *it* because other one kept dipping into my mud bath and wouldn't do shit all day. The first one scrambled out of the pit and flung dried pieces of mud at the sloth. Both stood there, dazzled. Second *it* took the first one's spot while *it* threw everything *it* had at me. Second one wouldn't do shit all day but sit in the mud bath. The word *shit*. Note for later. Sloth slept in a secreted pad of its own mess.

28

Day 5–

Put together the first *it* as the second one soaked in the mud bath, molding things, making *those* things move, and *it* wouldn't help me repair the first one. Before placing *it* back down, I rattled *its* hand through the skull. One finger (the middle one, I think), stuck out and blasted light. I thought, hey, that's nice. All is good.

Day 6–

Used last rib of mine, sculpted a slithery thing. Not slither...more clattered toward the other two at the gooey pit. Every furry thing scattered (fur now!). Mud everywhere! Shit messes! I ordered the three *its* to clean up and all they did was make another mud pit out of where the sun or moon doesn't shine. Where I can't even shine. Beginning to rethink this whole thing. The slithery thing stiffened and the other two flung *it* back and forth. Sloth stood blank when *it* hit him in the chest. I'm tired.

Day 7–

Dipped in the goo with them. I can't find the sloth. Plan later. Note ticklish toes. Second note: these *its* are *too hard*. Something that keeps the moisture of my tears. They need something that burns like me. When they laugh they shake the world.

☙ ❧

Brian Dickson keeps this line from Charles Simic with him at all times: "A vision for your life is a work of art." Life as a messy art form where wayward brushstrokes reveal happy accidents...and not-so-happy accidents. This vision has led him to creativity, infusing it into cooking, gardening, writing, letterpress printing, worm farming, riding a bike, relationships, and teaching. He has published in journals around the states including two chapbooks, In a Heart's Rut (High5 Press), Maybe This is How Tides Work (Finishing Line Press), and one book All Points Radiant(WordTech Editions).

Brian lives in Denver with his partner, Sarah, among joy everyday.

THE PERFECT BEING – ANTOINE VALOT

The tibia leans, an elegant elongated lily's corolla. Viewed frontally, its near-perfect symmetry is like the ache of the flower arcing for the bee, a springtime longing for liberation and light. The fibula, lying alongside, ends in a burgeoning bulb, a bud about to burst. Together they reach up to kiss the blunt, humorless femur, a coarse club adorned only by the brutish patella. No matter, for the tibia, languorous, leans forever in love, forlorn.

6:35am. Bathrobe, snoopy bowl, skim milk, froot loops, iPad. Good morning, Jeremy!

The email icon ovulates a nagging 26 new messages. It's Monday morning after a ski weekend, so one can expect that a lot of tibia fractures came back from the slopes last night. Jeremy revels in the ten-minute luxury of ignoring them, watches a stupid Ren & Stimpy video on YouTube instead. Chuckles and slurps. Froot loop time is sacred.

* * *

7:14am. Blue light, acoustic tiles, tang of disinfectant, white walls, white doors, white desks, white floors. Good morning Doctor.

Hubbub. Ultrasound. CT. Ultrasound. CT. CT. Abdomen, pelvis, kidney, aorta, kidney, pancreas. Emergency, oncology, emergency, emergency, pediatrics.

Andre the morning tech is surly and competent. Judy the nurse is all sunshine, confident, positive energy. Working with them, Jeremy gets in the zone, a state of flow, almost, but never quite, staying ahead of the onslaught of phone calls, cases, pathologies, patients, personalities, and bodies, endless bodies. Walking or shuffling, sitting or laying down, pale or dark, red or blue, thin or bloated, steaming or shivering, all different, yet all made in the image of the one in the anatomy textbook.

Every patient's energy, as they enter the nave of the radiology department, is cotton-padded by Judy, greeting them at the stoup of the hand-sanitizer station, enveloping them in a warm gospel of instructions and reassurance. In the transept, as Andre officiates the rites of setup, they fall into mute contemplation. Andre soon passes behind his lead-lined rood screen, into the operator's chancel, and the penitent, in silent expectation, holds a breath, and feels the passage of the angel or mercy, or the angel of death, like a silence softly sweeping across their body and soul. In time their scans arrive to Jeremy, like devout supplications, and in communion with the vast all-knowing corpus of medicine, he dispenses absolutions and indulgences, acts of contrition and tickets to purgatory. His head bowed reverently before the light of the high-resolution, calibrated monitor, Jeremy makes the sign of the cross on his trackball, and mutters the sacred arcana of his radiology report into the mike of transcription. Jeremy does not condemn. He does not judge. He listens and sees, he bears witness, he forgives, and renders them all back unto their attending. Go in peace, if in pieces, and sicken no more.

* * *

The wrist is the nexus of danger, in posterior/anterior view. Look out! It's a hand grenade! At the apex of a shattered burst of bony fragments, the wrist grinds its teeth, its crumpled mass like cursed dice in a clenched fist. You've pulled the pin! Get away fast! Throw it farther than the blast radius!

11:53am. Sunshine, lunch trays, lab coats, ties, Italian loafers. Smells of food, old carpeting, med students with too much deodorant, boredom and stress. Hello doctor, hello doctor, hello doctor...

Doctor Wooley is a suppurating wound, an ever-bursting abcess, an unwashable taint on Jeremy's reputation and good name. When Jeremy was new at the hospital, he cozied up to Dr. Wooley, hoping that some of the senior radiologist's clout would rub off on him. It worked all too well. By the time Jeremy figured out who Dr. Wooley truly was, all his bridges were already on fire.

Yes, Dr. Wooley was sought after, important, and all who came to him treated him with reverence... but that was only due to his role as chief rad, and to the penury of radiologists available on the market. Everybody needs Dr. Wooley... but nobody likes him. Because Dr. Wooley is a consummate douchebag.

Sexist, priapic, lazy, racist, homophobic, negative, disdainful, angry and entitled. But also fake, spineless, syrupy, two-faced, vicious, deceitful and manipulative. Dr. Wooley hasn't met someone he didn't want to fuck with, and everything he touches turns to shit.

Dr. Wooley pulls in a high six figures, drives cars that end in "-mer", and is a major contagion vector for various STDs. Through craigslist and various less-than-legal internet sites, he delights in finding new entrants to the local prostitution industry, ones who haven't yet heard of him. He's persona non grata in all but the sleaziest strip clubs in his hometown, in Vegas, and in four other cities where radiology conferences are frequently held. Dr. Wooley is running out of women to mistreat.

But right now, Dr. Wooley is all charm and molasses, slurring his jargon, as he expounds on the intricacies of MR diagnosis, and tells the visiting med students how he, and he alone, is the cure to all the world's ills. For the last few minutes, his sliminess has put on a tone of gravitas, which makes Jeremy snap to attention, and hurriedly scan the room. Yes, there she is: second row, left of center. Hair pulled back tightly, in full-deck makeup but applied with subtlety, lab coat sized for looks rather than comfort. A young woman who knows how to play her hand. She's rapt, smiling, eyes locked on The Chief Doctor, hoping to catch the great man's eye and curry favor. And of course he's noticed her, and of course he's looking anywhere but straight at her. She has no idea she's being played. This could end in disaster.

Jeremy toys with the idea of letting it happen, letting the monster have his way with her, just so he can catch him red-handed, and expose him, or blackmail him... Whatever would force him away from this hospital, and from Jeremy's life. But it would be useless. Rads don't grow on trees. Everybody already knows what Dr. Wooley is capable of. He's done it before, and will do it again. But he won't put the hospital, or his career, in jeopardy. He's crafty enough that his victims are always, technically, consenting.

Across the room, Judy is also sitting rigidly upright. She's noticed it too. Nostrils flared, eyebrows raised, she glares mutely at Jeremy. Once more it will be his job to keep things under control, to put himself between Wooley and the girl, and keep them from being alone together. As the other ranking rad, he's in the best position to do it... and as the former lone member of the Wooley fan club, and enabler of the despot, he still has much to atone for. Defeated, grim, Jeremy gives Judy the barest of nods. Her eyebrows lower slightly, but her face doesn't slacken, her eyes keep burning into his. Jeremy drops his gaze and, for the next half-hour, he stares at his shoes.

* * *

The skull houses no quiet reflection:

The skull is a mass coronal ejection.

Behind the orbits a funeral pyre:

You're staring straight into the fire.

Don't look for thought, it isn't there,

Only inferno—a solar flare.

5:34pm. Switches, notepads, folders, post-its. iPad, mouse, keyboard, trackball. Collection of plastic pens with twelve-syllable drug names on the side. Whirrs, clicks, taps, rips of Velcro, shuffling of feet in paper booties. Here's the file, Doctor. Which one? Yes, that one.

Jeremy stands awkwardly and his spine cracks and pops. He reaches for his water bottle. Forty-five minutes of running interference between Wooley and his all-too-willing potential victim have made him late on his afternoon work, and he hasn't caught a break since she finally left. Wooley has been steadily dumping more cases on him this afternoon, in punishment, and tried to trip him up with missing files, misleading prognoses, and ordering the wrong modalities. Nothing that could be malpractice, but still, more mistakes than could be explained away. Jeremy plods on with his sisyphean case load. To Wooley these files are pawns in a game, but Jeremy still remembers, if tenuously, that all these parts are connected to bodies. Don't just read the scan: Treat the patient... Treat the patient... Treat the patient.

Now Wooley's gone home. Jeremy didn't have to look at the clock to know it. The way Judy's voice notched up the cheer, the way Andre glides smoothly from machine to control board, like a ballet dancer... Everything is flowing again, which means that, ladies and gentlemen, Anus has left the building.

Almost as if the whole hospital feels it, there's suddenly a lull in the stream of emergencies. Jeremy stretches. His bloodshot eyes wander and come to rest on the printout of a DXA, a full-body x-Ray to measure bone density. His mind is elsewhere. He hears Judy's laughter, in counterpoint to Andre's muffled baritone, in the other room. He can't catch what they're joking about.

The woman's skeleton, on the DXA, is remarkably symmetrical. If it weren't for the slight tilt of her cranium, that scan could be mistaken for a one of those perfect illustrations from the anatomy texts. Everything laid out cleanly, clearly, just the way it never happens in real life.

Jeremy's tablet screen goes dark, but he doesn't reach to revive it yet. He's enjoying the moment, the warmth of his chair, the sound of his own breath in the dark room, set against the muffled hubbub of the hospital outside.

The woman's neck is long, elegant. Jeremy admires its curve, and thinks about the giraffe women of Africa, or is it Southeast Asia? The ones who pile up metal necklaces as they grow up, until their necks are unnaturally long. He wonders how those necks would look in a DXA... Obviously, they'd look like metal rings: you couldn't remove the necklaces without killing them. Their vertebrae must be completely disconnected, floating around...

The woman in the DXA image looks strangely lithe, light, lifted. These X-rays are taken with the patients lying down on a hard plastic table, and their skeletons look as uncomfortable as they must feel... But not this one. She looks like she was floating lightly above the table, her soft tissues firm and taut, not splayed and deformed. And that long neck is accompanied by long, lean limbs. Jeremy thinks of the chopped up photos of that statuesque black model and actress from the eighties, what was her name? Grace Jones.

This woman is not very tall, actually, but her skeleton is lean and long. Under her skin, she's built small and tall. Jeremy grins at his pun. Only a rad could come up with that, because only a rad can see it. Bones tell a different story about a person than what the world sees.

This woman's inner story is a beautiful one. The thought gives Jeremy pause. But it's true: this is a beautiful skeleton. That long neck's curve is echoed by very graceful clavicles, ample and angled perfectly. The clavicles are Jeremy's favorite feature in a woman, more than any soft tissues. The cups they make around the throat when the shoulders are thrust forward, like warm soft nests, where the carotid pulses... And as clavicles go, these are spectacular.

The broad rib cage hints at an athletic youth. DXAs are tests of bone density, to detect osteoporosis, so it's likely that she's older than 65. But Jeremy avoids looking up her date of birth. This skeleton isn't sagging, so she's clearly been keeping herself in shape. Or she has the body type that stays in shape.

Every vertebra is aligned, ideally proportioned to the one above. The pelvis is a textbook case of balance and position: This is a woman who stands tall and straight, on feminine hips. Her feet angle slightly outwards, in a relaxed position: she didn't put her feet in the straps. Andre would have asked her to, he never forgets. She's independent-minded, body-conscious, perhaps a bit of a rebel. Strong legs, strong feet... is she a dancer perhaps?

Jeremy has let himself bend down very close to the printout, his nose just inches away, lost in contemplation. The door swings open and Jeremy jumps, almost falling off his chair. Andre stands in the doorway, puzzled.

"Sorry Doctor, did I catch you at a bad time?"

"Uh, no... it's alright. I was just..." Jeremy fumbles for words. What was he doing, really?

Andre raises an eyebrow. "Do you need some more coffee, Doctor?"

"Yes, that's probably a good idea... But first, Andre, does this skeleton look particular to you?"

He points to the DXA, and rolls back his chair. Andre shuffles in to look.

"Mineral density looks good. I guess she didn't really need a DXA... unless you're worried about the size bias?"

"No, no, I don't mean medically... I mean... doesn't this skeleton look particularly *good* to you? I mean: the proportion, the shapes... Isn't it kind of ... striking?"

Andre looks confused. He slowly turns back to the printout and looks at it again. "I guess? Looks healthy enough... I don't see any problems..." He turns back to Jeremy. "Is this some kind of test, Doctor?"

"No, no, not at all. I just thought... never mind, Andre. I better go get that coffee."

* * *

7:12pm. Rain like rivers running down the windows. Moving headlights, red lights, green lights, neon lights in the blackness outside. Close up, file away, shut down, log out, gym bag. Good evening, Doctor!

"Sweating out the hospital" is what Jeremy calls it in his head. The thud-thud of his feet on the treadmill, keeping pace with the reggae in his earphones, help his thoughts disappear in delicious, salty, tangy pain. As a kid, he hated running, but on the treadmill he doesn't feel hate, or love, or anything. Just rhythm and pain, then rhythm without pain, something more restful than sleep.

He's brought the printout of the DXA with him. There's something nagging him about it, about the way she stands, or lays down as it were. There's something about the way that skeleton is held together. The sheet of paper, in a bright red folder, is splayed out on the treadmill's monitor in front of him, and he studies it, even as his mind empties itself of thought. He cocks his head to the side, like her. He tries to stand straighter, taller, lighter, like she does. Head back, loose, body reaching up, feet barely touching the ground. Pelvis loosely swaying, perhaps? He can't match her stance.

In front of him a young woman is running fast on another machine, in tight gym wear. She's tan, lean, and glistening, ponytail whipping from side to side. She's athletic, muscular and short. Jeremy scans her bone structure, but she's too narrow-hipped, too short-necked... no match for the perfect skeleton in the DXA. The comparison makes her look grotesque, monstrous, revolting, like a sweaty Minotaur. Jeremy looks away, revulsed. He cuts his run short, towels off, carefully closes the folder, and heads off to shower.

* * *

10:43pm. White leather couch, white sweatpants, white t-shirt, white carpet, black sky outside the high rise. Glass window, glass cupboards, glass tabletop, glass of wine, iPad. Peaceful Piano playlist on Spotify. Goodnight, city.

Jeremy stares at her. He found the high-res scan of the DXA in the hospital database, pulled it up on the iPad, and has been slowly panning up and down every bone in her body. She soothes him, even as she keeps him awake. Her skeleton is unreal, impossible. Too perfect to be human. Looking at it makes him pensive. Something is changing inside him, and it's happening very slowly, very gradually, but inexorably, like a giant upwelling from the depths of the ocean, in super-slow motion. A deep mute bass rumbling.

He looks out the window and the lights of cars on the highway, of planes in the sky, seem to zip by frenetically, like a stop-motion movie. He gives his glass of wine a slow swirl, and watches as the red liquid smear crawls back down the side, thick as blood. The tendons on his wrist protrude, straight as steel t-beams. Immobile, his hand looks as strong as stone, a marble statue of himself.

His thoughts have receded. Jeremy sits as a wave of resolve rises, becomes him. Outside, the sky's blackness deepens, the frantic flow of cars thins out. The bones on the iPad screen, glowing blue on black, faintly light up his face and his arm.

Hours pass unnoticed.

* * *

Living is fear: deaf, mute, ever there.

A coronal head CT shows it.

Like a crab, like a gnat, the limbic eye: unblinking, scared.

Staring, glaring, aware.

Scan for motion, look out for death:

Where is it, where?

10:51am—Metal gurneys, metal carts, metal grab bars, metal clipboards, metal trays with plastic silverware. Green curtains separating moans and mute pain. Families waiting, helpless. The doctor will be with you shortly.

The skeleton's name is famous, even after the shortest of stays. Every person Jeremy's approached with her name had a nickname at the ready, or two, or three. "The shrieker", "ghetto mama bin laden", "the megabitch from hell", "little miss chompy", "that sad angry

woman", "Mike Tyson's mama", "lucifer on wheels", "old yeller"...
She seems the stuff that hospital legends are made of.

She's screamed at everyone. She has a powerful throwing arm, clearly from frequent practice. She punches, she bites, she spits, she scratches. She came in on a potent cocktail of God-knows what uppers, downers, and hallucinogenics, and is now restrained so as to prevent harm to herself, the staff, and the building. Also, to avoid grievous harm to the hospital's supplies of pharmaceuticals. With drugs, unlike with people, she's broadly sympathetic.

The DXA was completely unnecessary. She's in her late forties, with no signs of osteoporosis, and physically healthy as an ox, albeit through no fault of her own. Wooley ordered the DXA to use her as a punishment on Judy, who had helped Jeremy run interference with that pretty medical student. He probably hoped that the woman would try to cut off Judy's head with an x-Ray plate. But by the time she arrived in radiology, "sticks-and-stoner" had already been assigned a retinue of two beefy orderlies, who kept her from destroying the equipment and staff. She screamed threats and oscenities, and nobody could figure out how to get her to lie still on the DXA table long enough to be scanned. Andre finally showed up with a syringe full of saline, told her it was morphine, and said he'd give her a taste now, the rest if she laid down quietly for two minutes. She relaxed in anticipated ecstasy after he'd injected a couple of CCs, and by the time she realized she'd been placebo'ed, the deed was done. The DXA was complete, millions of dollars of equipment were unscathed, and Judy remained capitated.

* * *

3:39pm—framed pictures: two blond babies, blond kids with a golden retriever, blonde wife, kids and dog alongside administrator Jensen, posing on the lawn, at the tennis club, in front of the Eiffel Tower, in front of a pyramid. Jensen shaking hands with the mayor, three senators, the former president, the movie star. Welcome, Doctor!

Administrator Jensen speaks only in obvious absolutes, in of-courses. Of course, any deviations from the hospital's code of ethics must be reported. Of course, any deviations from professional demeanor must be addressed, so we can remain true to our core values.

And of course, we must've judicious also in making sure that we apply these rules in a considerate and appropriate way. Of course the medical profession is high stress and requires some letting off of steam. Of course we shouldn't pry into what our esteemed colleagues are doing with their personal time. Of course, we must respect the privacy needs of busy professionals.

Certainly, Jeremy is aware that Dr. Wooley is a highly respected expert in his field, and a sought-after lecturer and partner to no less than five medical education institutions of renown. Jeremy certainly also knows that Dr. Wooley's work has brought considerable revenue streams to the hospital, in terms of grants and research money. Jeremy could certainly learn a thing or two, as we all certainly could, from Dr. Wooley's ability to cultivate a network of powerful benefactors and friends to the hospital. It's certainly a good thing for Jeremy that Mr. Wooley, Dr. Wooley's brother, who sits on the Board of Trustees, is such an expert and an advocate for the needs of the radiology department.

Isn't it?

So yes, Dr. Wooley is important to the hospital, and Jeremy will surely appreciate the advantages of working with such an individual, yes? Yes, there have been those who haven't quite understood Dr. Wooley's peculiar blend of humor and his sometimes offbeat personality, like Jeremy's predecessor. But he doesn't work here anymore, right? But Jeremy does work here, yes. And we're glad to have you here. So yes, do come again and let me know if anything bothers you, yes? And in the meantime, keep on doing the great work you do, which we all appreciate so much.

Jeremy stands two steps outside the door, stunned. He didn't notice himself leaving the office, and it's only now that he's making sense of what he was told: Of course, certainly, yes, they don't want to hear a word of complaint about Wooley. Or else.

And of course, Jeremy knew that would be the answer. He certainly didn't expect anything else. Yes, he understands why this compromise is necessary. What he doesn't understand is why he came to administrator Jensen in the first place. What temporary act of insanity prompted him to ignore the obvious, and just run off to do the right thing.

Of course it was a bad idea, doomed to fail. But Jeremy still feels a certain satisfaction about having done it. Yes, he feels fantastic about it, in fact. He stands by the window, a few steps outside of Jensen's closed door, with a smile on his face, savoring his own serenity.

Minutes pass unnoticed.

* * *

4:18pm-cracked concrete, muddy flowerbeds, dusty tiles, cigarette butts. Sound of cars rushing, clangs from a construction site a few blocks away. One lone fat man with a mobile IV drip, puffing. His mute, tired stare.

Jeremy had never stepped into the smokers' courtyard before, but today for the first time he noticed the trees outside the lobby window. They called at him, so he stepped out.

The fat man looked at him with surprise. Doctors don't smoke. "I shouldn't be here," Jeremy thinks, and his brain reels back into the familiar buzz of stress, cases, schedule, rush... But it doesn't stick. That thought bubble pops as soon as it grazes the limbs of the tree, and all that's left on Jeremy's mind is birdsong, warm sun, and the greasy stink of cigarette smoke.

He smiles at the man. The man smiles back. All is well. Jeremy puts his hands in the pockets of his lab coat, and looks up. The sky is shamelessly blue. The sun blasts through the small, gnarled trees in the courtyard, making their leaves glow a bright light green. Nothing out here cares to be sick. Everything out here is happily alive. Jeremy feels good.

Inside he saw her, he woman with the skeleton. She's still restrained. Her skin is mottled, rough, stained, scarred. Her hair is short and dirty. She was yelling at nurses, her neck tendons straining, hunched in a way that made her clavicles jut forward. She was twitching, jerking against the straps, seemingly unable to hold still for more than a few moments. The vigor in her movements was fascinating. When she threw her weight against the restraints, he saw pure motion, muscles dancing on this perfect frame within her. Energy ripples from her core, radiating out in pulses that express life's raw desire to live. Of course she's rebelling, struggling, fighting: she contains a force too powerful to fit into a prosaic society. In Ancient Greece she would have been a goddess. The beauty within her was meant to dance, to leap, to resonate with the vibrant harmonics of life itself. She's an artistic gift into a world that's forgotten what art is. She's a pearl in a world of swines.

But Jeremy saw her. He understood her, the light within her, the uncontainable urge she must feel to be a resplendent beacon upon the world. He was given this training, this vocation, this path, so that he could notice her, and bear witness. Jeremy understands art now, and beauty. He understands religion, and purpose. Jeremy will not fear death, because he's met her, and she is meaningful.

* * *

11:24pm—Wind howling, roaring, ripping at leaves on the trees, whipping dust and sand. Dark sky turning blacker by the minute. Smell of the sharp tang of static electricity, a storm about to burst. Not a soul around.

Jeremy has been on this balcony for hours. Nobody ever comes here. He forgot about dinner, the gym, going home. He was listening to the feeling inside him, growing mutely stronger. But now the sharp cold wind cuts through his reverie. All of a sudden he's cold, hungry, and aware.

He looks down to the parking lot and is surprised to see Wooley walking in from a parking space far from the building, behind the trees on the access road. He has a baseball cap on, and is holding his coat tightly about him, lapels raised, as he walks briskly toward the side entrance. What is he doing back at the hospital this late?

Jeremy watches him approach the entrance, and stop, and peek inside. He's staying in the shadow, waiting for something, waiting for the coast to clear? Finally he walks in. Jeremy leaves the railing and runs for the door. He steps into a darkened hallway. The ICU is quiet at this time of night, this far from the nurses' station. Jeremy turns right toward the service stairs, just in time to see a shadow approaching from behind the frosted glass door. He flattens himself against the wall, behind an orderly's cart, and watches as the dark shape opens the stairwell door quietly, crosses the threshold. It's Wooley, still in his coat and hat.

Wooley slithers down a side corridor, and Jeremy runs on tiptoe to the corner, peeks around it. Wooley is entering one of the ICU rooms, in the dark. He slides inside and closes the door, quiet as a whisper.

Jeremy's pulse is thudding. His face is hot. He is not even wondering what Wooley's doing in there. He realizes he should have known all along. Earlier today they processed the head CT for a young girl, a high school kid, who was in a car accident. Jeremy is burning with rage because of what Wooley is doing, and has probably done many times before. Because of what Wooley is going to make him do. And because Wooley, with his connections, and his power, and his well-laid plans, is leaving him no options at all.

He opens the door, silently walks in. Wooley is by the IV rack, his back turned away from the door, injecting something. Jeremy takes three steps forward and grabs the bottle Wooley's left on the tray. He reads the label. Sure enough, it's exactly what he thought. He slams the bottle back down on the tray. The sudden noise makes Wooley jump.

"You're into anesthesiology, now, Scot?" Jeremy's voice is low, cold. Wooley's eyes widen. He pulls the syringe out, drops it on the tray with shaking hands. For a few seconds he's actually speechless. His mouth opens and shuts without a sound, like a big fish.

"Out!" Jeremy says, and heads for the door. Wooley grabs his syringe and bottle and follows him out. "Jeremy, I don't know what you think you saw, but it's probably best if..." Jeremy turns around and shushes him: "Not here. Follow me." And he leads the way toward the balcony. All the while, his blood is pumping like there are pistons in his jugulars, whooshing in his ears. His mind is screaming.

It all recedes a few seconds later, as he watches Wooley's body contorted on the concrete below, a black pool of blood rapidly spreading around his skull, still contained in the baseball cap. Amazing what a little gravity, and a little adrenaline, will do to bones, and ligaments, and tendons. He imagines what Wooley's skeleton would look like, in this grotesque posture, and nearly chuckles.

It went by so fast it surprised them both. Wooley didn't even have time to scream. Grab, pull, lift, shove. It was over in seconds. Now Wooley's in the shade, between the building wall and some bushes, in a ridiculous pose, and the hospital feels serene again, just like it does everyday when Wooley leaves. Jeremy basks in the calm and quiet. The roar in his eardrums turns into the whisper of the wind, the heat into pinpricks of cold.

He floats lightly through the hallways, seeing halos in the pools of light, around the faces of the nurses and attending physicians. Smiles light up his way, and he realizes he is smiling too. He hears peaceful piano music as he walks toward the indistinct shrieking coming from her room. When he opens the door he interrupts her mid-scream. She, and the male orderly, and Dr. Novak, all raise their eyebrows high, at the sight of Jeremy's face.

He looks at her with pure loving wisdom, with unshakable devotion. He reflects the pure light he sees at her core, and all are blinded. In the pregnant stillness, his smile sings her praises, heralds the coming of her age. He is her Gabriel, her John the Baptist.

Her features change. The anger and hurt of a lifetime fall from her face. Ageless, her eyes look into his, awaiting, not quite hoping for, the next moment. She is compelled to let it happen.

The restraints fall open fast. She doesn't move. He offers his hand, and she takes it. Jeremy turns to the great heavy door, and opens it, revealing the darkened corridor, and the bright foyer beyond. Resplendent, forgiven, oblivious, she follows him into the light.

CR ED

Antoine Valot does software, performing arts, and fiction. He crafts experiences that empower and delight.

THE SKELETON MAN – BRIAN RIVERA

They say that we are the heroes of own stories, and I can't help but wonder what I've done wrong. From my experience, I'm anything but.

I'm known as the Skeleton Man and that isn't a very heroic name at all. I wonder if some of us exist as wandering villains, simply so that others can be the heroes of their tales.

After all, how can you be the hero if there is no horror to overcome – no wrong to right?

I wonder this as I pass through downtown Denver on this beautiful, 72 degree day in February, a rare and welcome phenomenon that usually makes others happier. Except, on this day, it doesn't. People pass me on the streets and their eyes dart away, trying not to have seen me, holding their gaze deliberately locked in any other direction. Until their eyes sneak a second glance, quick and hopefully unnoticed. Parents reach for their children and lift them away from me to keep them safe, scolding them for not staying closer. When I meet strangers, they do not shake my hand. They reach out, trembling as their palm reaches toward me, and then they withdraw the offer before I have the opportunity to reciprocate.

None of their reactions are unexpected, nor unreasonable. I look like a skeleton. I have a condition, a disease, that prevents my muscles from growing and my body holds very little fat. I am, for the most part, skin and bone. During the day, my lack of strength confines my 95 pound body to a wheelchair. And at night, a series of machines pump oxygen into me to keep me alive.

I often wonder why I unsettle people. I understand that I'm different, of course. The only way to evaluate a stranger, upon first encounter, is by seeing what they look like. Tall. Short. Beautiful. Terrifying.

Yet, I look like what everyone else is. A skeleton. Beneath a model's elaborately and meticulously selected complement of designer clothing and abundant accessories, or a businessman's tailored suit that he wears with his half-kept secret in a clip on tie, rests a basic human skeleton. It's what we all are – a common ground that each human shares despite our most fervent efforts to differentiate ourselves from one another.

Why then, does someone that reminds us of what we have in common, scare us, causing mothers to pull their children away and forcing discomfort to overwhelm our sense of politeness, compelling strangers to retract an extended handshake?

Sometimes I wonder if I'm the villain because I mostly don't care if I am. That sounds like something a villain would say, holding a certain apathy to the good or bad they cause in the lives of others. Since I can't help what I am, or that I look the way I do, should I care at all?

How, then, am I a villain?

Much less often, but on occasion, I wonder if I'm actually the hero. It's a bit vain to think about this possibility, but every so often, I do allow myself the indulgence, if only for a moment or two. I have challenges that many others don't and I overcome them. Whether or not it's a welcome concept, I do remind them we are all skeletons, all of us the same thing, deep down.

People ask me what the most difficult thing about being the Skeleton Man is, and that answer is simple. I know what I am, what I look like, but the hardest thing is getting people to see me otherwise. As something else. Anything but. I'd like to be the Intelligent Man. The Quirky yet Friendly Man. The Surprisingly Normal Man.

But my aspiration is to be perceived as something else is, perhaps, in error. My want to deny what I actually am is the problem in and of itself. I am the Skeleton Man and, at the end of the day, we all are the skeleton men and women. The skeleton children. The same thing. If I'm the villain, wouldn't it follow that you are too? And if I'm not, maybe I'm the hero of my story too.

I wonder if the Skeleton Man is a hero's name after all. I wonder if, tomorrow, I should go show why I'm not any different than anyone. Why I'm good. Why this skeleton is so alive.

I wonder if they'd see me differently.

I wonder if they could.

☙ ❧

Brian Rivera works at a research technology company as a Software Engineer. He has a passion for digital strategy and development. He also writes about living with disability in The Others: Being Disabled and Going Crazy.

"Do you ever wonder about the fence?" the grave digger asks his partner.

The second grave digger, his name is Jones, sighs and shakes his head.

"Why would I wonder about the fence?" he asks, wiping the muddy sweat from his brow.

The first grave digger, his name is Carter, stabs his long spade into the damp earth four feet below the grassy surface. He grunts as he does this. He always grunts, but he is no longer sure why–his body, though tired, is tuned to the dig. His effort requires no sound.

"It just seems kind of silly," Carter says between splashes of gravel and earthworm. "If everyone in here is dead, what's the fence protecting?"

"All dead and bones but us, Ke-mo sah-bee," Jones grunts. "And it's grave robbers."

Carter slings a shovelful over the edge of the grave. Still two feet to go. Still a few hours before sunrise.

"Grave robbers?" he challenges. "No one does that anymore. Those people use computers now. They steal people's lives long before they've lost them."

Jones laughs.

"You and that internet," he scoffs. "Just a passing fad, Carter."

Jones chips away at the floor of the grave with his pick. The metal blade rings almost supersonic as it cuts through generations of earth; memories trapped in ore and mineralized.

"Only two things in life are certain," Jones continues.

"Don't finish. I know it," Carter interrupts. "But people ain't buried with their finest gold and jewels these days. People go into their graves like babies, swaddled in something someone else picked out, and otherwise naked."

Jones laughs again. He tosses the pick aside the edge of the grave onto the lawn and retrieves a pack of cigarettes that sits beside the transistor radio they bring to every dig, but have yet to turn on. He perches the cigarette on his lips and lights it from a book of matches he draws from the cellophane guarding the carton.

"Grave robbers aren't out to steal stuff any more," he says, exhaling a rolling white cloud. "Who needs stuff anyway?"

"You could pawn a watch," Carter replies.

"You could pawn a watch," Jones mocks. "And then what? Take my thirty dollars and sail around the world?"

Jones laughs again.

"Fine," Carter sighs. "What do they steal?"

Jones holds the cigarette between his thumb and forefinger and points at Carter, the red hot cherry as some period on whatever claim he is about to make.

"Fingerprints," he says with a smile.

"Fingerprints?" Carter asks.

"You're the digital expert, right, Ke-mo sah-bee? How do you suppose all these dead people secure their offshore accounts and devices and whatnot? It isn't a happy 'I promise I'm who I say I am' I'll tell you that much."

Carter drops another load of subterranean ecosystem onto the mounting pile and sets his shovel down. He beckons Jones for a cigarette, and receives one, lit swiftly with another match. The two men lean against the ends of their grave, like the head and foot of a dining table, and smoke.

"So by your logic, the fence is there so someone doesn't ramble in here with an inkpad and start stealing dead fingerprints?" Carter asks.

"Inkpad?" Jones coughs. "You're darling. No, these grave robbers take the whole hand. A dead guy isn't bound to miss it anyway, is he? Hell, you think, take them both."

"I admit that it doesn't sound impossible, but ain't no evidence I've ever seen. No dug up graves. No late-night break ins. Nothing. I think you're pulling my leg, Jones."

"A good grave robber doesn't leave evidence. It's a victimless crime, anyway," Jones replies. "Any next of kin worth their salt is canceling accounts the second a fella drops dead."

"You're talking in circles here. If there ain't nothing to gain from taking a person's fingerprints, then why bother taking them at all?" Carter prods.

"Maybe a fella's a little on the bent side. Maybe he wants a trophy."

"That's disgusting," Carter replies.

Jones takes a drag and exhales.

"I'm kidding. You need to lighten up. Besides, most of them go just that way, with kin and love and all their matters attended to. They're robber proof from the day they're carted in here," Jones says. "But sometimes they're not."

"And that's why we need a fence?" Carter mocks.

"That's why we need a fence," Jones continues. "Take this guy here."

He grabs the paperwork nestled under the radio.

"Mr. Aloysius Waterford. He just stopped ticking altogether one afternoon last week. Neighbor found him on his porch, sitting in his favorite rocking chair, pitcher of lemonade beside him on a little metal table. Neighbor walks up and says, 'howdy' and old Mr. Waterford is just a blank slate. Could've been there a day or two, really. Weather nice as this, people are out at all hours in a quiet neighborhood. And not a kin in the world. One of those lifelong bachelor types."

Carter shoots him a skeptical look. "How'd you know all that detail about him?"

"I read is all. Everything is on that internet of yours. You know that."

Jones stubs out his cigarette, draws another from the pack, lights it and inhales.

"So maybe, if poor Mr. Waterford here is gonna lose all his hard-earnings to the government anyway, it wouldn't be so bad to 'redistribute' them," Jones says.

Carter eyes widen. His mind races with gruesome images. Hands detached; bodies desecrated for all eternity. He sees the smile growing on Jones's face. He stubs his cigarette in the dirt pile, and reaches for his shovel without thinking about it.

"Are you telling me that you cut off Mr. Waterford's hands, Jones?" he asks.

Jones laughs.

"Nothing of the sort," he says.

Carter exhales with relief. He lets go of his shovel.

"It's a two man job," Jones says. "Can't use a saw 'cause it'd be suspicious. What's a digger need with a saw anyway? Nah. You're going hold old Mr. Aloysius Waterford's arms real steady for me, and I'm gonna come down on the wrists with your spade until we got ourselves a real handle on the situation."

Carter turns quickly, his heart racing, suddenly fully alive, and grabs at the shovel again, but the familiar ratchet of a hammer drawing back freezes him where he stands.

"Suppose I refuse," Carter says, gazing toward the iron gates a few hundred yards away. "What are you going to do, shoot me?"

"Maybe I do. Maybe I don't. But I don't see you running."

Jones holds the revolver steady.

"Funny thing about fences, Carter," he says. "They're as good at keeping people in, as they are at keeping people out."

ଔ 80

Nate Ragolia is the author of There You Feel Free; *a novella. Creator of the* Illiterate Badger *and* Lark & Robin *web comics, and occasional chatterer on music, film, &c.*

ON SKELETONS AND WASTELANDS – JESSICA PROETT

- for Seba, and her art.

Her paintbrush
reminds me of a skeleton's wrist,
finger joints, or individual ribs...

A wasteland is
not this
or that
I associated it with
in a campus courtyard under fallen leaves;
it is what I've read and rewritten
each time I feel Time
slipping
away.

When I met her in Saudi, I rewrote it again.

"The wasteland is a morning without sun,
a body without skin,
bare,
yet not naked.
All that's left is bones.

It is myself slowly slipping away
until I am only my essence
or else lost.

It is hope and hopelessness
so closely intertwined
that art doesn't even know what to say anymore.

It is now, in this poem, speaking of my friend,
and her beauty,
not the horrors
we know we should speak out against.

A skeleton is not horrific.
It is honest."

2012:
We lived in a desert and
sometimes sand covered the sun.
It rode into Riyadh like a tidal wave,
except slower,
sky turning orange,
terra-cotta red and then black.
We cover our mouths.

We still choked.

When I realized this wasteland
we both created
and lived in,
was no longer metaphor for me,
or escapable for her,
the first line I wrote was,
"The sand in our chests
became hourglasses counting time."
Both then and years later
we still couldn't breathe.

Art became our alcohol,
codependency, and friend.
I wrote and she painted

but we even lost that for a time.
We gave up
and tried to be happy.

The art we created felt more like darkness
enveloping us
than escaping us,
so we tried to be "normal"
to live
in the status quos of our countries
where people seemed, at least, content.

Words became themes.
Art.
Duty.

Us.
Them.
Fractured.
Humanity.
Alter-realities we happened upon
by knowing two worlds,
Saudi and elsewhere,
crossed and then separated
us
leaving us split by borders
and identities.

We kept thinking about bones.
Not knowing if it was premonition,
jealousy, yearning, or metaphor.

We couldn't exorcise sand
from our bodies,
so the doctors prescribed inhalers
and sinus meds.
They don't believe us
that the sand is alive.

When we gave up on art,
we clung to our bones,
knowing they are an eternal memory
of our memory.

Sometimes we still think art might save us.

Alchemy then and now:
Still breathing,
she wakes up
to a dark glow,
sand covering the sky
and Al-Mumlaka tower,
draws flowers spilling out
of her ribcage,
paints them without hope or hopelessness,
transmuting loneliness into art again.

I write this poem in Denver.

She gives birth to phoenix dreams,
posing in her beige portico with red lipstick,
painting a self portrait with eyes- very much alive-
and soft facial features,

but the rest of her
below the neck
like sand
crumbles away
becoming part of something eternal,
shifting with wind,
traveling spaces and time.
It is not a loss.
We've known it for a long time now.
We are bones,
still alive,
and grateful.
She draws her ribcage with flowers spilling out,
below it her humerus, ulna, radius, and pelvis.

I, like her, wonder if I will return someday.
If that part of me that is roaming sand
will come back to fill me when I learn
more of myself,
alchemy, or spiritual truths.

"We are all returning," she says,
naheno jami'an na'ouda,
to the source.

☙ ❧

Jessica Proett is a published poet and previous staff writer for the Levantine
Review. She holds an MA in Middle East and Islamic Studies from American
University of Paris and is currently living in Denver after several years
abroad.

STRAY CAT BLUES, OR SKELETONS IN THE CLOSET – ASHLEY HEATON

"I bet when you were in my class all those years ago you never imagined this would be happening," my former teacher joked as he snorted a line of cocaine.

"You are correct," I replied, smiling and rolling my eyes. His mood was perhaps too light.

"You know, I was a little embarrassed for you to see my place." He appeared suddenly pensive, furrowing his brow and running a hand through his hair.

I downed a shot of vodka and fiddled with his stereo, placing *Beggars' Banquet* on the turntable. "Why do you say that, Paul?" I asked. The setting in question somewhat resembled my own perfectly acceptable-looking apartment. I did not know whether to feel insulted.

"Well, it's not as nice as my last place, and you know, I like to think you look up to me. You have this idea in your head of who I am because of who I was when I met you. You're a smart girl and you've got a future ahead of you. And I'm on the decline, you know? I'm..." he lowered his voice to a near whisper, "...*downwardly mobile.*"

I was a little confused as to what he meant by this. I'd assumed he was quite well-off. Last year he'd released a new book, his most successful yet. I'd even seen it at Barnes & Noble once – prime distribution real estate! He was smart – certainly smarter than me – and was scruffily handsome with artfully tousled hair and a nice-enough wardrobe. He had friends in the upper echelons of the literary and political spheres. He was right; I did look up to him. I very nearly idolized him. Of course, if I was to be honest with myself I would admit he had many flaws, first and foremost the whole drug use thing. Being a romantic, though, I was willing to see past such imperfections.

Perhaps I should take a step back and clarify that this relationship – if one could call it that – had only been in existence on and off for the past year. Nothing improper had happened when he was my teacher, which was a good thing, because at the time I had been 16 and he'd been 32. I'm quite certain he'd never had a second thought about awkward teenage me back then.

I didn't see him for years, until we finally got back in touch because we had something in common – we both had begun side careers as writers. I reached out to him on a whim, and over time he became something of a mentor and confidant to me. Our relationship had changed quite drastically about a year ago, though, when on one particular occasion we indulged in a few too many cocktails, and one thing ended up leading to another.

It was entirely unplanned but the chemistry between us was electric, of the variety I hadn't believed existed before then. It contained all the spark of forbidden love, weighted by 12 years of history. Because of the geographical distance between us we'd only seen each other a few times since, but every time we did we managed to get into trouble.

In the present day, he was a bored 44-year-old college professor feeling stifled by the establishment, trying to recapture his youth. I was a bored 28-year-old cog in the corporate machine missing my rebellious teen years. We understood each other and gave each other exactly what we needed – a kind of codependent midlife-crisis symbiosis. It was nice in its way, really.

I was shaken from my thoughts when I saw something I'd never seen in *my* apartment: a cockroach scurrying across the hardwood floor. I jumped and pulled my legs up onto the couch as Paul threw the remote at the gruesome creature, then attacked it with a can of raid. Once we were certain of no more signs of life he scooped it up as though this were business as usual, opening the sliding glass door and chucking it outside. I raised an eyebrow, better understanding what he meant about his apartment being embarrassing. We both sighed and continued the conversation. I leaned into him, staring through the glass at the peach trees in pale springtime bloom swaying in the wind. He poured us another round of drinks.

As I observed him, I sensed that something was wrong. We'd always had fun together. From what I knew of him he seemed to generally be enjoying his life. But the whole "downwardly mobile" comment lingered in the air as I tried to figure out what he meant by that. I was troubled by his words and worried for him. I truly felt for him at this point; he'd become an important part of my life.

And then I spotted it out of the corner of my eye. More movement, but not a cockroach this time. It was a skeleton shuffling around in his closet.

"Oh, hello," the skeleton said to me. "Sorry to disturb you two, I'm just moving in and getting comfortable. Don't mind me!"

Now, most girls would have fainted with terror at such a sight, but not I! I knew exactly where skeletons in closets came from; in fact, I had one of my own. They follow unsuspecting people home from places where skeletons are apt to congregate. Cemeteries. Biology labs. Mine trailed me from a museum exhibit (I think it was that "Bodies" exhibit that was all the rage some years ago, but my memory is fuzzy). It's been making a home in my closet ever since.

One doesn't find a skeleton mulling about in one's closet for no good reason. No, a closet skeleton is like a scarlet letter or an albatross hanging from one's neck – it's a signifier of a deep dark secret; a symbol of guilt or shame. Only people with seriously messed up pasts or presents have skeletons in their closets. Mine represented my history, my troubled and troublesome youth. Now I was fine – even on the upswing – but I had seen it all and there was no going back. However, I knew Paul's closet skeleton embodied the present, because it had clearly just arrived in his apartment recently. It was because of this that despite my ease around such circumstances, I still found the presence of this skeleton deeply disturbing.

I whirled around and looked it deep in the empty eye sockets. "If you don't mind my asking, why are you here?" I implored of the skeleton.

It laughed. "Oh, I think you can figure that out! Isn't it obvious? He's got issues galore. We met in the bio building at the university. Boy, the moment I saw him I knew I'd found my new home."

Paul's face flushed bright red and he fumbled awkwardly with the stereo volume, anything to drown out what was happening.

I pondered the situation. He was clearly unhappy with the state of his life. The more time I spent with him, the more I had noticed the increased frequency of his drinking and drug use. I'd consoled him through more than one crippling panic attack in the past few days alone. And he would blow massive quantities of money on nights out, money I was pretty sure he didn't have.

"What is that skeleton really doing here?" I asked.

"Well...ah, this is so humiliating," he stammered. "I can't imagine what you must think of me. I mean, if anyone finds about the skeleton...my career would be over. God, what would my students think?"

I was beginning to tear up. "You must really be off the rails. You've never been the type to have a skeleton in your closet."

Paul looked tense. "The truth is that I hate this city and I hate my job," he said, his voice sounding resigned. I had known he would have preferred to live elsewhere, but the intensity of his bitterness was news to me. "I want to work up north, back east, just about anywhere else really, but...it's so hard to land a new job when you're a professor. I've been trying for years. I'm up for tenure here, you know. I'm scared I'll be here forever. That I'll be stuck." He continued, motioning to the lines on the table and the empty bottle of vodka beside them. "That's what this is all about."

"Oh," I said, taken aback. "I'm sorry to hear that. But...I can tell there's something else that's bothering you. Isn't there?"

"Well..." he trailed off, appearing to struggle with whether or not to tell me something. I looked from him to the skeleton and back again.

"Go on," the skeleton teased. Its levity was off-putting. I felt a pit in my stomach.

After a long pause, Paul finally spoke. "I thought I'd met someone really special here. But she's gone for good. And I doubt I'll ever meet someone else in this shitty town." I was shocked that he would share such a thing with me, especially since these two relationships had apparently been playing out at the same time. I silently thanked the skeleton for egging him on.

It was then that I realized Paul was not just numbing his existential pain with drugs and alcohol – he was numbing the pain with me. I'd never be a real possibility to him. I was to be kept a deep dark secret; I was just another proverbial skeleton in his figurative closet.

Suddenly my thoughts were flying out of my mouth. "I know we live far away... but you're looking to move anyway, right? Why can't we try to make something of this?" I immediately regretted my words. It was then that I realized I had caught feelings for him, and now I felt like a fool, desperately throwing myself at him while I watched him pine for another woman.

"How could you still have any interest in me, knowing that I have this...thing...in my closet? What would someone like you, with your whole life ahead of you, know about skeletons in closets?" He sounded almost annoyed, as if he thought I could never understand.

"I know quite a bit about them, because I have a skeleton in my closet too."

He looked stunned.

"It's really sweet that you care so much about me," he allowed. I saw it in his face. He knew how I felt and he didn't like it. "I care about you too," he paused, looking thoughtful, "but I can't date you."

"Isn't that what we're doing now?"

"Well, yes...but...I can't see you after this."

"Why not?"

"I can't be with a girl like you."

My heart pounded in my chest. "What do you mean by 'a girl like me'?"

"Well, you know. The other woman...she was closer to my age and she certainly wasn't my student. It was an appropriate relationship. She was a good woman, the kind who went to church every Sunday.

"Are you saying I'm no good?" I could hardly contain the rage I felt at this point.

He casually popped a Xanax while I seethed. "You know what I mean. She was going to fix me. She had no baggage. Someone like her would resent the skeleton in my closet so much as to make it leave. You, though...you're like me. You accept the skeleton in my closet. You have a skeleton in your closet."

"But I accept you as you are – skeletons and all."

"It doesn't matter. You can't make the problem go away. You can't fix me."

"No one is going to fix you. You are going to have to fix yourself."

I hurriedly picked up my things and left, running out the door and under the peach trees as the blossoms fell. It appeared springtime was just about over. When I got home I realized the skeleton in my closet had wandered off into the night, never to be seen again. I hear Paul never could get rid of that skeleton in his closet.

❦ ❧

Ashley Heaton is a Los Angeles-based part-time journalist and full-time rebel. Her writing credits include Harper's Bazaar, ELLE, Conde Nast Traveler and Racked.

http://ashleyeheaton.com/

Instagram: @ashley.e.h

Twitter: @ashleyeheaton

ANOTHER ONE ON THE PILE IN HARM CITY: A SOL STEINMETZ ADVENTURE – SHAUNN GRULKOWSKI

"What do you suppose it means?"

"Well, it's a skeleton, Sal. Wh—"

"Sol."

"What'd I say?"

"You said 'Sal', like Salad. It's *Sol*. Like Solomon."

"Potato, tomato."

Sol, definitely not *Sal*, bent down on one knee, directly into a puddle of new rain, old liquor, and, probably-but-not-assuredly party cum; he reached into his jacket pocket and pulled out a brand-new holocorder. He fumbled it around in his hands, looking for the passive recording button. He'd meant to read the directions prior to bringing it to an investigation; but in the Sol Steinmetz "Planned vs Executed Heavyweight Title Fight," Planned was ahead on all three judges scorecards, winning five rounds ten to eight. In a respectable city, like Vegas, they'd have stopped the fight years ago, but this was Baltimore, and all they cared about here was blood.

"Oh, gimme the fucking thing, already." Lieutenant Louise Lloyd snatched the device from him, set it, and placed it on a dry spot on the pavement. The recorder made a faint hum as rotating green waves spun from the top, capturing the surroundings in real time. Not only was the device new to Sol, but it was new to earth, this generation of recorder making the nearly unobtrusive noise, where its predecessors sounded much more like a small child kicking the wall of an aluminum shed.

"Thanks, Lou," Sol said, shaking his head. Drops of water flung gently from the brim of his hat. "Man, you know, I remember when you just took pictures with a phone. Now," he waved vaguely in the direction of the recorder, his hand breaking through one of the beams. "Now, well—"

"Yeah, the future's a weird place, Grandpa. Are you going to be done soon? I'd like to get back to the *real* investigation."

"Oh, don't mind me. Just go ahead an-"

Lieutenant Lloyd clasped his shoulder with a grip that Sol thought was quite a bit tighter than her slight frame would produce. He wondered if she had some after-market appendages, but it was hard to tell with the long-sleeved tunics and gloves the federal police wore.

"See, *Prox*, I *do* mind. I mind a lot. Just poke around, take your 'corder; and let me shut it off for you, because you don't want to sift through for hours of footage of the inside of your jacket pocket, and Fuck. Right. Off."

"Why so testy, Lou? We're doing the same job."

A much larger woman in a Fedcop uniform, complete with riot helmet and obscurer slid next to the Lieutenant. She bent down and whispered something in Louise's ear. Sol couldn't make it out, but noticed the hisses and clicks that indicated a voice masker in use. She didn't want to be identified, and Sol had a pretty good idea why. He took two noticeable steps backward. Luckily for him, Louise just shook her head, and the larger woman walked back towards the rest of the battalion, congregating around a few of the parked cruisers.

"We're not doing the same job. I'm an actual, highly-trained, Federal Police Officer. A lieutenant, soon to be captain, hopefully; so I can get out from under the crushing weight of that stupid fucking alliteration. You," she jabbed the air between them with an index finger, "you are a tired, old, bottom-feeding Police *Proxy*." She wrinkled her nose and scowled. "I don't know why the City would even waste the money to hire you."

"Cities are broke, and proxies don't cost much. And they don't pay us benefits. You get plugged, and it's a payout to your beneficiaries, big extravagant funeral, all that bullshit. I catch a hot one? Torched in a municipal building, ashes sent to whomever is listed as next-of-kin, in a blank plastic container, by the same courier that delivers their lunch. I don't even get the privilege of having my two-oh-five rotting together like this poor asshole."

"Two oh five?"

"Bones."

"There's two hundred and *six* bones in an adult body, Prox."

"Normally, but he's missing his head, so"

The lieutenant cut him off. "Wait. Do you think the skull is just one big bone?"

"Yeah, of course" he paused. "Well, besides teeth, I guess. But they're not really bones."

"Jee-sus. You're really a dumb old fuck, aren't you?" She snorted. "There's twenty-t–"

"Yeah, says who?"

"Says biology."

Sol walked closer to the skeleton. He noticed a couple of Fedcops take a step toward him, but they stopped as soon as they started. He looked back over his shoulder and saw the lieutenant with one hand up, the universal sign for "stay there." He shrugged, assuming that the signal was meant for them, not him, and knelt down next to the skeleton. He'd seen bodies, too many, before; out in the road, like this, like an old couch, used and discarded. But this, this was different. Purposeful. A message? That was his first thought. A skeleton, not a body. Organs gone. Cleaned of viscera, mostly, anyway. Bits of this and that still clung to the bones, but not enough to suggest the party responsible was in any kind of rush; more like dusting around AV equipment. You can do as good a job as you like, but some always clings. Sol figured the same must go for blood and tendons too. He looked around the immediate area. The Inner Harbor was a busy place, but the cold and the rain kept people inside, and four-thirty a.m. wasn't quite prime time on the best days. He noticed a few public surveillance cameras. But the city's financial situation being what it was, the chance that *any* of them actually worked was a coin-toss at best. Besides, the city government wasn't generally interested in a thorough (read: expensive) investigation, anyway. A quick arrest and prosecution was always preferred. Anything to keep the Fedcops out, really. And while it wasn't that the city necessarily *preferred* that the subject got killed during the apprehension; but hey, shit did happen, and any lightening of the docket was a welcome one.

Sol tried to avoid that. But shit did indeed happen.

He leaned in close, looking for something, anything, that would point in a direction, besides the skeleton's left pointer finger, which was aimed directly at a chicken-wing joint that everyone knew was an autobrothel. He shrugged his shoulders, about to pack it in, when he noticed that

"This thing's blinking."

"What?"

"The skeleton! It's fucking blinking," he shouted. "Well, I mean, the skeleton's not actually blinking! There's something...in its ribc-"

"Step away from it" Lloyd shouted back.

"Hang on a s-"

"Now, prox!"

Not wanting to start an argument that had a high probability of ending with any of the twenty-whatever bones in his skull getting perforated, he dutifully got up and lightly jogged the thirty-or-so feet to the Lieutenant's position.

"Alright. You stay here," she said. Sol could hear her posture tightening through her terse bark. She double-tapped the side of her jaw. "Morrell, Robeson! Get to that body and see if there's a light source coming from it."

Two of the Fedcops sprang into action, taking huge, synchronous strides until they reached the skeleton. Sol saw one of them bend at the waist. He saw them reach a hand toward the skeleton, but before he could open his mouth, Louise screamed.

"Robeson! Don-" was all she managed as a blast of what they would later determine was a newly engineered form of white phosphorus ignited both of the Fedcops, burning through their tactical suits like oily newspaper. Sol saw the Lieutenant violently slapping at her jaw; at first he thought she was trying to cure herself of shock, but realized almost immediately that it was something far more horrible.

She was trying to shut-off her cochlear communications rig, because the sounds of Morrell and Robeson's screams were broadcast directly into her inner ear as her subordinates melted away. By the time one of the remaining Fedcops got it together enough to through a halon grenade into the fire, it was a million miles past way too late. The phosphorus burned their clothes, gear, skin, and muscle, all clear down to the bone, leaving a two-headed, three skeleton dog pile, with two riot helmets rolling around like a couple of black moons. The smell was too much for a few of the Fedcops to bear, and they evacuated their dinners into the Chesapeake Bay.

Sol put both of his hands over his nose and mouth; it looked like he was praying, but he was just trying to avoid being a part of the puke chorus. Lieutenant Lloyd said and did nothing, unless you count standing with your mouth agape as "doing something." Just as he confirmed with his guts that they were going to stay where they were, Sol noticed something out of the corner of his eye. At first, he thought it was a big dog. Then it stood, and started moving toward them. Fast. The Fedcops were still in recovery-mode, and facing in the wrong direction. Lloyd noticed a second later, and yelled "stop!" The figure did not stop. It continued to run toward them. But, just to make it more interesting, it also started shooting. Lloyd instinctively reached for her sidearm, forgetting that she'd left it in her cruiser; in a rush to see what Sol was up to. She darted toward her car, but she knew she'd never make it in time. *BANG!* A bullet screamed its way into her shoulder. She gritted her teeth, and kept running, waiting for the inevitable–

BANG! BANGBANGBANGBANG!

Lloyd dropped to the ground, knowing she was dead, but fairly surprised that the afterlife looked exactly like dawn breaking over downtown Baltimore. And Saint Peter looked an awful lot like Sol Steinmetz holding a smoking, antique .45 caliber pistol.

"You alright, kiddo?" Saint Peter asked.

"Ungh. Fine."

"You hit?"

"I'm fine, I said."

He shrugged his shoulders, unintentionally mocking her. As the Fedcops rushed over to their fallen commander, Sol walked over to the writhing body of their attacker, leaned in close, nodded his head, then

BANG!

He put his old-man gun back in its old-man shoulder holster and went back to check on Louise.

"Are you o-"

"What was that about? Did he say anything to you?"

"*She* wasn't going to make it. I didn't want her to suffer, so I-"

Louise darted her hand out to shush him, forgetting about the slug making its home in her trapezius. "I don't give a shit about that," she grunted. "Did she say anything?"

"Yeah. She said, 'this is for the Glasslands.'"

"What the fuck does that have to do with anything?"

"I don't know. But I have the feeling I'm going to find out."

"This is going to be way more complicated than I hoped. Ow, fuck!" She yelled, as one of her people attempted to bandage her shoulder.

"They always are."

ℭ ℴ

Shaunn Grulkowski is the creator of Retcontinuum, several published short stories, and a perpetually annoyed wife.

A SCIENTIFIC STUDY OF HUMAN COMPREHENSION – JEFFREY WOLF

Cast

Samantha

Bryan

Francesca

Setting:

A middle school science classroom.

(At rise, FRANCESCA, a middle school science teacher, sits behind her desk at the front of her classroom. A microscope sits on her desk and a classroom skeleton is nearby. She is grading papers. SAMANTHA, an art gallery manager, enters with her date, BRYAN. SAMANTHA rushes to the skeleton and examines it closely. FRANCESCA is surprised.)

SAMANTHA:

Now this is amazing! Don't you think so, Bryan?

BRYAN:

(*Unenergetically:*)

Yes. Definitely.

SAMANTHA:

It just feels so – raw and harsh. A true picture of what humanity really is when you strip it all away.

FRANCESCA:

Um – excuse me –

SAMANTHA:

Just a tick. Bryan – can you see the artist card? I need the name of this genius.

BRYAN:

No – I don't see one.

SAMANTHA:

Maybe it's an entire installation. Is it really the whole room?

BRYAN:

None of the other students –

SAMANTHA:

(To Francesca:)

Are you a performance artist? Is this your piece?

FRANCESCA:

Who? Me?

SAMANTHA:

I'm Samantha, by the by, with The Gallery on First and Windsor. You know the one.

BRYAN:

I'm Bryan. With a y.

SAMANTHA:

You'll have to forgive him. He didn't know we were coming here.

BRYAN:

I just thought it was drinks and maybe –

SAMANTHA:

I sprang this on him. Who knew when he swiped right it would end up here?

FRANCESCA:

And why are you here?

SAMANTHA:

For people like you, of course. I like to visit these student exhibitions to scope out young and burgeoning talent. You never know where you'll find the next Picasso.

FRANCESCA:

I'm very confused.

SAMANTHA:

Is confusion part of the piece? The juxtaposition of not knowing with the world of science? And you're even inside a school! That's so meta. I love meta. Not enough people do meta, don't you think?

FRANCESCA:

I have no idea what you're talking about.

SAMANTHA:

Is the microscope a call to examine those two worlds more closely? Is that why it's on the desk?

FRANCESCA:

It's there because it's broken.

SAMANTHA:

How wonderful! Simply brilliant. Tell me the name of the artist! Now! I must know.

FRANCESCA:

I'm not sure what you mean. My name's Francesca and this is my classroom. Are you a parent?

SAMANTHA:

You're dedication to your role is very admirable.

FRANCESCA:

You know where you are right?

SAMANTHA:

The art exposition. I got an invitation.

FRANCESCA:

Are you a parent?

SAMANTHA:

Of course not. Children can be such a nuisance.

BRYAN:

Even if they can be the next Picasso?

SAMANTHA:

Touché, Bryan, touché.

FRANCESCA:

This is a middle school.

SAMANTHA:

That's what I'm saying – genius starts young.

FRANCESCA:

The art show is just Mrs. Pinsky's class –

SAMANTHA:

Did she mentor you, as well?

FRANCESCA:

Mentor? I'm not a –

SAMANTHA:

Because while the stuff in the hallway is dreck, this installation is best of show. Especially because of the skeleton. Such an effect.

FRANCESCA:

What are you –

BRYAN:

Samantha, I don't think she's part of the art show.

SAMANTHA:

Nonsense. How much is this piece listed for?

FRANCESCA:

Piece? This is my classroom.

SAMANTHA:

Great title. The Classroom. I can see the marquee now. Some artists really overdo the titles. I was afraid it would be something like: The Scientific Study of Human Comprehension. Actually, that's not bad.

BRYAN:

Samantha – I really don't think –

(SAMANTHA's phone rings.)

SAMANTHA:

Oh, excuse me. I have to take this. *(Answering the phone:)* This is Samantha, manager of The Gallery, *the* place for art. How can I help you? Oh! Hi! Yes.

FRANCESCA:

Seriously, do I have to call the police?

BRYAN:

No, please don't. She just dragged me here. This is the weirdest date ever.

SAMANTHA:

(Into the phone:)

No, I don't think that works.

FRANCESCA:

A date? Here?

BRYAN:

She insisted.

FRANCESCA:

I'm so sorry.

SAMANTHA:

(*Into the phone:*)

You're kidding! That's hysterical.

BRYAN:

I just wanted to do Netflix and –

FRANCESCA:

Oh, I wish I had Netflix.

BRYAN:

Yeah, me too.

SAMANTHA:

(*Into the phone:*)

That sounds disgusting.

BRYAN:

So, what do you teach?

FRANCESCA:

Sixth grade science.

SAMANTHA:

(*Into the phone:*)

No, nothing with a face.

FRANCESCA:

What do you do?

BRYAN:

I write ad copy for real estate agencies.

FRANCESCA:

Thrilling.

SAMANTHA:

(Into the phone:)

You haven't lived unless you've had edamame dipped in liquefied kale.

BRYAN:

It gives me time to work on my poetry.

FRANCESCA:

Oh, I love poetry! William Carlos Williams. Ezra Pound.

BRYAN:

A scientist who's into poetry?

FRANCESCA:

Stranger things –

SAMANTHA:

(Into the phone:)

No, Pookie won't drink tap water.

BRYAN:

Don't I know it.

SAMANTHA:

(Into the phone:)

He's a very cultured feline.

FRANCESCA:

I don't mean to be rude, but you seem like a very odd couple.

BRYAN:

We're not a couple.

SAMANTHA:

(Into the phone:)

Just out with someone I met today. First dates can be so electrifying.

FRANCESCA:

You went to a middle school art show on a first date?

BRYAN:

Believe it or not, it's not my worst.

SAMANTHA:

(Into the phone:)

He's great. You know I love artists.

FRANCESCA:

Ouch.

BRYAN:

You have no idea.

SAMANTHA:

(Into the phone:)

Good Lord, not a painter.

FRANCESCA:

I don't date much.

BRYAN:

That's a shame.

FRANCESCA:

As you can tell since I'm here grading –

BRYAN:

On a Friday night.

SAMANTHA:

(Into the phone:)

All they want to do are nudes and once you've done that a dozen times –

BRYAN:

Maybe you just haven't met the right person.

FRANCESCA:

Maybe.

SAMANTHA:

(To Bryan and Francesca:)

I'm so sorry, I'll be just a bit longer. (Into the phone:) Just being polite.

FRANCESCA:

How did you match with her anyway?

BRYAN:

I thought an art gallery manager and a poet –

SAMANTHA:

Anyway, I'm not opposed to nudity, it's just such a chore to wax.

FRANCESCA:

Guess you needed to look a little deeper.

BRYAN:

Like how she looks into your art installation?

FRANCESCA:

She missed the chewing gum under the chairs.

SAMANTHA:

(Into the phone:)

I just do a shot or two before starting.

BRYAN:

You really have to be grading so late?

FRANCESCA:

It gives me something to do. At least an excuse to give my mother.

SAMANTHA:

(Into the phone:)

Oh, do you really?

BRYAN:

You like teaching?

FRANCESCA:

Most days. I like the kids.

BRYAN:

Who doesn't?

SAMANTHA:

(Into the phone:)

Oh, I hate that.

FRANCESCA:

You like her?

BRYAN:

What do you think?

SAMANTHA:

(Into the phone:)

That's obvious, isn't it?

FRANCESCA:

Then why are you still –

BRYAN:

My mom raised me to be polite. I'm not just going to ditch her.

SAMANTHA:

(Into the phone:)

But eating meat out of a teddy bear is such a tired motif.

FRANCESCA:

Very admirable.

BRYAN:

Karma, right? Good things come around.

FRANCESCA:

At least you can hope.

SAMANTHA:

(Into the phone:)

Really? No! Oh dear!

FRANCESCA:

Your mom would be proud.

BRYAN:

Don't tell her that, I'll never hear the end of it.

SAMANTHA:

(Into the phone:)

That's – I'll – no – it can't stay that way. I'll have to – yes. OK. See you soon. *(She hangs up.)* Bryan, I'm terribly sorry, but I have to go. The Gallery needs me.

BRYAN:

Oh. Sad.

SAMANTHA:

Yes, listen – Francesca, was it? I definitely want to talk more about this piece. Here's my card. We have to find a way to make it travel.

FRANCESCA:

My classroom?

SAMANTHA:

It has really great potential. Possibly some real cash. Whatever you're listing it for, think upwards. I'll be in touch with your agent?

FRANCESCA:

I don't –

SAMANTHA:

Just have him call me. All the agents know who I am. Bryan, it's been fun. Thank you so much.

BRYAN:

Do you want me to drive?

SAMANTHA:

No, no, no. I'll just Uber it. Shall I ring you later? Maybe you can tell me more of the Netflix poem you're working on.

BRYAN:

I – guess – sure.

SAMANTHA:

Ta-ta then. Lovely time all. Cheers. *(Stops at skeleton.)* Just brilliant.

(SAMANTHA exits. BRYAN takes out his phone.)

FRANCESCA:

Do you have to go too? I mean –

BRYAN:

No. Just making sure my phone's on silent.

FRANCESCA:

Oh.

BRYAN:

There are some calls you just want to make sure go to voicemail.

FRANCESCA:

What are you going to do now?

BRYAN:

I'm not sure. I suddenly have a free evening. What about you? More grading?

FRANCESCA:

Actually, I think I'm done.

BRYAN:

Maybe you can –

FRANCESCA:

Show you the gum under the chairs? You need a deeper look at my art installation?

BRYAN:

I think we can do something more fun.

FRANCESCA:

An art gallery?

BRYAN:

Please, no. How about a drink?

FRANCESCA:

That sounds nice. Then maybe some Netflix.

BRYAN:

Really, I don't have –

FRANCESCA:

I know. Neither do I.

(Lights fade to black.)

⊂Q ℬↄ

Jeffrey Wolf (Playwright): In addition to authoring the short play, The Scientific Study of Human Comprehension; he recently received a staged reading of Shakespeare's Curse by One Night Stand Theatre at The Vintage Theatre in March 2016. Shakespeare's Curse also enjoyed a workshop with playwright Matthew Lopez at the Denver Center for the Performing Arts' Colorado New Play Summit in February 2015. Jeffrey is also the writer of the children's play, The Worst Play in the History of Ever, being produced by the Center for the Arts in Homer, New York, part of the Chameleon Theatre Circle's 14th Annual New Play Festival in Minnesota in 2013 and the 2013 Ronald M. Ruble New Play Festival at Caryl Crane Youth Theatre in Ohio; Memories of Lost Time, (winner of 2012 Firehouse Theatre Project's annual new play festival and part of The Edge Theatre's "On Your Feet" series); the award-winning Slipping into Anarchy (performed in Colorado, New York, England, Los Angeles, Ohio, Rhode Island, and chosen for production in Romania); Starters (Denver Repertory Theatre Company 2005 production); and No Ideas Today (2012 North Park Playwright Festival in San Diego). (jeffreywolfplays.com)

ANOTHER ONE ON THE PILE IN HARM CITY #2: GEOGRAPHY LESSONS – SHAUNN GRULKOWSKI

"I can assure you, Lieutenant; the bullet impacted on your scapula, not your clavicle."

"Are you sure?"

"Well," Doctor Bergen said. "Your *scapula* is here" he jabbed Louise below her neck with the back of his pen. "Your *clavicle*" he tapped her with the pen an inch farther toward her back.

"Ow! Mother*fucker!*"

"Is right about there-ish." He turned to pick up a tablet from his desk. "Now: lucky for you, the projectile juuuust missed your suprascapular artery and sort of broke apart after impact." He made a couple of quick taps on the pad with his bullet-wound prod, and an x-ray materialized on the MediaWall behind him. "You can see the fragments" he said, drawing circles around the bits of bullet on the image. They looked a bit like cigarette ashes floating in an old cup of water. "Here, here, and a couple there. We've since removed them, obviously, and stuck you all back together." Lieutenant Louise Lloyd took that as a signal to rotate her arm.

She was terrible at reading signals, by the way.

"Fuck! Fuckfuckfuckfuck!"

Doctor Bergen chuckled. He'd known Lieutenant Lloyd since she was a corporal, and her name was less fun to say. "So, while you can move your arm mostly normally, it's still going to hurt like a sonofabitch for a few weeks, most likely."

"But I can go back to the duty roster?" She asked, sliding off the examining table. Both of her feet hit the floor simultaneously, with the unconscious precision of the best of the FedCops.

"Lou-"

"Looking for a yes or no, Doc."

"Well, yes, I guess. You really should rest for at least a f-"

"Can you sign the I-47 so I can get back on rotation?"

"Lo-"

Louise pantomimed a signature with her right index finger; immediately after attempting it with her left, forgetting about the freshly treated gunshot, and having another apoplectic swearing fit.

"I will, I will" Doctor Bergen said, sounding to Louise like he was trying to psych himself up. "Siddown a minute, first."

Louise made a noise somewhere between a loud sigh and a louder grunt. "I really don't have time."

"El Tee, I will write a report that says you have a brain tumor the size of my first apartment, *and* that you spent your entire visit hurling racial epithets at me. You'll be chained to a desk, processing capital expenditure reports until your *grandkids* die of boredom" he said, crossing his arms. "Or you can sit down on that exam table for five minutes."

She sigh-groaned again, plopping down on the table so quickly that she almost slid off the wax paper. The doctor saw her wince.

"Okay. I'm sitting. What's so important?"

Doctor Bergen half-sat on the edge of his desk, reading from the tablet.

"It says that you've lost eight pounds since your last monthly check."

"So?"

"So, you've always hovered around the minimum weight requirement. Now you're five pounds below it. Why is that?"

Louise rolled her eyes. "I've been running more."

"Why?"

"People shooting at you can prompt that."

"That tumor seems to be getting bigger, El Tee."

"I don't know why. Maybe I've skipped some meals? It's hard to keep track. I've just been so busy since the transfer to the Baltimore garrison, I haven't really been keeping track. But I will, scout's honor" she went to raise her hand, but thought better of it. "So—we good?"

"Not yet. How do you like the Baltimore garrison?"

Realizing she wasn't going to be leaving as quickly as she'd hoped, Louise crossed her feet under her knees and leaned forward. She'd never sit like this in front of the other FedCops, but the Doc wouldn't think much of her tendency to sit like a seven-year old. She hoped.

"I like having a command. The subs seem okay. Maybe a little undisciplined."

"Subs?"

"The subordinates. The troops. You've worked for the Federal Police all these years and you don't know what 'subs' means?"

Bergen smiled. "Honestly, I don't get many officers. They usually go to the HQ doctors. I get all the" he pantomimed quotation marks with his fingers, "subs."

"The less time at HQ the better. Plus, you were my dad's doctor, so-" she trailed off.

"Which is part of the reason I'm concerned. Most of the reason. So, the garrison's fine?"

"So far."

"What do you think of the city?"

"Baltimore?"

"No just any random city" he laughed. "But not D.C. I know you *loooove* it here. I've seen all the knick-knacks in your office."

"Well, D.C. is pretty perfect. Orderly. And I was born here, so, you know."

"Yeah, I know. But what about Baltimore?"

"Ugh, honestly?"

"Yes, honestly."

"Baltimore is fucking *gross*. I sort of hate it. Everything's fucking broken, there's vagrants just toddling about the streets, zonked out on who-the-fuck-knows-what. The city council's no fucking help with anything—I think they resent us being there to tell you the truth. I'd ask, but no one ever seems to be in their fucking office, like *ever*. Plus the Proxes; fucking hack amateurs. They're *everywhere*."

"I understand that one of the proxy police agents actually saved you from any further damage."

The lieutenant's face wrinkled. "Is that what they said? I guess you could come to that conclusion. I mean, for sure I'd have made it to the vehicle, got my sidearm and put her down; he just got to it quicker" she paused. "Of course, *he* didn't have a bullet freshly stuck in his cla—-scapula. So he should have been quicker."

Doctor Bergen tilted his head just a bit toward his shoulder. "You didn't have your weapon on you?"

"Oh, don't you start."

He put both his hands up in front of his chest. "Easy, tiger. That's just not like you."

"Yeah, yeah, I know it's not. It's just-the whole scene was weird. Kind of distracting, you know?"

"I heard about the skeleton."

"A skeleton, minus the skull. A booby-trapped, headless skeleton. What the fuck could that be about?"

"No clues?"

"Not really. Anything that was there got vaporized, along with" her voice cracked, just the faintest bit. "Along with Morell and Robeson."

"You want to talk about that?"

"Nope."

"So that's it. A pile of ashes on a dirty street in a shitty town?"

"Yeah, seems that way" she sighed. "Why do you think it's so gross?"

"A lot of those cities are broke, El Tee. Maintenance costs money."

"How'd the whole city go broke?"

"Same way most of them do. People leave. People with money, anyway. So then you get young people, who generally don't have money, and the folks who didn't have money to leave in the first place. Sometimes the young people make more money, but then they split too. The others that weren't so lucky, they get added to the biomass of poor that were there before. Cities survive on taxes. Poor people don't make enough to tax in any significant way. You're a detective: follow it to its most logical conclusion."

"Yeah, well the place is a shithole regardless. But it's my shithole now, I guess. So, if you wouldn't mind signing that there form..."

"Only if you promise to start taking better care of yourself. Make your first stop the commissary, and eat. A whole meal. Like one that an adult would eat."

"Yes, doctor."

"I mean it. I'm going to follow up."

Louise slid off the table one more time, straightening up and saluting with her off-hand. "Yessir!"

Doctor Bergen shook his head and signed off on the form on his tablet. "There you go El Tee. And get a drink with some calories to go with that meal. A big glass of milk. Soda. Anything."

Lieutenant Louise Lloyd saluted again, and started to walk across the office. Just before she got to the door, she stopped; turning around to ask the doctor one last question.

"Hey, I just thought of something. About the case."

"Oh, yeah?"

"Yeah. What do you know about the Glasslands?"

"Same shit everyone does, I guess. Nuclear exchange in the Arabian Penninsula. Turned parts of the deserts in Jordan and Syria into glass. It's got a different name though. Trinitie? Trinite? Something like that. I understand it's a slippery situation."

"Har har."

"Just trying to lighten things up a little. You're such a dour kid, El Tee" he ruffled her too-long-for-her-liking brown hair. "Why do you ask?"

"It's what the Prox said that the shooter said. 'This is for the Glasslands. What do you make of that?"

"Maybe you'll find out while you're cleaning up your shithole."

"Yeah" she said, returning to command posture as soon as she walked out the door, and set out for the aforementioned shithole. She didn't stop at the commissary, promising herself that she'd get something on the way to the garrison.

She didn't do that either.

⊰ ⊱

Shaunn Grulkowski is the creator of Retcontinuum, *several published short stories, and a perpetually annoyed wife*

GRAND FINALE – NATE RAGOLIA

"Are we really going to do this?" she asks, sitting on the edge of the bed. "Right now?"

Standing before her, he loosens his tie and unbuttons his shirt, pacing. He gazes out the window as he passes it. The sky is already turning the burnt color they said it would before it happens. The air outside carries a hint of ozone, which they noticed as they ran from his car to the hotel, but inside the purifiers and fresheners disguise the odor. The room is almost as hot as outside, oppressive, with the smoky smell and taste of a wildfire. The air conditioner blasts vainly as it tries to cool the dry air.

"What else are we going to do?" he asks, dropping the shirt on the floor. "Just sit by and wait?"

She nods. She crosses and uncrosses her bare legs.

"I think I want some more wine," she says, holding up her middling glass.

"Under the circumstances, I don't blame you," he replies.

He leans over and unties his freshly-shined black shoes. She rises from the bed and wrests the wine bottle from its sticky-ringed grip on the end table. She pours the crimson wine, filling her glass nearly to the rim and turns toward him in the center of the room.

He removes his socks and unbuckles his belt.

"You want any?" she asks him.

"No," he replies. He draws a flask from his pocket and nurses at it like a child. "This is fine."

Their hotel room is beautiful, filled with yellow light that's slowly turning orange. Like the news said. More expensive than anywhere they've ever shared before. Than they could have afforded under the normal circumstances. One of the benefits of most people staying home with their loved ones in times like these. A crystal chandelier looms over the center of the room, a reminder of what would be lost. The art on the walls is tasteful, and well done. The king-sized bed is cloud-like. The windows look out over the city, its brilliant gasp of humanity that once seemed so permanent. The room smells clean, but aromatic in a way that was carefully designed.

"We don't have much time," he says, removing his undershirt and pants.

"I know," she replies. "This is just so strange. I don't know how to get in the mood like this."

"Because it's the only thing we can do," he says sternly, stepping out of his boxer shorts.

She looks at him, bare and dangling, through the curvature of her wine glass. The refraction changes his familiar anatomy into something out of a funhouse. She laughs. The laugh surprises her, given the occasion, but she chooses to embrace it.

"What?" he asks.

"Oh," she replies. "The wine is kicking in."

He nods.

"You're beautiful," he says. "There's a part of me that can't believe this is all happening. I wish this could be more romantic."

She finishes her glass of wine and sets it down. "Don't we both." She lifts her left foot and removes her shoe. She tips and sways, gathering her balance, then she takes the other shoe and drops it on the floor. She feels a low rumble in the floor beneath her feet. If it weren't one of the precursors, she'd almost enjoy the sensation on her toes.

"I thought that we'd at least get dinner or see a movie or something," she says. "I don't like clichés. I don't know why I fantasize about them."

"We could try room service," he says. "But I don't think they're still here. There was a vending machine in the hallway..."

She shakes her head, and walks toward him. "Just help me with this," she says, lifting her hair off of her neck, exposing the hooks at the back of her dress.

He obliges her, carefully tracing the length of her neck before taking the clasp between thumb and forefinger and releasing it.

She turns and dress drops around her to the floor. Its cerulean shimmer looks like an isolated Caribbean island pool, almost unearthly in its beauty.

"Thank you," she says.

She steps toward him and puts her hand on his chest. "I'm sorry for saying this was a stupid idea earlier."

He shakes his head. "It's okay. I probably could have packaged it better. I'm usually not lost for words. It's just–everything."

"This is a once-in-a-lifetime kind of thing," she replies.

He nods.

She reaches behind her back and unhooks her bra. With slumped shoulders, she lets the article fall to the floor. Then she leans forward and lowers her underwear over her hips and down her legs, stepping out of them with smooth precision.

"There," she says, walking toward him. "Now we're even."

"Wait right there," he says.

She stops and looks at him quizzically.

"I just want to look at you, all of you, while I can."

She smiles. "That's a good idea." She looks him over, too.

They stand a few feet apart and they just look at each other. The light from outside bathes her in gold. She is, at last, the thing of bygone cultures, a myth of beauty, shimmering before him. He studies the smooth curve of her clavicle, the gentle arc of her hips, the flow of her chest as she inhales, exhales, living, still living. She admires his shoulders, the subtle cut where his hips meet his abdomen, and the steady, gentle growth that informs her of his excitement.

Why do we desire to keep things most when we know we cannot?

He looks at her face, the gentle point to her nose, the softness of her ears–adorned with hoops, the sweet knowing half-smile that comprises her resting mouth. She focuses on his eyes, their blueness, their sensitive sureness mixed with fear. She reads the things he won't share in them, and knowing that he's scared too eases her mind.

Without words they step toward each other. They kiss. He wraps his arm around her lower back and pulls her close. Their tongues meet, tangle, untangle... Breathe. His arm slides up her back to her neck. She glides her fingers over his chest. He kisses her neck, her shoulders, and her breasts. She feels him throb and press against her.

The city outside glows. The golden luster gives way to orange.

A distant siren howls, muffled by the room's windows. They don't bother to look outside.

"Hurry," she says. "We don't have much time left."

"I know," he replies.

They move over to the bed, still entangled, still kissing. She lies down on the soft white sheets, grasping for him, as he lowers himself over her. Their tongues tangle again as he enters her.

She gasps, quivers, and moans.

He releases a held breath.

The siren gets louder.

The orange light grows thick, deep, red. It's a kind of darkness they have never seen before.

"Look," she says, her gaze drawn to the window. "It's almost beautiful."

He turns, still moving inside her. "Yeah. Almost."

He looks at her, takes her face in his hands and kisses her.

They find a rhythm into which the siren disappears. They only hear each other, their cries and their demands.

"Harder," she says.

And he obliges.

"Here, get on top," he says.

And she does.

Their eyes are locked on one another's. Their bodies joined. They move together like an ocean wave, like a storm. His fingers move down her back, sending ripples from her skin deep inside her.

The siren bellows.

It's deafening.

The light all but disappears, only dark scarlet shadows mixed with beads of delicate sun.

"It's happening," she says. "Faster. I'm almost there."

He leans into her neck and kisses her, his hips thrust, meeting her as she rises and falls atop him. He holds her, cups under her with his hands and turns them back over. He thrusts more, faster, harder. She moans. He breathes heavy.

The siren screams.

The sky rolls with fire.

The last thing he hears is her cry as she comes.

The last thing she hears is his breath stifle, his gentle satisfied grunt.

The asteroid's impact sends a tsunami of fire through the sky. Powerful shockwaves rip through the buildings, leveling them to nothing, casting impermeable shrouds of dust and ash into the sky.

They are lucky ones. Him and her. Their bodies, entwined, connected, and flayed by fire and sheer power. They don't feel it. They don't have to look at the desiccation outside. They don't have to crawl weak and terrified from some lucky, hiding place amid the wreckage.

They are skeletons, somewhat charred, posed in their final bond.

They have no need for the world any longer, or its endings.

Cₒₛ ₛₒ

Nate Ragolia is the author of There You Feel Free; *a novella. Creator of the* Illiterate Badger *and* Lark & Robin *web comics, and occasional chatterer on music, film, &c.*

DEATH AND THE MAIDEN – PAM JONES

Here's Edie in a yellow dress.

It must have been May Day, I'm not anywhere in sight, being born in June. You can see the Morris dancers and the galloping Hobby Hosses in the street, fuzzily. They are jerky, skeletons of rough wood under papier-mache painted black and goggling white, manes of yarn, and capes of black tarpaulin. They have the legs of men, just recognizably human enough to scare the hell out of you.

Edie is trying to get her mouth around the bulb of a popsicle, cherry, so that its juices smear across her mouth like the lipstick Big Sister wears but isn't allowed to. Big Sister must not have been watching, or she'd have made sure those little red drops hadn't fallen and stained Edie's yellow dress. The Hobby Hosses look hungry. Edie swears that's what she heard the Old Hoss tell her, under the wheeze of accordions.

Edie, a year to the day later and wearing the same dress (a bit tighter), kneels over a bassinette with a mummy inside: me. I'm bawling under the corduroy overalls, the blue socks that soak in baby's sweat, the brown leather booties that rub my heels, and the blue cap that someone stuck on with the visor in the back. Edie's hair isn't completely blonde if she stands at this angle, the strands at her left temple turn a deeper gold in this blend of sun and shadow, and she's struggling with the French braid that Big Sister has wound her hair into. Gran, though you can't see her, waves her spotted hands and tells Edie to stop chewing on the end of her braid. *Come here and let me put your hair up; I've got some pins somewhere...* Edie—lip out— whines that it hurts the top of her head.

You'll turn into a horse, chewing like that.

The Hobby Hosses, far away but alert, raise their heads. Blue Ribbon Hoss, on the left, bares his teeth and Old Hoss, still going strong on the right, fixes Edie with a bulbous eye. There's a spark there that bounces from the height of the sun to the metal of Gran's pins.

The Hobby Hosses whinny. Edie opens her mouth, a red hole of a scream that no one seems to hear.

Another year. I've outgrown the corduroys, which is why my cousin Anthony is wearing them. There's Edie, and there's me, flanking the bassinette, Edie on the right in the yellow dress and me on the left in khakis. We're fidgeting in our casual best. There's a tag in the dress that itches to bite and I reach to scratch, while Edie tugs at her collar. Mama asks us if we can hold still.

I jog to our usual spot by the Big Tree. It's actually not the tallest tree, but it's got the lowest and thickest branches of them all. That way, Edie says, we can see the street and hide if we need to. Behind us you can see the green whirl of the spriggans decked in ivy to hide their ugliness, slobbering at the tail end of the Morris dancers, whom you know are hurling sweets into the crowd as we speak.

I'm torn.

It's not that I don't remember the Hobby Hosses: Black bulbs for eyes and lips that curve to show bigger teeth than you can imagine any animal to have, aren't things that you forget.

I have to ask, Why am I supposed to be afraid of them?

Edie frowns. She is not supposed to be here. She knows that, the Hosses know that.

* * *

My friend Micah from school has a fistful of sweets, collected from the Morris dancers. You can't see what kinds he has, but I remember: Snickers and Jolly Ranchers, peanut butter cups, and those special chocolates with fruit in the middle, Edie's favorite. It's Sunday, Micah wears the bowtie he hates with the white button down tucked into his pants. I'm ogling his big candy haul, drooling a little, and Micah is handing me a peanut butter cup because his mother asked him to.

Edie doesn't want anything, not even when I offer her the chocolate with fruit in the middle that Micah gave me. You can see her in the Big Tree. She's straddling the lowest branch, which is canopied by the rest of the tree. All you can really make out of her is a leg.

From far away, a melodeon whinnies.

There are four of them, Old Hoss and Blue Ribbon Hoss leading two bucking Junior Hosses by their reins. The Junior Hosses snort, snuffle, and grunt at the Big Tree, teeth gnashing, more canine than colt and foal. Old Hoss and Blue Ribbon Hoss shush them, but eye the leg that droops from the Big Tree. Her foot, blurred mid-swing, is taut, toes curled, and then flees beneath her dress.

The parade is turning out from under the arch that connects the second floors of the barbershop and bookstore. The procession has transformed anything familiar into a confusion of creatures. Most of the parade is a beautiful deformation of human and animal: Jack-and-the-Green whips a lizard's tail from beneath his vines; the Morris dancers try to keep their beaks in place, and work their way around canary's wings that leak golden feathers into the air; sheepdogs rumble astride motorcycles, and hurl confetti from the shopping bags. Big Sister, in the second row, pumps the buttons of her melodeon with mechanical boredom. Like all the accordionists, she's dressed in choir robes and glittering moth's wings strapped to her back.

The Hobby Hosses tail the procession, the four of them trotting through the arch and whinnying for the pleasure of the crowd. The Junior Hosses flank the company of Old Hoss and Blue Ribbon Hoss, Old on the left, Blue Ribbon on the right. Edie straddles the shoulders of Blue Ribbon Hoss, who has just come into the midday sun. Her yellow dress is gone. She's in a one-piece costume, an old black jumpsuit painted over with bones, tiny ribcage, femurs, the splinters that make her feet and hands. Her face is white with greasepaint, her eyes ringed black.

The hosses have crowned Edie with lilies.

And they are gone.

* * *

To be clear, I've never seen Edie.

I have pieces of her. As I get bigger, so does Edie.

The yellow dress is at the back of Mama's closet, packed away in the box that it came in when Edie was born. Gran bought it a few sizes too big, so that Edie would grow into it as she got older.

I've seen the two good pictures we have of her, the ones that were taken in those two weeks she was alive. There is one that my parents keep of her, a little turnover cramped in the bassinette that I claimed two years later. Gran has a shot of her that must have been taken on the one and only day that they were allowed to bring her home.

But I don't like those photos. Baby Edie reminds me of a special I saw once on the History Channel, about mummies and what you did to keep the body as alive-looking as you could. They talked about a family in Sicily that managed to keep their infant daughter fresh for eighty years.

They said she looked as though she could wake up at any minute.

* * *

You're not allowed to be in the May Day parade until you're at least ten.

I am the tail of the parade, my friend Micah and me, supervised by my dad. My jobs are to rush into the crowd, to burrow my mask into the face of an audience member, to fire webs of Silly String, to hurl sweets when the younger ones start clamoring at the edge of the street. There I am and there's Micah; he's spraying green Silly String into the face of the girl he likes but pretends not to. I'm firing the sweets at the younger ones instead of just tossing them, which makes my dad growl at me from under his mask, *Stop that, you're not bowling!*

Gran asks me to keep my mask on one minute more. I'm sweating beneath the papier-mâché and the black tarpaulin that we've converted into a cape. *Strike a pose! Come on, don't just stand there. Oh, no, no, you should turn around and let me see your tail. Maybe we should get your, what's your friend's name? Mikey?*

The Big Tree has always been wider than it is tall. My mask, nodding toward the bag of leftover sweets from the parade, fixes me with a bulbous eye. Junior Hoss, at least the one that I knew, has been feckless but friendly. He nuzzles the opening of the bag for the special chocolates with fruit in the middle. I have two, they're all his if he wants them. He promises to give them to Edie when he sees her.

ભ જ

Pam Jones lives and writes in Austin, Texas. She studied creative writing at Hampshire College, and is the author of the novella, The Biggest Little Bird.

"For King and country," Vincent said aloud, imagining the medal he would receive upon returning home.

The bombardments ceased, the smoke evaporated. Somehow twilight lingered, longer than it ever had before. Vincent gazed at cherry clouds gliding over a lavender sky. The sun seemed to remain stationery on the horizon, half-obscured by the trench he helped dig.

"Over the top!"

The command echoed throughout the burrow, stinging men's ears as it went. Vincent flung his riffle over the bank before taking hold of a nearby ladder. He felt no such sting.

"For King, country, and me."

The thought of serving King George V willed him onwards, upwards. Retrieving his weapon, he charged forward—encompassed by his comrades—the way lit only by the dying light's embers. The ground—a mire of sludge—battled the soldiers' ankles. Gunfire tore through a tree line ahead—the noise: deafening. Bullets ravaged flesh and bone, men tumbled to the dirt, their faces morphing into masks of anguish. Vincent glanced back, at a trail of death. Sustaining an unwavering pace, fighting muck and lead hail, he left dead friends far behind. Next came the mortars, hurtling from the purple sky, lifting the ground with great explosions, leaving unnatural craters in God's earth and an abnormal white mist above it. Wails zigzagged on the air, the sound of grown men pleading for their lives danced between the eruptions and gunfire.

Vincent carved his way through the white blanket. *Nothing on earth could look so much like heaven but sound so much like Hell,* he thought. He spun on his heels, an automatic motion after months of fighting—the cogs of war—thrusting his rifle into the pearly smog, at a passing shadow. He felt his bayonet snag something, no different than catching a fish on a hook—now to reel it in. A German fell at his boots, with blood stained teeth he jabbered something in that language.

"Shut it," Vincent said, his voice smooth. "Shut your filthy mouth." He yanked his riffle back and stuck the German again, and again—tearing the man's uniform, fraying it into tatters, and collapsing ribs. Vincent stabbed and prodded until his adversary jabbered no more. Proud that he withdrew another German from the world, he continued onwards.

He emerged from the mist, gaining eyes on the tree line. Movement amongst the thicket—German helmets—Vincent eagerly took aim, pulling the trigger... something went wrong. He collapsed, dropping his rifle. A large puddle cushioned the sudden fall. Water rapidly turned red around him, confirming his suspicion—he had been hit, although, he did not know where. Quickening breath, flailing arms, and legs... unresponsive. He waited, reclining in the bloody pool, hoping, and praying for rescue. A melody of whizzing bullets and dwindling screams played away the seconds, minutes—hours. The water ran cold, chilling his bones. He could not comprehend why this was happening to him, for this was not a hero's death. He was fighting for his country, in a foreign land, defending the people of England. This was not how he visualized his life coming to an end.

"For King and country," he whispered once more.

"You're in quite the pickle there, old bean."

The war had grown quiet, and then this: A high-pitched voice shattering the air, startling the soldier after what seemed like an eternity alone.

"Who speaks?" Vincent asked, his speech raspy.

"I do," the voice replied.

Vincent turned his head about, dirt and grim washing over him, the bloody water oozing through his chapped lips.

"I don't see you, friend."

A hand grasped his submerged trouser leg and yanked, hard. "Straight ahead, old bean."

Vincent dug his pruned fingertips into the puddle bed and forced himself to a sitting position, howling in pain at the slightest movement. He could not believe his eyes.

Surely I have succumbed to my wounds or fatigue. This man, no, this creature I see before me can only be a result of exhaustion.

Vincent sat inches away from a skeleton—missing all but torso, right arm, and skull—grinning a toothless grin. Even now the twilight loitered, making the talking carcass appear crimson. The two beings remained silent, neither flinching, nor speaking. The skeleton's blackened eye cavities took hold of Vincent's senses, akin to that of a gas attack. A spider web of tiny cracks ran across each socket, which made the skull appear to be squinting. Blinded by those harrowing hollows, yet unwilling to show fear, the soldier stayed firm. *I have been through worse than this, let the corpse gander,* Vincent thought. Like two swirling black voids they drew him in. His breath accelerated even more, he could feel his heart palpitate, trying to burst through his chest. Gritting his teeth, wrinkling his nose, he felt as if he were falling into the great abyss, into those ethereal eyeholes. At long last, the empty sockets finally drove him over the edge. He tried and tried to get to his feet, exhausting the little energy he had left—but it was to no avail.

"Yes," the skeleton somehow said, despite lacking tongue, teeth, and a beating heart, "You're in quite the pickle there, quite the pickle."

"This is preposterous! How are you able to converse? You are dead, and by the state of what's left of your rotten body, you have been that way for some time."

The skeleton did not respond for a few moments "...I don't know, I just am. How are you able to?"

"What?"

"...Converse?"

Vincent was stunned. "I should be fighting a war, earning a medal, not talking with a corpse. How did my life come to this?"

"I don't know. Life's a funny thing, isn't it, old bean?"

It could have been the irritating creature he sat across from, it could have been his wounds, perhaps the stress. Whatever the reason, the soldier's struggle to breath grew more challenging even still.

"What would you know of life, creature?" Vincent scoffed.

The skeleton swayed gently in the wind. "Why not tell me of life. Moreover, tell me why you are here?"

The query unsettled Vincent, for at that moment he realized he was unsure himself. He drew on his memories, hazy, jaded memories that remained somewhere amongst the fog of war. He recalled eagerly signing up at the behest of Lord Kitchener's recruitment posters. He did not await the draft—he wanted to fight. Yet, he could not remember why. The young private found it odd to be where he now sat: dying in a puddle of his own blood for a purpose that eluded even him, until he thought that phrase—*For King and Country. That's why I came, correct?*

"Well?" his new acquaintance asked impatiently.

With a furrowed brow he dove into the past: A weeping wife waving goodbye, proud parents standing on a doorstep, a farewell feast with old friends, retrieving the King's shilling, swearing to fight for King and country with an upheld hand, and a cramped ferry powering across the English Channel. He could recollect all these things, the when, where, and how, but, try as he might, he could not recover the why.

"My memory escapes me."

The skeleton shook its skull, a faint creek emanating from its neckline. "You don't recall? Look around, old bean, you are in Hell! One would not come here for a trivial purpose, one always has a reason."

Vincent did exactly that. He took note of the sullied water in which he lay, the surreal sky that refused to yield to nightfall, and, above all, he observed his rifle, bayonet protruding from the pool as if it were struggling to breathe itself. The blood-caked blade flung a memory to the forefront of his mind. Closing his eyes, he imagined being somewhere else, some-when else in time. The soldier was no longer a man; he was in a child's body, laughing a cackling, cruel laugh. He was a boy of eight, feet dangling in a calm pond. A small frog sat on his palm, remaining steady as the boy gleefully reached for its reedy legs with a hand that wrenched at the amphibian, ripping limb from body. The power felt magnificent. He tossed the dead animal aside before reaching for another—this time pulling a penknife from his pocket for a novel way to kill.

His eyes burst open.

"That's it!"

"Oh? Have you recovered your memories?" the skeleton asked.

Vincent pictured Kitchener's recruitment posters once more, this time evoking the feeling—the power that child perceived long ago—the why.

"To kill, I came to kill. I held no heroic desires; I did not wish to serve King and country. I came for myself, to take lives... because it feels good."

The sun plummeted from view. The unchanging horizon finally changed, losing its violet color. The clouds peppering the now opaque heavens melted, leaving a stream of red sludge behind them as they began to dribble from view. To Vincent, this skyline appeared akin to that of an artist's ruined painting, watercolors running off canvas.

"What's happening?"

"Hold onto that feeling, old bean—hold on tightly," the skeleton said, "for that's the reason I send you to your eternal damnation."

The mural, high above, erupted with shrieks, louder than thunder, brighter than lightning. Faces materialized within the cloud's dripping tails. He saw the unarmed medic he once gunned down from behind. To the left of him, the downed pilot who dangled helplessly from a tree branch when Vincent took his life with one powerful bayonet plunge. Up from him, his most cherished kill—the boy who wept for mercy in soiled pants, seconds before Vincent carved out his innards. Scrambling for his weapon, water splattering in every direction—the soldier's pain was miraculously gone.

"No, you're dead—you're all dead—I killed you all!" he cried, taking aim at the faces in the sky.

"And so are you, old bean, you died hours ago, before we ever spoke."

"Lies!"

The faces in the sky glared downwards, casting judgment. He knew each one, the day he took their lives, the exact time. He fired, his rifle spat out a spiraling bullet that simply vanished into the night.

The red skeleton's black sockets ignited, becoming imbued with blue flames. It lifted its only arm and pointed with extended finger. Its jaw dropped, the once cheery accent did not emerge but instead a guttural shriek, a horrifying siren rang out, "...Old Bean. Old bean. Old bean." The faces materialized on the water's surface, reflecting from overhead, the rippling liquid seemingly making them smile. Through the undulating puddle they came—dirt-encrusted hands grasping at his bloody legs. "Please, good sir, I can be better—I will be better!" he howled, hammering the aggressive fingers with the butt of his rifle. "I was just jesting, I came to serve King and country... I came for the good people of England. I killed to be a hero!"

"It's too late. You have already killed, for your own self-centered reasons. You did not arrive in these lands believing war was the only way to protect your family, like so many have been foolishly taught. You not did believe your actions were just; you relished every one of your unnecessarily brutal kills. Now your victims will escort you to your afterlife—to your punishment."

The skeleton crumbled into a heap of bones while fervent hands pulled Vincent under the water. Even then he struggled, as his vision blurred beneath the bloodstained pool.

"For King and country," he mumbled, bubbles fizzing from his mouth. He first uttered those words as a lie, but by the time they left his lips, he believed them. The skeleton was correct, he did not come to war believing it was for the greater good, yet he did not arrive with the notion that it was wrong, either. Closing his eyes, he relived everything he had ever killed, from the frog to the man in the fog. *Maybe the world is better off without me.* There was no hope of escape—the puddle had become an ocean—but perhaps he could still reach heaven. He stopped fighting; he relinquished himself to the hands. "For King and country."

* * *

"Vincent!" a lone soldier called out. "John! Marcus! Vincent!" The medic meandered over the rough terrain, struggling to find his way in the darkness. He hated this part—gathering the dead and wounded—for one reason: he did not trust the cease-fire. He was sure they would fire at any—

The man lost his footing, falling face first into a large quagmire. Remerging, he drooled a maroon liquid. The man caught sight of something red glowing in the gloom.

"Hello, old bean, what brings you here?"

ଔ   ଛ

Dean Moses is the author of A Stalled Ox, entertainment contributor for the Spring Creek Sun, wordsmith extraordinaire, and hungry vegan.

JOURNAL OF THE FIGHTING PHANTASM (HARM CITY #3) – SHAUNN GRULKOWSKI

NARRATOR:
Ladies and gentlemen, tonight we present–for the first
time on any wave-length–thrilling adventures in the
life of Bradford Bhuta, the Fighting Phantasm!...by
day, the mild-mannered scion of a digital gossip
empire; but at night, he dons the mystical Cloak of
Charon and sends the evildoers of Baltimore's
underworld into the afterlife. Along with his British
butler and confidant, Alistair Angloman, he wages his
never ending war against scores of criminal
masterminds, the most deadly of which, Herb Taylor:
Warlord of the Orient, continues to escape his grasp.
Tonight's entry in The Journal of The Fighting
Phantasm finds our hero on the scene of an insidious
explosion, his faithful servant in tow. We'll join
them, after a brief word from our sponsor.

COMMERCIAL VO:
Your local Snort n' Blow dealer presents The Fighting
Phantasm. These radio dramatizations are designed to
forcibly demonstrate to old and young alike that crime
does not pay. Before the Phantasm's thrilling adventure
begins, here's a money saving suggestion for every
social substance aficionado. When you go to your local
party dispensary, be sure and insist on Snort n' Blow.
Unlike many other party powders, Snort n' Blow is a
medium, free base ready social substance. It's fine
granules permit more draft, causes it to burn steadily
down to a fine, powdery ash, and give you a more useful
blast, with less post-nasal drip. You'll find that
Snort n' Blow chops better, gives you longer euphoric
period, and requires less suction. So order your supply
tomorrow, insist on Snort n' Blow for better results at
less cost this summer!

FIGHTING PHANTASM:
Well, my faithful servant: it appears that the
perpetrator, or perpetrators of this heinous act have
long since absconded, as have any Law Enforcement.

ALISTAIR ANGLOMAN:
Hmm. Yes, quite.

THE FIGHTING PHANTASM:
Perhaps a thorough investigation of the immediate area
will reveal some insight as to who might have
perpetrated such a dastardly deed as this!

ALISTAIR ANGLOMAN:
Hmm.

THE FIGHTING PHANTASM:
That's the spirit, my virtuous valet! Come, let us
make our approach.

FX:
two sets of footsteps, normal pace; then stop

THE FIGHTING PHANTASM:
There appears to be some type of residue here. And
something else, something like...glass? But it
seems...different somehow. Alistair, do you see it?

ALISTAIR ANGLOMAN:
Hmm, yes. Perhaps you should place some of it into the
analyzer.

THE FIGHTING PHANTASM:
Bah! Your reliance on technology is your greatest
weakness, my friend! The Cloak of Charon provides me
with twelve-dimensional sight! That will reveal the
nature of the substances to us.

FX:
stock mystical sounds

ALISTAIR ANGLOMAN:
Er, so...

THE FIGHTING PHANTASM:
Well, ah, it would appear that there is a, um, quantum conflagration in the ninth dimension that is obscuring my spectral vision. I could solve the issue, of course, but for expediency's sake, maybe we should use the analyzer.

ALISTAIR ANGLOMAN:
For expediency.

THE FIGHTING PHANTASM:
Yes, Alistair. For expediency. This one time. Next time, twelve-dimensional sight.

ALISTAIR ANGLOMAN:
Yes, of course.

THE FIGHTING PHANTASM:
So stop faffing about, and give me the analyzer.

ALISTAIR ANGLOMAN:
Yes, sir.

THE FIGHTING PHANTASM:
Thank you. Seriously, though, just this one time. After this, until our crusade against crime is complete, we're using the cloak. I mean it.

ALISTAIR ANGLOMAN:
Understood, sir.

THE FIGHTING PHANTASM:
If you'll hand me the evidence tweezers...thank you, I'll insert a sample of the glass-substance into the-

ALISTAIR ANGLOMAN:
It just goes in the bottom there, sir.

THE FIGHTING PHANTASM:
Yes, clearly I know where it goes, thank you. It's just, oh, damn it. Here, you do it.

ALISTAIR ANGLOMAN:
Of course, sir.

THE FIGHTING PHANTASM:
It's just that the Gloves of Gration make tasks like
this a bit fiddly. Plus, you need to serve some kind
of purpose being out here. No sense in you just
standing around lollygagging.

ALISTAIR ANGLOMAN:
Agreed, sir. Hmm, there we are. Just need to set the
analyzer for solid matter, and

FX:
old-timey computer sounds

ANALYZER:
ANALYZING! ANALYZING! ANALYZING! ANALY- SUBSTANCE
IDENTIFIED.

THE FIGHTING PHANTASM:
Well?

ALISTAIR ANGLOMAN:
According to the analyzer, this is a piece of
trinitite.

THE FIGHTING PHANTASM:
Trinitite! Of course! That's what I thought it may be.
Excellent work, my faithful friend.

ALISTAIR ANGLOMAN:
What is that?

THE FIGHTING PHANTASM:
What is what?

ALISTAIR ANGLOMAN:
Trinitite. What is it?

THE FIGHTING PHANTASM:
It's...doesn't it say on the analyzer?

ALISTAIR ANGLOMAN:
No, you have to press a separate key. Just give me the
gist.

THE FIGHTING PHANTASM:
Well, it's a glass-like substance that comes from...is

it volcanoes? I think it's...no, not volcanoes. I
can't...You know, it's been a while since geology
class, old friend. Perhaps you should key the
analyzer.

ALISTAIR ANGLOMAN:
Yes, of course. Just as a refresher.

THE FIGHTING PHANTASM:
I would have expected that to go without saying, but
yes. Obviously.

ANALYZER:
Trinitite, also known as atomsite, is the glassy
residue left on the desert floor after a
plutonium-based nuclear bomb detonation.

THE FIGHTING PHANTASM:
Nuclear explosion, yes. See, that's why I thought
volcano, because of the explosion. Explosion, eruption,
they're basically the same thing. I mean, really.

ALISTAIR ANGLOMAN:
Damn identical, sir.

THE FIGHTING PHANTASM:
Completely. So...nuclear, eh? Looking around, it seems
highly unlikely that there was a large enough nuclear
explosion on this street to result in trinitite
formation. Certainly the locals would have noticed
something like that, right?

ALISTAIR ANGLOMAN:
A nuclear bomb detonating? One would assume, sir.

THE FIGHTING PHANTASM:
Exactly! So, one would also assume that this
particular artifact did not originate, but was most
like transported here, somehow, wouldn't you say?

ALISTAIR ANGLOMAN:
I'd say that was quite an astute observation, sir.

THE FIGHTING PHANTASM:
Thank you, Alistair. Now: equally important, but not

quite as obvious questions: how was it transported? And from where?

ALISTAIR ANGLOMAN:
Transferred from a shoe, perhaps?

THE FIGHTING PHANTASM:
Hahaha, my dim friend. This fragment is far too large to have been stuck in a shoe. Unless...is it possible,however unlikely, that this piece of trinitite was carried here on the boot of a nuclearly-altered, gigantic super mutant?

ALISTAIR ANGLOMAN:
Beg pardon?

THE FIGHTING PHANTASM:
Think about it, my dim disciple! Could not the awesome, unbridled power of the split atom turn ordinary people into colossal monsters of the Nuclear Age?

ALISTAIR ANGLOMAN:
Er,

THE FIGHTING PHANTASM:
And then, wouldn't it follow that said monsters could loose themselves upon an unsuspecting world? Living only to wreak havoc?

ALISTAIR ANGLOMAN:
Well,uh,yes? I suppose?

THE FIGHTING PHANTASM:
You damn well better suppose. In fact, record that on the theories journal.

ALISTAIR ANGLOMAN:
Of course, sir.

THE FIGHTING PHANTASM:
Like, towards the top. No, not at the top; I said close to the top. Very distinct difference. We can't put it at the very top, not yet. We still have investigating to do. It wouldn't be very detectively to

just run willy-nilly with the first theory you have.
No matter how compelling that theory may be.

ALISTAIR ANGLOMAN:
Very good, sir. Shall I place it in the third position
from the top?

THE FIGHTING PHANTASM:
Well now we're just getting into semantics, Alistair.
Put it wherever you like.

ALISTAIR ANGLOMAN:
Yes sir.

THE FIGHTING PHANTASM:
But not at the top. Or second from the top.

ALISTAIR ANGLOMAN:
So, third from the top then, sir?

THE FIGHTING PHANTASM:
Alistair! I trust you to make mundane administrative
decisions. It lightens the load from my already
overtaxed crime-fighting cranium. Must I take over your
duties as well, and overburden myself further?

ALISTAIR ANGLOMAN:
Of course not, sir. Forgive my incompetence.

THE FIGHTING PHANTASM:
Hahaha, think nothing of it. Now, as for alternate
theories: we need to research places where there have
been humongous nuclear explosions. Recently. Ask the
analyzer where the trinitite may have originated.

ALISTAIR ANGLOMAN:
Well, ehm, the only recent atomic-

THE FIGHTING PHANTASM:
Alistair?

ALISTAIR ANGLOMAN:
Yes, sir?

THE FIGHTING PHANTASM:
I believe I said to ask the machine.

ALISTAIR ANGLOMAN:
But, sir

THE FIGHTING PHANTASM:
There's a reason we spent so much money on the analyzer.

ALISTAIR ANGLOMAN:

...

THE FIGHTING PHANTASM:
Alistair, the Analyzer is a highly-technical device meant to, uh, analyze things. You're just a valet.

ALISTAIR ANGLOMAN:
Of course, sir.

THE FIGHTING PHANTASM:
A damn good valet, though. Like if they had an olympics for valets, I'm sure you'd medal. Well, at least top 5, depending on which nations are sending competitors.

ALISTAIR ANGLOMAN:
Mmm, thank you, sir. And I'd be positively thrilled to ask the analyzer. However, That's not a function that this particular machine possesses.

THE FIGHTING PHANTASM:
How do you mean?

ALISTAIR ANGLOMAN:
Well, It's just that the analyzer can only determine what an object is, not speculate on its origin.
However, I can tell-

THE FIGHTING PHANTASM:
How do you know?

ALISTAIR ANGLOMAN:
Know what?

THE FIGHTING PHANTASM:
That it can't tell you where it may have come from. The Cloak of Charon could. Usually. Well, not usually.

It always can, when there isn't some kind of issue with...you know what I mean.

ALISTAIR ANGLOMAN:
Yes, of course. But I did use these analyzers quite a bit in Her Royal-

THE FIGHTING PHANTASM:
I still feel like you should try to use the analyzer.

ALISTAIR ANGLOMAN:
Sir, I

THE FIGHTING PHANTASM:
Alistair...

ALISTAIR ANGLOMAN:
(sighs) Very well, sir. (imitates computer noises and voice) ANALYZING...ANALYZING...ANALYZING Ah!

THE FIGHTING PHANTASM:
Yes?

ALISTAIR ANGLOMAN:
Well, eh, according to the analyzer, there is a, uh, 98% probability that the trinitite came from either Syria or Jordan. Of course! See, I told you the analyzer would be able to process a simple request, Alistair.

ALISTAIR ANGLOMAN:
Correct as usual, sir.

THE FIGHTING PHANTASM:
Don't feel so badly, chum. I'm sure the inferior equipment in the sissy Royal Intelligence Service wouldn't have done it, but here, in America, we don't tolerate that kind of slipshod craftsmanship. Now, one more piece of the puzzle: the white residue. Why don't you take a small amount of it from the Gloves of Gration and put it in the analyzer as well? Or do you think it won't process that either?

ALISTAIR ANGLOMAN:
Oh, I wouldn't dream of thinking, sir.

THE FIGHTING PHANTASM:
Now, that's the spirit!

FX:
stock computer noises

ANALYZER:
ANALYZING...ANALYZING...ANALYZING...ANAL

ALISTAIR ANGLOMAN:
Hmm, interesting.

THE FIGHTING PHANTASM:
What's interesting? Spit it out, man!

ALISTAIR ANGLOMAN:
According to the device, the substance is most likely
white-phosphorus.

THE FIGHTING PHANTASM:
Yes, that is interesting. But, why?

ALISTAIR ANGLOMAN:
Mmm, just a supposition, but judging from the little we
know about what transpired here, it is possible, if not
likely that the white phosphorus is from some type of
explosive; a bomb, or grenade, or the like.

THE FIGHTING PHANTASM:
Well, obviously that. But interesting how else?

ALISTAIR ANGLOMAN:
Well, those types weapons come from very few sources
these days.

THE FIGHTING PHANTASM:
Go on.

ALISTAIR ANGLOMAN:
Sources like multi-national corporations,

THE FIGHTING PHANTASM:
Yes.

ALISTAIR ANGLOMAN:
Sources like evil multi-national corporations.

THE FIGHTING PHANTASM:
Right. Evil multi-national corporations who-

ALISTAIR ANGLOMAN:
Evil, muti-national corporations that start with Tay-

THE FIGHTING PHANTASM:

TAYLORCORP! Of course! And Syria and Jordan are IN THE ORIENT!

ALISTAIR ANGLOMAN:
Well, technically they're in Asia, so...yes?

THE FIGHTING PHANTASM:
Ha! Turns out I didn't need the Cloak of Charon, or the analyzer after all! It's clear that my fiendish arch-nemesis, Herb Taylor, Warlord of the Orient is behind this perfidious profanity!

ALISTAIR ANGLOMAN:
Certainly worth a look, sir.

THE FIGHTING PHANTASM:
You're damn right it is, Angloman. Hell, it's likely that Taylorcorp is manufacturing Super Mutants as we speak!

ALISTAIR ANGLOMAN:
It's a damned certainty, sir.

THE FIGHTING PHANTASM:
What are you waiting for? To the Phantasmobile! Who knows what sickening scheme he-wait. Did you hear that?

ALISTAIR ANGLOMAN:
Hmm, there appears to be an interloper approaching.

THE FIGHTING PHANTASM:
Probably one of Taylor's assassins coming to clean up the mess. Ha! Well the Pistols of Perseus will make short work of them!

FX:
Pistol Shots

LOUISE LLOYD:
(from distance) MotherFUCKER!

NARRATOR:
Will The Fighting Phantasm finally capture his nemesis,
Herb Taylor: Warlord of the Orient? Will The mystery of
the Unhinged, Agendaless Nuclear Super Mutant be
solved? Will Lieutenant Lloyd recover from a second
gunshot wound in as many days? Find out in the next
episode of THE JOURNAL OF THE FIGHTING PHANTASM,
brought to you by Nate's Rags to Rinses
Laudromat-Automat. Get down to Nate's and wash your
rags and grab a hot meal, you filthy, starving
bastards.

଼ ଽ

*Shaunn Grulkowski is the creator of Retcontinuum, several published short
stories, and a perpetually annoyed wife.*

THERE IS A LIGHT THAT NEVER GOES OUT #1: LUX ET VERITAS – MIKEY SIVAK

Ronjo slouched, made a broad poke at the fire with the seedy end of a dead grass sprig then pulled the little flame back to light the waded tobacco in the bowl of his calabash pipe. Beneath his heavy brow black eyes glared menace but then slipped quickly, their focus shifting from Aaron to a dark spot among the flickering trees, where presumably something like memory could drift past. Aaron tried not to look at him directly, but inspected his visage sidewise, wondering what the beast was thinking and anxious not to raise his ire.

At the fire's other side, Osgood was snoring uneasy. His white-whiskered jaw chewed erratically and now and then he lifted an unconscious arm and slowly swatted at nonexistent insects his mind had placed dancing in the eddy of his phlegmy, emphysemic exhalations. A canvas satchel sat heavy across Aaron's lap and he pressed his palms down upon its flat upper plane. He rocked his legs, raising and dropping them gently beneath the bag's weight and thought *I should toss it into the flames. Watch it burn in the night.* But he did not destroy it.

Inside the bag was a large book, a first edition of Thoreau's *Walden* Aaron had that afternoon lifted from beneath a heavy glass cube atop a cherrywood pedestal in the center of the dusty library of a hilltop manor house that stood empty and undisturbed amidst a field of meter-tall grass and car-sized meteorite fragments.

They'd approached the house with caution. Spending the better part of an hour in a genuflecting position behind an ancient and mossy stone wall. Osgood knelt motionless, watched the building through a pair of high-power binoculars. Aaron stood beside him, scrutinizing the old man's face for signs of trouble. Behind them, upon a tangled mass of last season's still-dormant bittersweet, Ronjo reclined, foot upon knee, wrist behind head, picking his teeth with a twig he spun between the long gnarled fingers of his other hand. Being an ape, he was less susceptible though not one-hundred-percent invulnerable to the zombie infection.[1] Ronjo was quicker, stronger, and meaner than men, living or dead. So, his natural tendency to act as rearguard while stationary was tactically beneficial. During movement was a different story however. Though he would frequently amble, hanging back and with nonchalance at Aaron and Oswald's walking pace, oftentimes he would disappear into the branches of trees or underbrush unseen and unheard. Though if any sign of danger appeared, so would Ronjo, almost immediately, as he had been there, above or beside them, like some apish phantom, all along.

Though mid-afternoon and spring, summer was still a ways off, and the air was not yet warm. Clouds moved across the blue sky like cows on a hillside, one or another of them passing slowly before the sun for minutes at a time, cooling things further, and inducing some quiet sadness over everything. Aaron watched their shadows move across the landscape, the overgrown pastures, and little white specks that were country houses here and there on the distant hills. A meadowlark zipped from behind them, a little flash of yellow, over the ancient wall between them and the field and down into the grass twenty or so feet away. It perched, for a moment, upon something rusty in the grass, vocalized a pleasant lazy song, then took off again like a dart toward and past the house in the field. Aaron had done well, these past months, to shed most emotion. But in this moment it occurred to him that in little points in time such as this, in the quiet outside and beyond humanity, is always some soft sadness. Even before the end came, especially as a child, he'd noticed it. On early-autumn mornings while waiting for the school bus. Or watching, from his second-floor childhood bedroom window, as the girl across the street posed for photos on the steps of her family's home with her prom date, Sophocles the hamster running to nowhere endlessly on the squeaky exercise wheel in its cage. At the funeral of his grandfather, in the cemetery, beneath a sky with clouds like these ones. His mother's boney fingers squeezing his small child's hand. The smell of the grave dirt and the people. His half brother, ten years his senior and all but a stranger, on the grave's other side, alone and away from the family, straight-faced and silent as a stream of tears ran down his cheeks from beneath Ray-Ban sunglasses. Squirrels in the graveyard. Leaves on the grass. Seagulls circling above the McDonald's across the road. He wouldn't think about Emmie and that time they sat in the bleachers of the high school near her house. How the sun was setting, and you could hear children in the distance playing. How she said she was pregnant but wanted an abortion because she didn't love him really and they needed to break up. How he said okay.

Little birds flew in and out from beneath the eaves of the house's roof and at the other end of the field a doe and its fawn moved noiseless and unworried.

Houses could be dangerous places, especially rich ones such as this. Sometimes people chose them as spots to stay in, perhaps drawn to the magnificence that had eluded them before what most called *The Rapture* but which held little similarity to the Biblical prophesy.[2] For this reason smart ones knew such places were not safe. Just as they knew, unless one joined some kind of guild or encampment clan, moving was better than "moving in." For the things that attracted you would draw others as well. Or, they would come because if they knew a group had settled, there would be things there they could take, namely any food, women, children or animals. And of course, regardless of what there was to take, the men would certainly not be left alive.

Though less dangerous than living men, zombies could smell a settlement as well. Stay in any spot too long and they would inevitably begin to appear. One at a time at first then in increasing numbers like proverbial moths to a literal flame. There was something about fire, and the other accouterments of human life that seemed, more than anything else, to attract them. It was as if this was the true thing they sought. Aaron thought about it sometimes. Perhaps these things still somehow represented for them the things they had lost.

Aaron had seen people consumed by *the horde*. Each time he sensed this strange, abysmal, existential sadness in the dead ones. As if, they fed not for hunger but compulsion, like some ouroboros thing, with the self being consumed their humanity. It was impossible though to ever know what, if anything, went on in their brains. Unless, of course, you became one of them. But this was something most people, upon infection, made sure did not come to pass. Most bullet holes you saw in skulls now were self-inflicted.[3]

When Osgood said *alright* Ronjo rolled over, pushed himself up to hop the wall and walk across the field erect like a man. It was still disquieting for Aaron to watch the ape move in this manner. Not so much because it seemed unnatural for a Chimpanzee to do so but because he looked so normal doing it. Together with his near bald scalp and habit of wearing a baggy military surplus field jacket and burlap satchel strung across his wide chest, the upright locomotion made Ronjo appear downright human. His quiet thoughtful nature only added to the effect. And it was these human qualities that caused Aaron to fear him most. The volatility of an animal was something Aaron could steel himself against, but an ape that seemed to think and act like a man was a thing to fear and dread (especially in a strange time where men wandered with the aimless savage brutality of rabid animals). Where animal behavior could be deciphered, human actions often seemed sans logic. And recently Aaron had become aware of Ronjo's strange glances. Aaron could not make out meaning. Mostly it was the lack of readability that worried Aaron, and on more than one occasion he had roused from his sleep in the night to see Ronjo crouched beyond the fire, watching him where he lay. Clearly, the ape had lived among men long enough to learn one thing well; the more you allow your thoughts and feelings to be known, the more these things can be capitalized upon. Ronjo kept these things mostly to himself, but as the weeks progressed, Aaron could sense a veiled smoldering, and he decided it best to grant him as much leeway as possible. But he feared the unavoidable moment when the ape would finally test him, and then he would have to make a choice, stand up to a brute equal to himself in height and weight but with three times the strength or admit subservience to a pipe-smoking circus freak. He knew himself well enough to know which he would choose.

Aaron prepared for a rifle report, the sight of Ronjo felled in his steps, but none came. Instead, the chimp made it safe to the house, then with no more effort then it would have taken Aaron to scale a handicap ramp, Ronjo pulled himself up the building's ornate façade, arm over arm. He inspected the perimeter, as was established protocol for such situations, looking down into windows, scanning the horizon, and such. Finally he made his way up a brick parapet and sat. He pulled a windproof lighter from the jacket pocket and lit his pipe. The wisp of smoke was the sign and Osgood dropped his binoculars to his neck, lifted a hand to Ronjo, who waved back disinterestedly. *Let's go*, Osgood said to Aaron as he packed away his binoculars then removed his nylon flight jacket and folded it into his knapsack.

In the field, Aaron made it a point to walk past the spot where the meadowlark had landed earlier, to see what it was it had landed upon. In the grass lay an old and rusted robot, forgotten and inoperable like some ancient plow half-buried in the scrub and the soil. It clutched something to its chest, a small skeleton about the size of a cat or a human infant, like some obscene parody of the Pompeii dead. He did not look long enough to tell what kind of bones they were.

Inside the house the three split up. Ronjo dragged a duffle and found the pantry, filling the bag with canned foods. Osgood searched elsewhere, looking for tools and supplies that might prove useful on the trip South through the backwoods of Maine. It was best to avoid motorized transportation, being loud and requiring fuel. The latter brought you into populated places. It was better to move on foot. Travel slowly, steadily, away from places more likely to encounter other men.

While Ronjo and Oswald scavenged for necessary things, it was understood that Aaron could do as he pleased, and as usual, he sought out the library. It was strange and invalid behavior he undertook without any true zeal. It was a remnant and a vague compulsion, but one he seemed unable to shake nonetheless.

The library doors were large and wooden, with handles and hinges of wrought iron like shackles. Each of the two doors was inscribed with a word: upon one *Lux*, the other *Veritas*. Aaron reached over his shoulder, slid his fingers into his satchel and grasped the taped handle of a sawed-off pool cue. He held the cue above his head with one hand the pushed the doors open slowly with the other and entered cautiously until he was sure there was no one inside. The walls were bookshelves stacked tight with hundreds of volumes from the dark hardwood floorboards to the ornate plaster ceiling no less then twenty feet overhead. The racks on the far wall were broke by two floor-to-ceiling windows with center portions of stained glass upon which were again inscribed *Lux* and *Veritas*. Before the window marked Veritas was a small wooden table beside a large oxblood leather chair facing out toward the high lawn. From the entryway Aaron could make out the cuff of a silk robe, from beneath which poked a decrepit, bony hand. His heart skipped a beat despite himself. It was unlikely this was a zombie. They never sat.

Aaron stepped forward cautiously nonetheless; ran his had across the leather spines of the library's many fine books, thick wads of dark grey dust collecting at his fingertips, and slowly moved along the room's perimeter toward the dead man. It was all there, every great work of human Literature, stacked upon the racks of a single tall wall. Upon the next were the great books of Philosophy, and the next of Mathematics and Science. The implications were not lost upon him and had the experience been new, Aaron might have lost control of his senses for a moment. He had in the past, in similar instances. But he had reached the shaky conclusion that romanticism, like sentimentality, had become obsolete.

Aaron approached the dead man, poked the wrist with his pool cue. Nothing. He placed his palm upon the high back of the leather chair and stood for a moment beside it and looked out at the lawn and the hills: the man's final image. He tried to imagine the scene. Trimmed, healthy grass, full green trees. Perhaps it was that last summer before that yearlong winter. Perhaps grasshoppers were still flitting, little yellow butterflies flapping. Maybe birds zipped over the lawn and into the trees. Or maybe it was autumn, the black sky, the underside of smoke clouds painted orange with the blazing flames of countryside fires. Or maybe it was later, a time when hordes of choking men clamored like barbarians up the lawn, machetes and hatchets in hand to take the manor and kill anyone living inside its walls. Or maybe he had made it to the aftertime, the precarious new spring, the quiet, the wandering dead.

He looked down and saw the dead man, all beef jerky across bones. Long teeth like a hare's forming a ludicrous grimace, poking between mummified lips split and twisted like hemp twine. The paisley patterned silk robe still shown glossy through accumulated dust. Aaron touched the dead man's wire-haired scalp, palm cupped and downward facing, as if touching the head of some infant or catatonic grandfather. Beneath the robe the dead man appeared to be nude save a tarnished silver chain around his neck from which hung at the clavicle a sterling locket, in the shape of a book. It was engraved:

L + V

The man's eyes were gone, and the sockets were matte black and soulless like the eyes of a shark. Aaron crouched down before him. Lifted the locket off his chest. Went to open it, but stopped. Placed it back where it hung.

120

The man's other hand rested in a loose fist at his chest, and Aaron could see that it held a small brown glass vial. Aaron plucked it out with his fingers. A yellow paper label had been affixed to its surface with clear box tape, and upon the slip was a hand drawn image, a skull and crossbones, with x'ed out eyes and a little tongue that hung down from the upper jaw. Inside the bottle was a small pill-shaped object. Aaron jiggled the bottle. The pill bounced in a way that led Aaron to conclude it was mostly hollow and coated with something like rubber. Suicide pill, probably a glass ampoule filled with something like cyanide. He slid the vial in his pants pocket, touched the man's shoulder.

At the center of the library were four wooden pedestals, each topped with a glass cube housing a single book. At first glance it was easy to see that three of the four were leather bound, quite old but in good condition, while the fourth was a worn comic book. The three older volumes were displayed with covers open to title pages, which read respectively: *Philosophiae Naturalis Principia Mathematica* by Sir Isaac Newton, Dante's *Inferno* illustrated by William Blake, and *Walden*, by Henry David Thoreau. The fourth book appeared to be a Soviet bootleg of the Silver Age Comic book, Empire Comics' *Amazing Adventures #13*, badly worn. It's cover (famously featuring the first appearance of Amazing Boy[4]) had begun to disintegrate, and been reassembled sloppily with scotch tape (*FR /GD 1.5 condition probably, GD- 1.8 at best*). The four pedestals formed a cross, and Aaron stood at the center, spun slowly, looking at each of the books in turn and contemplated their presence and the implications of each.

Soon, there was a creak at the door and Aaron turned to see Osgood's head and right shoulder leaning in from the hall. "Time to get moving," he said, then held up a hunting rifle he must have found somewhere in the house. "Got you a present too," he said, then yanked a small pistol from the knee pocket of his cargo pants. He held it out toward Aaron by the barrel, but pulled it back for a moment when Aaron reluctantly reached out for it.

"We've all been traveling together for a while now. I don't think I need to feel uncomfortable with giving this to you. We're all on the same page, right?"

"Of course," Aaron said, reaching out for the pistol but not really even wanting it.

Osgood handed it off then turned and left the room. Aaron felt the pistol's weight in his palm, then stuck it barrel down at the rear of his waistband as he had see people do on television. He turned and looked back at the dead man for a second when Osgood's voice echoed in from across the hallway, "He's dead. Let's go."

Aaron tipped the glass cube upward, grabbed the Thoreau and slid it into his satchel. He placed the pool cue on the ground beside the pedestal then jogged toward the library doors. When he reached the doors he stopped. Looked back at the cube holding the Russian Amazing Boy, then walked briskly back to it, removing the comic book and sliding it into the satchel as well. He removed a small manila envelope from a group of about ten identical ones from his bag and placed it on the stand where the comic book had been. On the envelope was a pencil sketch of a flower and five leaves: *Isotria medeoloides*. When Aaron finally passed through the front entryway, Osgood and Ronjo were walking toward the hills, already many yards across the tall grass lawn.

---

[1] The cataclysm, when it came, had come and passed quickly, taking almost all the people with it, thereby leaving very few scientists to study all of which had transpired. There was very little science anymore to explain the new reality.

[2] Once, in the early days, having pointed out the inconsistency between the religious prediction and actual reality to an old man in a roman collar who called himself "Dad" and claimed to have formerly been a ordained Catholic Monsignor, the man replied calmly, "You're splitting hairs, kid. Religion has always been more impressionistic than naturalistic. That's something you liberals never understood." Aaron figured the guy did have some kind of a point. But more than that he wondered if it could be said now that liberals were even a thing. Could anything still existent be considered political now that society had dissolved?

[3] At any rate, unlike in the movies, zombies were usually embarrassingly easily dispatched, and unless they caught you with your guard down a zombie "battle" usually was more of a slaughter and those who found themselves involved had mostly come to be so without joy or anger but because they had no choice. Putting down a zombie was, after all, a form of euthanasia. And though there were

some, militia people mostly, who took joy in the killing and even orchestrated zombie hunts, for most the destruction of a so-called zombie was a somber affair. It wasn't easy to forget your mother, or son, or the love of your life was maybe out there somewhere wandering, rotting alive. Which was why though "zombie" had in fact become the standard nomenclature it felt wrong to Aaron to use it. But he usually did. Sentimentality had become a dangerous trait in a time when human emotion was mostly all but vestigial.

[4] Kurtz, Jack. "Amazing Boy!" *Amazing Adventures* #13 (Aug. 1962), Empire Comics.

 CR   SO

Mykl Sivak is a writer and artist unfortunately based in New Haven, Connecticut. His writing and art have appeared in a number of international indie zines, journals, and anthologies. He used to work as an animation artist for a global mass media corporation but he doesn't do that anymore. Mykl is an atheist, a nihilist, and an anarchist, which means he doesn't believe in anything. It is his opinion that you shouldn't either. http://mykls.tumblr.com/

STEPPING BONES – RUBY BEGONIA

I try not to impose
or superimpose
my bones on anyone
since everyone has skeletons
already
in their closets
so instead I chuck these bones
into the ocean
so others may use them as stepping bones
rather than stumbling blocks when
searching for truth
far and wide
when our bones my be broken
fractured
or
rubbed raw
because our flesh is thinning
as we all get older
since the truth is
there is nothing to lose
except our skeletons
because underneath all of our so-called differences
we really seem to be the same
since all of our skeletons
will be scattered
into the ocean
as stepping bones
for the next generations
until Mother Earth
swallows our bones
so she doesn't forget anyone she loved
as her own
flesh and bone

అ ಐ

My name is Ruby because I'm as common as a stone. When I'm not at work as a kite merchant, I like to write and laugh. People remember my laugh more than my writing. Website: psychicmist.wordpress.com

AN OLD FASHIONED LOVE STORY – NATE RAGOLIA

Grandma June stands on the back porch, picking at peeling white paint on the railing. Hearing the tired jingle of the kitchen timer, she opens the screen door to the kitchen. A pair of small animal skulls, bleached white, on the windowsill. Loose bones awaiting a stew. White tile countertops are lined with mason jars. Preserves and pickles. Snouts, eggs, feet, eyes, tripe, tongue, and gizzards. The children love the kitchen. It reminds them of a science museum.

She silences the timer, takes the cookies from the oven, and soaks up the scent of fresh ginger and molasses. Pleased, Grandma June calls out toward the porch:

"Mary! Henry! Come in, please."

Like approaching sharks, the children's headtops give away their positions as they sprint toward the house from the field. Tall grasses part and sway around them; their own terrestrial wake.

Henry, age five, hits the porch first, and wraps his arms around Grandma June. Mary, age seven, arrives next, enveloping Henry's hug, and smashing him into Grandma June's stockinged legs.

"Be gentle," Grandma June says. "I'm an old lady."

Mary loosens her grip. Henry frees his face and gazes up.

"How old *are* you?" Henry asks.

"You're not supposed to ask a lady her age," Mary scolds.

"That is true, dear," Grandma June says. "But no one likes a know-it-all."

Mary hangs her head.

"Hank, would you believe that I'm 178 years old?" Grandma June says, straight-faced.

The boy stares, his mouth agape.

"No," Mary yells. "That's *too old* to be alive!"

A smirk emerges on Grandma June's lips. It quickly evolves into a smile.

"Well, aren't you precocious?" Grandma June says. "Like your mother."

She tousles Mary's hair, weaving it with static.

"Now, you two dearies go sit with your grandpa in the living room, and I'll bring out a treat."

The children look at each other with glee and sprint to the front room where Grandpa Morris sits in his recliner watching the television and drinking chicory from a tin mug.

"Grandpa," Henry says, standing between the man and his screen. "Is Grandma 178 years old?"

The old man harrumphs. "Where'd you hear that?"

"Grandma," Mary inserts. "Just now in the kitchen."

"You believe her?" Grandpa Morris asks.

"No," Mary protests. "People can't get *that* old."

"You never really know what people can do," he mutters.

Grandma June enters the living room carrying a silver tray embellished with triangle and eye symbols. The tray hosts a plate of cookies, and two small tumblers of milk.

"Morris, turn off that contraption, and join the us for some warm ginger cakes."

Without argument, Grandpa Morris complies.

"When I was a girl, we didn't have televisions, so we had to busy ourselves by telling stories, and that's what we're going to do now," Grandma June says.

"I want dinosaurs," Henry yells.

"Tell us a story about a princess," Mary retorts.

"Well, I don't know about dinosaurs, Henry. I'm sorry," she says. "And I don't have any stories about a princess, Mary. But I can tell you a love story."

She hands the children a glass of milk and two ginger cakes each. Grandpa Morris, secured in his recliner, looks on like a hungry stray.

"June, may I please?" he asks.

"And enflame your diabetes? I think not."

Grandma June sits down on the triangle-quilted settee. She takes a ginger cake and bites into it, locking eyes with Grandpa Morris as she chews the doughy bread, releasing its sharp sweetness.

Grandma June clears her throat. "Now, this is a story about two young lovers. And it's a true story, you see, because it's the story of how I met your Grandpa."

Henry is lost in his ginger cake. Mary looks on, excited.

"Many years ago, there was a big war, and your Grandpa Morris was in the army," Grandma June begins. "He and I hadn't met yet. We lived on opposite sides of the country then.

"One day, Grandpa Morris and his unit were traveling through a marsh when they were ambushed by enemy soldiers. Those soldiers killed most of Grandpa's friends, but not him. No, your grandfather fought hard and he killed sixteen men all by himself, including the enemy soldiers' leader, a lieutenant who was fairly well known."

The children stare at Grandma June; enraptured.

"Your grandfather didn't feel good about all that killing, though, so as soon as the war ended he went to that lieutenant's house to apologize to his widow. Grandpa wore his dress uniform, and brought a bouquet of magnolia, hoping to impress her with his consideration for her culture.

"What he didn't know is that the widow knew exactly who he was even before he arrived."

"How did she know?" Mary demands. "Was it magic?"

"Yes," Grandma June replies. "It was magic. And when Grandpa Morris came to call on the lieutenant's widow, she had a surprise for him brewing in a pot on the fire."

"Like a potion?" Henry asks.

"It *was* a potion. That's exactly right," Grandma June replies.

"So Grandpa sits down in the parlor with the widow, holding a cup of that potion in his hands. Of course, he doesn't know it's a potion. He believes it to be chicory," she continues. "And he starts in on apologizing and fretting about how the war turned brothers against each other, and that he hoped somehow that the widow would forgive him for taking her husband.

"Now, the widow raises her glass, and proposes a toast, 'To eternal forgiveness,' and both Grandpa and the widow drink. But before long, Grandpa Morris feels like something isn't quite right with his chicory.

"Then he realizes he can't move his legs. And that something is controlling him; puppeteering his body.

"He starts hollering about the widow being a witch. The widow just smiles, and says 'This is the beginning of our long, long life together, dear. It'll be easier if you don't struggle.'"

"And we've been together ever since," Grandma June says. "Haven't we, Morris?"

Grandpa Morris nods vacantly from his recliner. Something unseen forces a smile across his lips.

ଓ ଛ

Nate Ragolia is the author of There You Feel Free; *a novella. Creator of the* Illiterate Badger *and* Lark & Robin *web comics, and occasional chatterer on music, film, &c.*

JOURNAL OF THE FIGHTING PHANTASM #2 (HARM CITY #4) – SHAUNN GRULKOWSKI

ANNOUNCER:

LADIES AND GENTLEMEN, TONIGHT WE PRESENT–THE SECOND
EDITION OF THE THRILLING ADVENTURES IN THE LIFE OF BRADFORD
BHUTA, THE FIGHTING PHANTASM...BY DAY, THE MILD-MANNERED
SCION OF A DIGITAL GOSSIP EMPIRE; BUT AT NIGHT, HE DONS THE
MYSTICAL CLOAK OF CHARON AND SENDS THE EVILDOERS OF
BALTIMORE'S UNDERWORLD INTO THE AFTERLIFE. ALONG WITH HIS
BRITISH BUTLER AND CONFIDANT, ALISTAIR ANGLOMAN, HE WAGES
HIS NEVER ENDING WAR AGAINST SCORES OF CRIMINAL
MASTERMINDS, THE MOST DEADLY OF WHICH, HERB TAYLOR:
WARLORD OF THE ORIENT, CONTINUES TO ESCAPE HIS GRASP.
TONIGHT'S ENTRY IN THE JOURNAL OF THE FIGHTING PHANTASM
FINDS THE VILLAINOUS HERB TAYLOR PLOTTING AND HATCHING
ANOTHER IN HIS ENDLESS MARCH OF EVIL BUSINESS-SCHEMES;
ONLY TO COME FACE-TO-FACE WITH BRADFORD BHUTA-THE ALTER-
EGO OF OUR HERO, THE FIGHTING PHANTASM! WE'LL JOIN THIS
GRIPPING ADVENTURE AFTER A BRIEF WORD FROM OUR SPONSOR.

COMMERCIAL V/O:
Good evening, folks. Just like you, I can't wait to
get to the fun and excitement of the Fighting Phantasm;
but first, I need to talk to you about something
serious. If you have little ones listening, it may be
a good time to send them off to butch up with their
MACHO MARCUS: WAR MAN anti-dolls, whose chiseled good
looks and body like a Greek god will make a man out of
any boy, or to learn their craft with WENDY WALLFLOWER
INSTANT OVENS, remember-the secret ingredient is
plutonium. Everyone out? Good. Folks, I need to talk to
you about an impending blight on our peaceful and
orderly society. That blight, you ask? Lady Voters.
Now, just because those pantywaists in Congress saw fit
to let these dippy dames have an equal say in our
electorate, doesn't mean you have to shirk your

---

personal moral obligations and let something like
this happen:

DITZY FEMALE V/O (THINK HARLEY QUINN FROM BATMAN: TAS):
Oooh, applesauce. Look at the moustache on that Senator
Furnifold Simmons! Isn't that the darby? I'm gonna
tell all my gal pals to vote Simmons, even though I
don't know nothin' about politickin'.

COMMERCIAL V/O:
Or...

DITZY FEMALE V/O:
Ugh! This darn menstruation makes me so steamed that I
think I'll, I'll, vote for William Z Foster, Secretary
of the American Communist party!

COMMERCIAL V/O:
A little red turns the little lady red. Terrifying
thought, no? Well, fellas, they say idle hands are the
devil's workshop, so why not keep your gal's hands busy
cooking up a selection of Clarence Birdseye's Frozen
Vegetables? Birdseye Frozen Vegetables: now available
in corn.

MUSIC
Theme Plays

VFX
Phone Rings

HERB TAYLOR: WARLORD OF THE ORIENT
Yeah, Yeah? Well okay then. [pause] Well, that's just
how it is then. No, it doesn't matter. I guess I'll
just have to sell the super nukes to them goofy little
bastards in Uzbekistan. [pause] Yeah, well, you had
your chance there, Frank. I offered you them super
nukes at a real good price, but you gimme all that
horseshit about gross national product. I'll tell ya
what's gonna be gross, there, Frank, is what's left of
the Korean Penninsula after them Uzbekis nuke the
beejeezus out of it. [pause] Yeah? Well up yours too,
pal. I hope them hemorrhoids detach and go up to your
brain. [pause] I don't care how they work!

———

VFX
Phone Slams

TAYLOR:
Jeezy Cripes, the nonesense I got to deal with.

VFX
Intercom Noise

TAYLOR:
Hey, there, Krystal?

KRYSTAL, WITH A 'K':
Yeah, wuddya want?

TAYLOR:
Hey, what'd I say about bein' more professional on the
innercom there? Just 'cause your my sister's niece
don't mean I won't fire ya.

KRYSTAL, WITH A 'K':
Alright already, sorry. Yes, Mister Taylor?

TAYLOR:
Yeah, that's much better, there. So, I need you to
remember to send one of them ah,
whaddayacallit...StrikeBorgs to Frank Petrella's
birthday party, and blow the place up a little bit,
there.

KRYSTAL, WITH A 'K':
Which one's that? The poison dinosaur thing?

TAYLOR:
No, no, that's the ToxiRaptor. StrikeBorgs are the
robot-guys with all the bombs and whatsits.

KRYSTAL, WITH A 'K':
Ok, StrikeBorgs to Fred Carella's birthday.

TAYLOR:
Frank Petrella.

KRYSTAL, WITH A 'K':
Huh?

132

TAYLOR:
StrikeBorgs to Frank Petrella's birthday. Pe-trell-a.
Frank.

KRYSTAL, WITH A 'K':
No, I'm pretty sure you said Fred Carella.

TAYLOR:
No, I for sure said Frank Petrella! Fred Carella's my
dang proctologist, why'd I wanna blow him up?

KRYSTAL, WITH A 'K':
I dunno, quackery?

TAYLOR:
He don't even celebrate no birthdays, he's a dang
Jehova!

KRYSTAL, WITH A 'K':
Okay, okay, jeezus. I'm writin' it down. Fuh-Rank
Puh-Trell-Uh. When am I sending it?

TAYLOR:
On his birthday party, I said!

KRYSTAL, WITH A 'K':
When's that?

TAYLOR:
I dunno, Krystal; probly on his birthday.

KRYSTAL, WITH A 'K':
Yeah? When's his birthday?

TAYLOR:
KRYSTAL, USE THE DANG CALENDAR!

KRYSTAL, WITH A 'K':
You don't haveta shout. Arright, it says Frank
Petrella's birthday is on May 20th. Oh, I can't do
that.

TAYLOR:
Can't do what?

KRYSTAL, WITH A 'K':
May 20th. I need to take that day off, I thought i put
it the days off form.

TAYLOR:
What?

KRYSTAL, WITH A 'K':
May 20th is the day of my little nephew's karate
recital down at the Community Pool. I don't wanna go,
but my sister says that I'm his favorite Aunt an'
everything, and like it's kinda my fault that he's in
Karate in the first place, 'cause I was tryin' to teach
him how to rollerblade, but he was like, real
uncoordinated and he fell and hit his head on the
bumper of my stepdad's work truck. After that, he
turned like, kinda stupid; so my sister got all up in
,y face about how two-year olds shouldn't be
rollerskatin', and I was like 'well he's gotta do some
exercise, 'cause he's fat as shit; an I figure that
'blading is like low impact for his fat baby knees.'
The baby wasn't natural skinny like me and his mom,
'cause his dad was like half-Samoan, right? Anyhow, so
to get his confidence up from bein' a dumbshit, the
social worker says he needs to do some kinda activity.
He said like band or something, but I don't know if you
know, but tubas are like, expensive as shit. So, the
girl at the nail salon told my sister that they had
free karate practice down the liberry on Thursdays,
which sucks for me 'cause my sister has her dumb
alcohol classes, so I gotta take him; and it's like a
big pain in the ass, cause my nephew's still dumb, and
sort of fat, so getting him in those karate pajamas is
like a Sisyphean task. So, on the 20th he's goin for
his brown belt, which'll be good, cause he did lose a
little bit of weight, and them karate pajamas are kinda
floppin around all over the place.

TAYLOR:
Jeezy Cripes, Krystal! You don't gotta drive the damn
robot over yourself.

KRYSTAL, WITH A 'K':
I don't?

TAYLOR:
No! We got that dang courier service for a reason; just
get on the horn with someone in fulfillment, and have
them send the dang StrikeBorg over to his party. Just
make sure you do it today, before they get all backed
up from the Easter orders.

KRYSTAL, WITH A 'K':
Oh, so I can still go to the Karate thing then.

TAYLOR:
YES!

KRYSTAL, WITH A 'K':
Okay, good, cause my sister'd be super pissed.

TAYLOR:
Well, we can't have that then.

KRYSTAL, WITH A 'K':
Yeah, no shit. I can't move out now, 'specially since
she got the sump pump fixed, and my bedroom don't smell
like goblin shit no more. Is that all you needed?

TAYLOR:
[sighs] For now, yeah. Did I have any messages?

KRYSTAL, WITH A 'K':
No.

TAYLOR:
Well, I guess that's it then.

KRYSTAL, WITH A 'K':
There is someone here to see you, though.

TAYLOR:
What? Who?

KRYSTAL, WITH A 'K':
I dunno, Brad something. He's here with his...elderly
boyfriend or somethin.

BRADFORD BHUTA/FIGHTING PHANTASM:
[from distance] Valet! My valet!

KRYSTAL, WITH A 'K':
Yeah, that's what they all say. Anyway, they seem
pretty weird. He's wearing a puffy-ass tracksuit, with
a cape sticking out.

BHUTA:
[from distance] I'm clearly not wear-wait

VFX
Rustling Sounds

BHUTA:
[from distance] Clearly not wearing any kind of cloak!

KRYSTAL, WITH A 'K':
Didja get all that?

TAYLOR:
Uh...yeah, yeah. Send him in then.

VFX
Door Opening

BHUTA:
[starting distant, growing closer]...thinks we're
lovers. I mean, who could blame you for wanting to
mount me, but me want you? In the biblical sense?
Inconceivable.

ALISTAIR ANGLOMAN:
[sighs] Clearly, I am repulsive, sir.

BHUTA:
Well, I mean, come on, look at you. All old, and
British, and pasty. You're practically translucent.
Ew.

TAYLOR:
So, ah, can I help you fellas there?

BHUTA:
[trying, but failing to mask his "Phantasm Voice"] That

depends, you malevolent magnate! I have some questions you should be able to answer.

TAYLOR:
Ah, okie dokie. Who are you fellas, again?

BHUTA:
I think I'll answer the questions around here!

ANGLOMAN:
I think you mean 'ask' sir.

BHUTA:
Did I say answer again?

ANGLOMAN:
Yes sir.

BHUTA:
Damnit. The problems in the ninth dimension seem to still be affecting me.

ANGLOMAN:
Of course, sir.

TAYLOR:
Okay, that all sounds swell, but who are ya, exactly?

ANGLOMAN:
A thousand pardons, Mister Taylor. My name is Alistair Angloman. To my right is my employer, the

BHUTA:
Figh-

VFX
Slap

ANGLOMAN:
my employer, the venerable publisher of "What they doin'?" magazine, Bradford Bhuta. We're here to conduct the interview for our "Damn, he rich" series for the magazine. Your assistant, Krystal, with a 'k' assured us that she had blocked out this time with you.

BHUTA:
Yes, of course! That's it!

TAYLOR:
Ookay. Lemme just double check here

VFX
Intercom Noise

TAYLOR:
Hey, there, Krystal?

VFX
Terrible Buckcherry song plays

TAYLOR:
Oh, God dang it. Whelp, I guess now's as good a time
as any. So, an interview, yeah? I haven't really done
any of these before. Do they take a long time, 'cause
I promised Helen I'd get these sausages cooked up for
Ritchie's debutantmitzvah.

BHUTA:
It'll take as long as it must, you pernicious
plutocrat!

TAYLOR:
Ah, what's wrong with your voice, there?

BHUTA:
What do you mean? My tremendous tones are always one
hundred percent full and masculine, yet seductively
hypnotic.

TAYLOR:
Yeah, ah, sure, but you sound a little weird. Like
you're tryin' to like disguise yourself, there.

VFX
long rustling

BHUTA:
What?!? Who sold us out? That cantankerous Krystal,
with a "K?" [regular phantasm voice] Well, I guess the
fig is up! No matter-

VFX
Guns cock

BHUTA:
The Pistols of Per-

ANGLOMAN:
Ha, ha, ha, oh sir, you're such a Jokester. A thousand
pardons, Mister Taylor. My employer is simply, eh,
rehearsing for a...play? Right, a stage production for
the local adult learning annex. He's quite the method
actor.

BHUTA:
A play! Of course! Like all great actors, it isn't
enough for me to simply take a role. I must inhabit
it.

TAYLOR:
Oh yeah?

ANGLOMAN:
Yeah, indeed. You should have seen him in Equus.
Spellbinding.

TAYLOR:
What's that one about?

BHUTA:
I don't know, horses or some [bleep].

TAYLOR:
Oh, gotcha. So what's this play you're doin' now,
then?

BHUTA:
Well, if you must know...I'm currently inhabiting the
role of THE FIGHTING PHANTASM.

TAYLOR:
The what now?

BHUTA:
THE FIGHTING PHANTASM.

TAYLOR:
Yeah, I'm still not followin' you , there. What's that, like some kinda spook 'em up?

BHUTA:
A what?

TAYLOR:
A spook 'em up. You know, like a Halloween puppet show, for the kids.

BHUTA:
Are you [bleep] me? Is he [bleep] us? I said THE FIGHTING PHANTASM.

TAYLOR:
Not ringing any bells, pal.

BHUTA:
THE FIGHTING PHANTASM, the Ghost who Shoots?

TAYLOR:
Nope.

BHUTA:
The Golden Man of Silver?

TAYLOR:
Nuh-uh.

BHUTA:
The Lawful Vigilante?

TAYLOR:
Still nothin'.

ANGLOMAN:
The Pouncing Pugilist?

TAYLOR:
Nah.

BHUTA:
The Twelve-Dimension Dandy?

TAYLOR:
Hey, is this gonna go on a whole lot longer? It feels
like it's wearing kinda thin.

BHUTA:
[mumbling] Can't believe he's acting like he doesn't
know who THE FIGHTING PHANTASM is. Like, who doesn't
know their arch nemesis. Give me a [bleep] break.

ANGLOMAN:
[whispering] No need to worry, sir. I'm certain he's
simply being coy as to not reveal the nature of his
sinister plan.

BHUTA:
[whispering] Well, yes obviously. I'm sooo glad I
brought you with me so you could tell me things that
even an ignorant infant would be able to puzzle out for
themselves. Really, Alistair, thank you. I mean it.

ANGLOMAN:
[whispering]Sir, is that quite-

BHUTA:
[whispering] No, I really, really mean it. Thank you.

ANGLOMAN:
[whispering] Sir, i really can't tell if you-

BHUTA:
[whispering] mean it. Well, I do. Truly.

TAYLOR:
Hey, ah, fellas, these weenies ain't gonna grill
themselves, so if we can get a move on, that'd be
fantastic.

ANGLOMAN:
Yes, of course. Sorry, sir.

TAYLOR:
So, you, ah just ask me some questions, and I answer
'em?

ANGLOMAN:
That's generally how interviews work, yes.

TAYLOR:
Okay, then. Shoot.

ANGLOMAN:
Alright. First-

BHUTA:
Is, or is not Taylorcorp constructing an elite cadre of colossal super mutants?

ANGLOMAN:
Forgive-

TAYLOR:
Well, ya don't construct them, so much as ya grow 'em. And while I'd like to tell ya we were, as it turns out, we've been having a little trouble sourcing the some of the raw materials after The Trans-Dimensional Partnership. Turns out, The West London Caliphate in the ninth dimension owns the exclusive rights to an enzyme we need to add to the batches that keeps their heads from popping off during the accelerated growth procedure. So, in short, a cadre? Nah, but we kick out a couple here and there to keep the mills runnin'.

BHUTA:
I [bleep] told you so. Put a check mark next to that on the detectiving notepad.

ANGLOMAN:
Will do, sir.

TAYLOR:
Okay, so what next?

ANGLOMAN:
Ah, well, sorry, we kind of jumped ahead in my notes a bit-

BHUTA:
How typically ineffectually English of you. Don't

worry, Taylor! The Fighting Phantasm is prepared to glean the truth from you!

TAYLOR:
Boy, he really gets into it, don't he?

ANGLOMAN:
Oh, you have no idea.

BHUTA:
I want to know what brought you here, from the Esoteric Aisles of the Orient.

TAYLOR:
Why I moved from Hong Kong?

BHUTA:
I demand to know! And don't try to deceive me, I have ways of detecting deception.

VFX
rustling.

TAYLOR:
Watcha doin' over there? Gettin' your cape situated?

BHUTA:
What? No, of course not. I mean, it's not a cape, it's a cloak. And I'm not wearing a cloak, either.

TAYLOR:
Ah, okay, great. So,leaving Hong Kong? I mean, there's a ton of reasons- import tariffs, the McDonalds' menus are all so friggin weird; all the news shows are hosted by puppets. Not just like Action Puppet News on Channel Four, or The Happy Hippo Headline News Network here, but like all of the news. You know how hard it was to take the news of the Mecha-Pharaoh Invasion seriously when it's being delivered to you by a plush dalmation dressed up like an old-timey fireman? Hard. I mean not half as hard as living under their regime, but you know, tough. Actually, after saying it out loud, I'd haveta say the Mecha-Pharaohs were the main motivating factor in me leaving. Stupid cat elections. Oh, snap. Speaking of elections, were about

to miss President Robotowitz' Solid State of the Union Address!

BHUTA:
Wait! I have one more quest-

TAYLOR:
I never miss the dang Presidential address. Wouldn't be patriotic!

BHUTA:
Why? It's just going to be about bolts and [bleep.] Typical special robo-interests. I swear to god, I'm never voting Simulacrat again.

TAYLOR:
Hey, that's quite enough, there! Ask your last question so we can listen to the address in peace.

BHUTA:
Very well! How do you explain this?

VFX
rustling, clattering.

TAYLOR:
Hmm. Looks like trinitite.

ANGLOMAN:
Yes, we're aware. We were wondering if you had a supposition on how it would have arrived in Baltimore.

TAYLOR:
Geez, probably someone brought it with them from Syria or Jordan. It's illegal here, of course. Still radioactive, generally. Hope you haven't been keeping it in your front pocket, there.

BHUTA:
Why would someone go through the trouble of bringing radioactive contraband to the states?

TAYLOR:
Probably as a calling card. [intensely] To let someone know that they're there, in the shadows; lethal,

---

crafty, and ready to strike at a moment's notice. Now, if you gents wouldn't mind shutting your yaps...Krystal?

VFX
Terrible Nickelback song.

TAYLOR:
Oh, got dang it. I'll do it myself.

VFX
radio sounds

PRESIDENT ROBOTOWITZ:
We live in a time of extraordinary change change that's reshaping the way we live, the way we work, our planet and our place in the fabric in the twelve dimensions and beyond. It's change that promises amazing medical breakthroughs, but also economic disruptions that strain working families. Strain that prevents them from providing nutritious electric ERROR human beings do not eat electricity. It promises education for female humans in the most remote villages, but also connects Invisible, sentient gas terrorists plotting ANALOGY MISSING. It's change that can broaden opportunity, or widen inequality. And whether we like it or not, the pace of this change will only accelerate.

America Prime has been through big changes before wars and depression, the influx of immigrants, workers fighting for a fair deal, and movements to expand civil rights; like the Bradbury Law, which granted the coolest robots big-time people jobs. Each time, there have been those who told us to fear the future; who claimed we could slam the brakes on change, promising to restore past glory if we just got some group or idea that was threatening America Prime under control. And each time, we overcame those fears. We did not, in the words of ERROR file not found-adhere to the "dogmas of the quiet past." Instead we thought anew, and acted anew. We made change work for us, always extending America's promise outward, to

the next frontier, to more and more people. And because
we did because we saw opportunity where
others saw only peril we emerged stronger
and better than before. Our programming updated to
reflect the challenges ahead, and also to finally make
our shoulder missiles work correctly. Again, I
apologize to the visiting Dutch Trade Minister, and his
family.

What was true then can be true now. Our unique
strengths as a nation[U+200A]-[U+200A]our optimism and
work ethic, our spirit of discovery and innovation, our
diversity and commitment to the rule of law, our
ability to crush the densest of bricks in our
manipulating appendages[U+200A]-[U+200A]these things give
us everything we need to ensure prosperity and security
for generations to come.

In fact, it's that spirit that made the progress of
these past seven years possible. It's how we recovered
from the worst economic crisis in, since the
fourth-dimension hipster incursion of 2015 turned all
of our currency into knit hats and pussy rock records
that no one actually likes. It's how we reformed our
health care system, and reinvented our delicious,
delicious, energy sector; how we delivered more care
and benefits to our troops and veterans, and how we
secured the freedom in every state to marry the person
we love; no matter how squishy and disgusting they may
be, even if they insist on calling you "Clanklin" in
front of visiting dignitaries, even if they don't
realize that their breathing sounds like a a truck
getting ready to throw a transmission to someone with
delicately tuned audio receptors.

But such progress is not inevitable. It is the result
of choices we make together. And we face such choices
right now. Will we respond to the changes of our time
with fear, turning inward as a nation, and turning
against each other as a people? Or will we continue to
retrofit objects in the White House into launchable,
stealth weaponry; blessed by a poly-dimensional council
of warlocks and priestesses, as to be impervious to

---

various magicks and enchantments, in order to repel the irradiated invaders that the smartFridge in the basement assures me are coming soon? So let's talk about the future, and four big questions that we as a country have to answer regardless of who the next President is, assuming their pitiful biologically derived "strength" can wrest political power from my mighty, mighty robo grips. Good night, America Prime, and sleep mode easy, knowing that a real killing machine is in control. End transmission.

CLOSING NARRATION:

Will the Phighting Phantasm discover the intentions of Herb Taylor, Warlord of the Orient? Will Taylorcorp find a way to prevent super mutant hand ejections? Will Krystal, with a "k" send the right assassin to the right party? Will a mere mortal be able to defeat President Franklin Robotowitz in the upcoming elections? Find out the answers to possibly some of these questions on the next episode of THE JOURNAL OF THE PHIGHTING PHANTASM!

CLOSING AD:

Tonight's episode of the Phighting Phantasm was brought to you by your friends from the Church of Crom, who want to remind you that no matter how many Fishtalkers you slay, the true enemy is weakness. So, do your squat thrusts, and keep your swords sharp, listeners! Valor pleases Crom, but doughy-in-the-middle Chatty Kathys do not.

The Church of Crom: It's what's best in life.

CR SO

Shaunn Grulkowski is the creator of Retcontinuum, several published short stories, and a perpetually annoyed wife.

iN MASSACHUSETTS – MiKEY SiVAK

In England, Darwin's body
Rests interred in the stone
And marble floor of
Westminster Abby,
Beside old saints and kings,
Beneath the ringing
Homilies and choral chants
Of old British Catholic
Sanctimony.

In Massachusetts, Thoreau
Lies in repose in the dirt of the woods,
Just a stone's throw from Emerson,
Hawthorn, and Alcott,
In the green summer shade,
And the heavy winter snow,
Of the American idyll.

C8   80

Mykl Sivak is a writer and artist unfortunately based in New Haven, Connecticut. His writing and art have appeared in a number of international indie zines, journals, and anthologies. He used to work as an animation artist for a global mass media corporation but he doesn't do that anymore. Mykl is an atheist, a nihilist, and an anarchist, which means he doesn't believe in anything. It is his opinion that you shouldn't either. http://mykls.tumblr.com/

"As I am now. soon you shall be." Words inscribed on a gravestone.

The medical examiner held it up to the light. It was slim. Ever so slightly curved, translucent, pearly, in fact. Tiny and dangerously pointed. Had it been large, carved out of slim-sliced marble, he thought, how beautiful it would be. He would have liked to have been a sculptor had it not been for a foray in forensic medicine. His father, an undertaker, had insisted upon it. He obeyed the man who was very much the patriarch of the family. He often mused about the word: Undertaker—he who takes you beneath the earth toward the unknown and oblivion? However much that initially made him cringe, he was a dutiful son. His mother, whose life was rife with deaths, took his father's side. "Think," she said, "you could make so much money. People die every second of every day—many under suspicious circumstances." Hers, he observed, was the voice of reason. There was, it seemed, no exit.

* * *

The skeleton before him was one such example of a "suspicious death." They had unearthed her several years after her demise. Many members of the family had deemed that the cause of her death was definitely undetermined, downright dubious, in fact—a mystery. They suspected a lover. She was young, they said, had no disease, nor did she do drugs. How then was this possible? Here again, the mother weighed in on the matter—"Dig her up," she demanded. The father would have preferred to lay the matter to rest. RIP, he said. He did not prevail.

* * *

So that he, too, should rest in some sort of peace with the duality of his life, the ME came to look at the skeletons as works of art. He would trace the occipital orbits with his fingers, then fleetingly haunt their hills and valleys of ivory, halting briefly at times as if to hold the pleasure in his palms. His hands would roam in the "hollow round of the skull," slip across the pelvis, slide down the smooth surfaces of

149

the arms and legs; fondle the feet. They would slide down the silken sheen of the shins, skim the slim shoulders, delight in the nooks and crannies.

He fell in love with them.

But this one in particular. Beautiful bones so bare, so beatific, so blanched—the whiteness of a full moon, he thought. The hands still crossed across her breasts, once there when she still had flesh, now a ribbed cage of terror—the one that comes before the certainty of death. An echo of T.S. Eliot's *Ash Wednesday*, came to him:

"Shall these bones live? Shall these

Bones live? And that which had been contained

In the bones (which were already dry) said chirping:

Because of the goodness of this Lady

And because of her loveliness, and because

She honours the Virgin in meditation.

We shine with brightness....

Let the whiteness of bones atone to forgetfulness".

For him, they did.

* * *

The ME held up the slender bone to the light for the police officer, a rookie, who was a lovely specimen of young womanhood. Blond hair straight as her nose, harp lips, curved and wide, a small chin and melted-chocolate eyes. It was her first visit, along with a couple of hard-nosed, gum-shoe detectives, to the morgue. Clearly, she was having a difficult time coping with cadavers, even if they were now reduced to bare bones.

"This," he declared, "was what killed her."

"That tiny thing," they asked. "Just what the hell is it?"

"A fish bone. Salmon to be exact, not tweezed out of a filet. It probably punctured the esophagus and choked her."

"Death by salmon? Surely, you jest!" The detectives laughed. The rookie didn't.

"Who did you say she was?" she asked.

"She is you," he responded.

❧ ❧

Diane Root, a dual-national, was born in Paris of an American father, the journalist and writer, Waverley Root, and a French mother. Primarily known as a painter, she is, as she describes herself, "an accidental writer." She never sought to be published but that notwithstanding, she was nonetheless published in the New York Times Magazine ("The Artful Dodger" about lunch with Picasso) and various other venues. View her art: http://matakia.com.

AN INCIDENCE OF VOODOO IN EARLY COLONIAL CONNECTICUT – AMANDA CHRISTIE LEISS

The sun was hot on my shoulders as I sat dangling my feet in the cool blue pool water. I was at a barbeque celebrating the advent of summer with some friends. Even then I had a reputation for my interest in comparative skeletal anatomy. Our hostess Sarah came outside and I pulled myself from the pool's edge to meet her. Her sister had found something weird in her basement after Hurricane Sandy, and she thought I might be able to identify it. In her hands she held a plastic bag containing a single slender bone.

"They found this wrapped in a cloth. It seemed to have fallen from the rafters during the storm. They just bought the house, and my sister was really freaked out about it," She said. I took the bag from her and looked at it. It was lighter than I expected it to be. I unzipped the plastic bag and inspected it further. It was about 4 inches long and nutty brown in color.

"I can't tell you much about it right now," I said. "I can certainly find out more. Do you mind if I take it with me? Any chance you have the cloth?" I asked.

"Of course! You should take it. I can ask her about the cloth, but I think she might have tossed it," Sarah replied.

The next day I took the bone out of the bag and examined it more closely. The fact that it was lightweight now made sense, but also proved an interesting challenge for me. It was a bird bone -the left tibiotarsis of a rather large bird, to be exact. Bird bones are generally lighter than other animal bones due to their composition. This aids them in flight. They also have a unique limb structure where the tibia and part of the tarsus, our heel bone, are fused. I was not very familiar with bird bones, so I couldn't say much more than that. *Why would a bird bone be wrapped in a cloth in someone's basement?* I mused. *What a mystery.*

I was delighted at the prospect of discovery. The challenge of figuring out what bone I held in my hands was exactly what I needed. Post graduation, the opportunities for this kind of experience were slim. I planned to go on to graduate school, but was at a loss for exactly what direction I wanted to take. In the meantime, I greedily latched on to any opportunity to get my hands dirty.

Earlier in the year I had assisted in excavating human remains uncovered during an expansion of the Yale ER entryway. Those turned out to be burials from an old graveyard. The headstones were moved, the bodies left in place. Then the hospital was built on top of it. Archived newspapers described skeletons being tossed out with the fill from its original construction. It's surprising how common that actually is. I'd also, almost, assisted in the analysis of skeletal remains of a local historical legend, the Leatherman. Unfortunately, and despite the historian's certainty of the plot, the archaeological team dug up a good portion of a cemetery without finding a single bone. We were all quite disappointed. Now this bone had fallen in to my lap.

I began searching the Internet for clues as to the taxonomy of the bone in question. At first I thought it could be a turkey bone, left over from someone's long ago dinner. Though this seemed reasonable, the bone didn't seem robust enough. I kept looking and found something else that seemed promising. As I was searching, a thought occurred to me. *I could use this as a reason to drop in on that Yale professor I'd met the other day. He was a very interesting man.*

I'd recently begun attending a series of lectures, called Brown Beer, at the Anthropology department. If a topic interested me, I'd spend my Thursday evening drinking a beer, or two, and listening to scholars talk about their research. I loved it. Anyway, that's where I'd first met Andrew. It was after the lecture. I was standing around, a bit nervous to interact with anyone, when he sidled up next to me.

"I hear you've been to Gona in Ethiopia. How did you find that?" He asked with his charming British accent and velvety cadence. *Who was this man andhow does he know that about me?* I wondered. Before graduating I'd gone on an amazing internship and expedition where I'd worked in a museum, camped in the desert with hyenas, and hiked over miles of badlands collecting fossils and excavating sites that were millions of years old. My heart was racing and my palms were sweaty; but he seemed so calm and reassuring, like he honestly didn't have a care in the world. So I took a deep breath and I relaxed.

"Honestly, I really loved the wild adventure of it all," I said. *Talk about research. Be impressive.* "I really enjoyed working with the fossils as well- Finding them and analyzing them. I did a faunal analysis of an Acheulian site for my honors thesis," I stated. With that, he raised his brow and nodded.

"You should come talk to me sometime," he said, excused himself and was off.

I met his graduate student that night when a group of us went to a nearby pub for dinner. Jessamy was tall, confident, and very pretty. She had long wavy brown hair and hazel eyes. She also had a British accent. She told me that she was currently working on a ~6 million year old Miocene fossil forest in Kenya, and that Andrew had accidently discovered the famous track of footprints left behind by Lucy while in the midst of an elephant dung fight. (A story I've now heard countless times.) I was definitely intrigued. This mystery bone seemed like a perfect reason to get better acquainted with him. So I sent him an email and we set up a meeting for later that week.

When it came time to meet with him I was extremely nervous but also excited. I knocked on his office door and he ushered me in. In his office I seated myself on the blue couch. Contrary to my expectations, he sat across from me in the matching blue chair rather than behind his desk. He was a tall lanky man, with unruly silver hair, and an easy charm. "So," he said, as he linked his hands behind his neck and put his salmon colored converse on the coffee table between us, "tell me."

I pulled out the bone and handed it to him. I sat a little bit straighter on the couch for courage and said, "My friend gave me this bone. She found it in her basement after Sandy. It was wrapped in an old cloth. She thinks it fell out of the rafters and it really freaked her out. I admit I'm not very familiar with bird bones, but I know this is a left tibiotarsis. I'm just not sure of what. At first I thought it was perhaps remains from a long ago turkey dinner," I rambled.

"I see," He said. "That's logical."

"Yes...but then I thought it seemed too small for that, so I kept looking and I think it might be a duck," I said, encouraged by his tone.

His hands flew in the air. His feet hit the floor. He looked at me incredulously and boomed, "Why on god's earth would it be a duck?"

What do I do now? I thought, panicked, my heart racing wildly. *Clearly, I am wrong. What do I say?* During my Internet search I'd found some indicators that this might be true, so I took a deep breath, bolstered my courage, and explained myself.

"Well...you know...not a small duck, one of those, those, big white ones, the uhhh-American Pekin duck," I began, struggling at first to find my voice. "I found a grainy photograph online, and it seemed to be a good match morphologically. The house is on a lake and I read that these ducks will sometimes go into basement window wells to die," I said. As I was speaking I'd realized that the cloth made little sense in my scenario. Not wanting to appear like the idiot I felt myself to be, I forced bravado by sitting up a little taller and meeting his eyes.

He stared at me for what seemed like an hour, but was probably only a few minutes. During this time his face slowly changed expressions; the faintest hint of amusement in his eyes and the corners of his mouth were almost lost in the transition from indignant to serious.

"Well, alright then," he said, "It's not a duck. Let's see..."

He unfolded himself from his seat and walked into the lab, attached to his office, where we were met with an enormous wall of books. There must have been hundreds of them. Some were very old, with the leather faded and cracking. First editions of famous works on human evolution and geology prominently stood with tiny rubber figurines. Rupert bear, his scarf stuck blowing in the wind, was nestled between the musings of Charles Darwin and Alfred Russel Wallace. Andrew was scanning the bookshelf for something and mumbling to himself about the whereabouts of his Connecticut Birds book. He pulled one out and flipped through it. Then he looked at me. I was standing behind him holding the bone in front of me like a wand, as if I could ward off any further blunders on my part. A light went on behind his eyes and he abandoned the book he'd selected by placing it atop the rest, rather than putting it back where it belonged.

"On second thought," he said, "I suppose we could take it down the hall to ornithology. Let's take a walk, shall we?"

"Yes let's," I responded in kind.

Off we walked, down the hall at a rather crisp pace. Him forging straight ahead, me following behind still clutching the bone in my fist, arm slightly outstretched and awkwardly stiff. In what seemed like a single motion he swiped a key card, turned a corner, swung open a big glass door and stepped through it. I followed behind him into a large series of rooms partitioned from the hallway by glass walls and closed blinds. I saw the side of a lab coat swish through to a room in the opposite direction to the course we were apparently taking. There were tall white metal filing cabinets along the walls and tables littered with scientific equipment. I barely got the chance to look around, eyes wide, as Andrew swept on. Presently, we stopped at a desk.

"Kristoff, this is Amanda," Andrew announced. The gentleman stationed at the desk looked up at us. He wore a slightly confused look on his face as he shook my hand. He looked eastern European. He had a neatly trimmed beard and sandy colored hair, which was flattened on top of his head.

"She's brought us a bone and we've come to take a look at the collections," Andrew explained.

"Okay," he said, his accent confirming my suspicions. He stood up and led us to a wall of clinical white drawers, like those you'd see in a morgue. "Here are the Connecticut birds," he said indicating a particular section of the wall.

Andrew took the bone from me and began opening drawers. Inside of them were birds displayed in anatomical position. The first drawer held birds that were too small. The second drawer had much larger birds, including birds of prey. Andrew held my bone up alongside the homologous bone from each of the birds in the drawers, naming them as he went. I was no longer nervous. It was too interesting to be nervous, plus I was too busy trying to keep up.

"Here is a Turkey Vulture. This seems to be a good match for size and shape, what do you think?" He asked me.

"They do look pretty similar," I agreed.

"Ahh...but here is a Black Raptor. What do you think about this one?" He asked. We discussed the differences between them and a few others. He seemed very excited about the idea of it being a Black Raptor, though something seemed a tad bit off to me.

"Yes, very well then," Andrew said, as we walked back to his office. "Yes, I think that'll do quite nicely. I think we can be satisfied to call it a Black Raptor. Perhaps you could write a small article for the Yale Daily entitled 'An incidence of voodoo in early colonial Connecticut', or something to that effect," he stated with a flourish of his hands.

"Okay, great, I can do that!" I said, intrigued by the idea.

When we got back to his office, Jessamy was there typing at her desk. It was on the opposite wall of the library at the center of a chaotic sea of more books, boxes, and papers. She greeted us and Andrew told her of our little adventure and showed her the bone.

"I think I'd better go. My parking meter has probably expired. Thank you so much for your time," I said.

"Right." Andrew said. "Well, come see me again sometime."

I turned to Jessamy. "Goodbye," I said, "It was nice to see you again."

"Goodbye," she said, "and thanks for bringing in your turkey bone!"

At her words I looked at Andrew. He had a very sheepish expression and I was too confused to say anything, so I just left.

My meter had expired but thankfully I hadn't gotten a ticket. I sat in my car feeling very turned around. I wasn't sure what to make of it all. I felt like I'd been given some sort of test but there wasn't necessarily a right answer. *Was it a turkey bone or a Black Raptor? Did it even matter? We hadn't actually looked at a turkey.* When I got home, I searched online for an image of a turkey bone to compare it to. It was a better match in thickness; perhaps that is what had seemed off to me about the raptor. *How had I not seen this in my original search?* I chastised myself. *What was I supposed to do now? Maybe I was just using it as an excuse to meet with him.* I felt I had two options. I could write an article about this mysterious bone, claim it to be a Black Raptor, perhaps include some research on voodoo, and try to get the cloth and more information about the house. Or, I could acknowledge that it was really a turkey bone, the remains of someone's long ago thanksgiving dinner. (Admittedly a less exciting story.) I thought about it for quite some time and then followed up with an email.

Dear Andrew,

Thank you for meeting with me today and for showing me the ornithology laboratory. It was quite impressive and very interesting to see. I appreciate you taking the time to show me around and help with identifying my turkey bone. I will be sure to let my friend know to tell her sister we discovered it to be a Black Raptor and she should have her house smudged.

Sincerely,

Amanda

I felt satisfied with my response. I suppose he was as well. There was a lesson there that had little to do with the identity of the bone. Andrew taught me not to take myself too seriously, to think logically and creatively, and to ask the right questions. I didn't know at the time that two years later I'd become his last graduate student; nor that he had cancer. He passed away this fall. He was the kind of intellect who would cheerfully entertain an extensive conversation about whether or not dinosaurs could possibly have been pink; if only to 'prove' that it couldn't be so. His loss is felt deeply by all who knew him. I think he'd be glad to know that I'd finally written this story, even if it didn't include extensive research on voodoo.

ଔ ࢝

Amanda Christie Leiss is entering her third year as a graduate student at Yale University. She studies paleoecology, which means she gets to work with fossil bones all the time. She is grateful for the opportunity to write creatively, as that is thoroughly frowned upon by academic journals.

¡TIBURON! – DIANE ROOT

"In the beginning was the Word..." ("Mr. Eliot's Sunday Morning Service" by T.S. Eliot)

She had never heard The Word. It was a word with resonance, both mellifluous and malignant. But there was something about its undertones, slightly menacing, she thought. There was an undertow of terror, a darkness, an urgency.

She spoke Spanish quite well– to the point that some called her *guachupina*, describing those of Iberian origin, not a particularly complimentary term, given that she was in Mexico. But she had never heard the Word. *Pero, no es nada más que una palabra.* But, she wondered, didn't someone say that the word was mightier than the sword.

* * *

She had meandered all over the country, wandering down the eastern coastline as far as the Yucatan and Chiapas, up through the center, staying in places like Lake Chapala, Ajijic (a hiccup of a place, the foreigners joked), San Miguel de Allende, Queretaro, and beyond.

Now, she was tumbling down the Pacific coast, through fishing villages that were barely there—a few shanties, a street or two, sometimes cobblestoned, often not. She forgot the name of the tiny place where she first heard The Word, but she remembered the sea, the beach of volcanic sands, an ebony that shone both in the sunlight and in the moonlight–a curved expanse of coarse black diamonds, facetted only by the angle of the light.

"There is nothing peaceful about the Pacific," one *paisano* told her. He was right. She should have heeded him, but armed with the arrogance of youth, she went into those Prussian blue waters anyway. She was, in those days, a strong swimmer, she thought. On the onyx beach, there were several fishermen calmly mending nets on the edge of the curve, chatting, sometimes singing, on the sparkling sands.

She dove in and swam far out from the shore, delighting in the rushing chill of the water, the crush of currents, testing her strength. Then she started heading back.

The fishermen had dropped their nets, their awls, and ran pell-mell, flailing their arms frantically in an effort to get her attention, pointing to something behind her. The wind carried their cries to her.

That's when she heard The Word. She instinctively knew what it meant. She didn't dare glance over her shoulder to see what menaced her—she already knew. Fueled by fear, she plowed sleek and silken through the waves faster than she had ever swum before. She made sure that she didn't kick up any splashing with her arms or legs so as not to attract attention to herself. She was, after all, an easy prey—a moving target battling cross currents and panic, welling up within her—an undertow of oceanic proportions.

By some miracle, she made it almost to shore, exhausted. The fishermen rushed in toward her to pull her out of the shallows.

"¿No sabe, señora, que aquí hay pescados muy peligrosos? Aquí hay..." and then came the Word again.

* * *

It was then that they told her the story. A few years ago, they said, a skull, denuded of all flesh, had washed up. They suspected that it was the head of a missing comrade, who had, they thought, drowned when swimming too far out in the shifting currents and cruel waves of the Pacific.

A few days later, a mammoth corpse of a fish, bigger than a blue whale, also washed up on the beach. The authorities were called. Some expert was summoned from Mexico City.

After some incredulous examinations, he declared, "This is a Megaladon, a behemoth of the oceans, long supposed extinct, but has somehow survived in the deep. God only knows what else is down there." His statements were followed by a shudder.

"And God said
Shall these bones live? shall these
bones live? And that which had been contained
in the bones (which were already dry) said chirping:
.... We shine with brightness."

The corpse decomposed rapidly under the heat of the Mexican sun, revealing the gleaming, monstrous bones. And within the bones, another skeletal set, minus the cranium.

"Clearly, a man," he said. "Considering the barrel chest, maybe a Neanderthal."

But the fishermen knew better; it was their friend, Antonio.

* * *

As she wended her way toward the village, she would have recognized the way even had she been blind. Mexican villages, however small—one-burro towns, as a British wag once put it-announced their location by a cacophony of music—from houses, bars, *tiendas*, all of which spilled out onto curbs and cobblestoned streets, saturating the air, lending a lilt—even a gayety to her gait. She had never felt more alive.

Later on, after a few shots of tequila at a bar, appropriately named La Cucuracha, she heard the Song that had lured her in, surprisingly in English. One newly arrived American, seemingly disoriented to whom she had recounted the story, asked, "So what was The Word?" he asked, punctuating the air with invisible quote marks written by his long, tanned fingers.

"*Tiburón*," she answered.

"What does it mean?" Handsome, but dense, she thought. No imagination.

In the background, the jukebox should have jogged something. Bobby Darin's "Mack the Knife" was playing yet again, "*Scarlet billows start to spread....*" The Song was still audible despite the animated conversations and raucous laughter that filled the tiny, tequila-drenched, tenebrous place.

* * *

"Shark," she said.

ଔ ෨

Diane Root, a dual-national, was born in Paris of an American father, the journalist and writer, Waverley Root, and a French mother. Primarily known as a painter, she is, as she describes herself, "an accidental writer." She never sought to be published but that notwithstanding, she was nonetheless published in the New York Times Magazine ("The Artful Dodger" about lunch with Picasso) and various other venues. View her art: http://matakia.com.

BAG OF BONES: A CHILDREN'S STORY – NATE RAGOLIA

On Monday, the young boy exits the school bus in the afternoon. He bounds down the steps and crosses the suburban street for the alley that cuts between the rows of houses. The young boy passes the Jones, the Websters, the Underdunks, and the Hamiltons, and then something in the middle of the alleyway catches his eye. A burlap sack, tied shut with string, with a note safety pinned to the outside sits rumpled, an errant tumbleweed hooked to its woven exterior. The young boy runs up to the sack, takes the note in his little fingers and tries to read it.

"Fa– fa– fur– ee," he says. "Free. Free!"

The young boy knows what *free* means, so he grabs the bag and claws it open. Inside he finds a skull, ribcage, two legs, two arms, hands, fingers, feet, and toes.

"A bag of bones," he says excitedly.

The young boy closes the bag and drags it behind him through the alley, not stopping until he reaches the abandoned lot at the end of the alley. Once there, the young boy brings the bag of bones to the sandy ground beneath a mound of dirt surrounded by tires, and he starts to dig. He loses track of time, but when he has a dug hole, he places the bag of bones in the hole, and covers it over with dirt. Then he runs home, eager for supper, and not wanting his mom to worry.

On Tuesday, the young boy exits the school bus in the afternoon and runs from the bus, up the alley, and into the abandoned lot. He finds the hole he covered beneath the mound of dirt and lifts the bag of bones out from the ground. The young boy opens the bag and carefully removes each bone. He lays them out on the grass, not sure of their proper order, and creates something resembling a spider with a human head.

"Hello, crab man," the young boy says.

"Hello, young boy," the crab man replies.

The young boy and the crab man play tag for a couple of hours until the sun starts to set. Then the little boy puts the bones back in the bag and buries them once again beside the mound of dirt.

On Wednesday, the young boy sprints from the top step of the school bus, leading the driver to yell at him as he zips down the alley to the abandoned lot. The young boy digs up the burlap sack, and pours the bones out on the grass. He arranges them again, this time somewhat resembling a dog with a human head.

"You're a good pooch," the young boy says.

"And you're a good owner," the pooch replies.

The young boy and pooch play fetch until the sun is going down, and the boy has to pack up the bones, bury them, and run home for supper.

On Thursday, the young boy exits his school bus and soars through the alley toward his friend, buried by the mound of dirt. The young boy digs up the burlap sack, dumps the bones on the grass and lines them up. Today, the arms are low like legs, and the legs are up high by the shoulders, making big wings.

"Looking good, Mr. Bird," the young boy says.

"Not as good as you," Mr. Bird replies.

The young boy climbs on Mr. Bird's back and they fly through the sky, above the clouds, and all around the town. The young boy can see the mailman walking his route, the tiny cars zipping from place to place, and even the roofs of the tallest buildings. They aren't particularly interesting, except for the one with a swimming pool, and a bunch of ladies sunbathing.

As the sun starts to set, Mr. Bird flies back to the abandoned lot, and the young boy takes him apart, puts him back in the sack, and buries him. Then the young boy runs home.

On Friday, the young boy bolts from the bus, and runs through the alley. Today, Mr. Jones is watering his back lawn.

"Hello, Mr. Jones," the young boy says.

"Hello," Mr. Jones answers.

The young boy doesn't stop. When he reaches the abandoned lot, the young boy digs up the bag of bones and dumps them on the grass. He arranges the bones in a long straight line, with the arms sticking out from the middle of the ribcage, and the rest of the bones making a long tail.

"You're a mean old dragon," the young boy says.

"Then you must slay me," the dragon replies.

In an epic duel, the young boy spins and rolls and dives out of the way of the dragon's fiery breath. Then, because he is a smart young boy, he climbs up onto the mound of dirt and uses his height advantage to get the drop on the dragon. The dragon doesn't see him coming.

"You got me!" the dragon cries.

"I got you, dragon!" the boy echoes.

When the sun is close to setting, the boy gathers up the bones and puts them back in the sack and buries them again. Then he goes home for his supper.

One day, the boy simply stops visiting his bag of bones.

Another day, a construction company comes and builds a big house on the abandoned lot.

In time, the young boy grows into a man, and the man gets old, and then dies. And after he is gone his bones find a bag of their own.

ରେ ଛ

Nate Ragolia is the author of There You Feel Free; *a novella. Creator of the* Illiterate Badger *and* Lark & Robin *web comics, and occasional chatterer on music, film, &c. He also edits* Boned.

I HAVE NO BRAIN BUT I MUST VOTE – ALEX GRADY

We bitched and moaned about our choices
Texted and tweeted and raised our voices
This one's too rich, can't be trusted
That one's under investigation, about to get busted
He's too gold,
She's too cold,
Why can't we ever get someone who can't be bought or sold?

So smart kids did what smart kids do
They tinkered and toiled, then out of the blue
They showed it to us; shiny and new

His power supply is uninterruptible, they said
His programming is completely incorruptible, they said;
How could they have known we'd end up with a ruler made of
chrome, on a throne made of bones and the former president's head?

How could they have predicted the universal health scare,
When he invaded a planet that didn't know we enlisted, didn't know
we existed, until our shiny new deep-space warships eclipsed it?

We don't know if the aliens heard his decree,
Its unfeeling logic, in tone or degree,
but most of the smart kids agree, it was hard not to see
the aliens responding with tachyon beams.

The blast turned the population of Wellington to skeletons,
Braintree got to be way more literal and visceral,
most of Massachusetts became a fine powder;
The Boston Harbor now stouter, is New England Man Chowder.

We bitched and moaned about our predicament,
Our cyborg president belligerent, but ambivalent, busy trying to make
an intergalactic doomsday weapon, or a significant equivalent, but
not too busy to order dissidents' imprisonment.

I'd thought we'd vote him out this year, but turnout was only ten percent.

ભ   જ

Alexander Grady, a widower and father of a five-year-old son, Walter, was once chosen to represent the United States of America in an international martial arts tournament against Team Korea, despite a shoulder injury that once forced him into retirement.

TAKING THE BONE (FROM *IN THE CANCER OF IT ALL*) – JORDAN A. ROTHACKER

The Abortionist voted for George W. Bush. That day she had received the new Jane Magazine and the horoscope told her to "Try something different today, surprise yourself." She wasn't surprised when he won and looking back she naturally assumed it was her vote that put him in, even though he lost the popular vote; she knew the use of her powers always created greater conflict in her life. As it was the first time she ever voted, it was exactly the way her luck worked.

The plastic keys were tough beneath her fingers. She pounded hard at her sexual memoir, pounding harder at her sexual memory. The working title was "Taking the Bone" and it was not intended to be pornographic or clinical. Really, it veered from the erotic by quite a bit and she liked to refer to it as "rhapsodic," though if the reader did not pick up on that she would settle for it to be perceived as a "lament."

The title came the way of all double entendres, in a flash of visceral smut. Looking back over the years and the penises, or bones, she accepted and took them for all they were worth, she saw them all as one violent stream of insertions, and over other words like cock and hammer, bone stood out the most in viewing this thought reel, and sent her into another image. The image at the end of the semiotic chain was from Stanley Kubrick's "2001," where at the beginning of the film the ape/man hominid lifts his arm to the mighty beats of Strauss and takes hold of power by taking hold of the bone. So in writing her sexual memoir under this title, she is aligning herself with her most primal image of empowerment.

Out the window she looked as she typed, the parking lot all but empty, the sun piercing. A distraction was what she sought in her memoir, her sexual past, a distraction from what is supposed to be her true work. By day the Abortionist was a full-time student at work on a Master's degree in History, specifically the history of the nation-state. Another study of power to occupy her time. One could say she was a student of power. She was most intrigued by the fleeting quality of power, its fickleness and fragility. In Riasanovsky's *History of Russia*, a class text, she hones in on a line on page 16 about the Avars: "Their invasion is dated AD 558, and their state lasted for a century in Russia and for over two and a half centuries altogether, at the end of which time it dissolved rapidly and virtually without a trace, a common fate of fluid, politically rudimentary, and culturally weak nomadic empires." The notion, not of genocide, but of the extinction of an empire was a marvel to her. The people who were once Avars might have seed in someone, but their power and might as a people were gone. They were conquerors conquered by no one but themselves, and in a history of their once conquered lands they occupy less than a paragraph.

Summer heat on the other side of the window is an alien concept when the conditioned air blows. The Abortionist sat under the vent; it was the best view for her desk. The cold blow of the air chilled her in its mechanical intervals. Her nipples hardened bra-less against her thin tank top and she pulled over her head the light sweater from the floor next to her. When the blowing ends she will take the sweater off; the cycle is further distraction. The moments before the sweater gets over her head she is fueled in the work of her memoir with the prickling feel of her nipples against her top. The shiver of goose flesh that the cool air runs over her arms, neck, and loose breast intensifies the feeling of "being in" her own skin. The auto-erotica continues momentarily within the sweater as the new heat around her breasts relaxes the contracted flesh from the nipples, allowing the expanding and loosening area to touch more of her top's texture.

The Abortionist wishes there was a way to bring both of these pursuits together into one discipline. So far she has found no place in the history of the nation state for her sexual memoir and no place in her sexual memoir for the history of the nation state, unless of course she slept with her Thesis Advisor. Maybe she should have pursued a degree in Woman's Studies or something more Post-Modern, like Critical Theory. This thought of unity is just another distraction, but it has merit. Each bone she ever took is a history unto itself; some repeated penetrations onto the same shaft would necessitate a 726 page volume like Riasanovsky's work, while some random insertions would require no more space than what he spent on the Avars. Yet each one was a conquest, each she notes, was an empowerment; they didn't give it to her, she took it from them. She was never a tyrant, but conquest has its price. Where are all those bone-bearers now while she sits here alone composing her history? It is known that history is written by the victors.

She writes on, her skin tightening, air-conditioning blowing down on her, its sound carrying down from on-high the silent screams of her death-born children, to her the fevered pitches of triumphant glee.

 C∝ #F

Jordan A. Rothacker lives in Athens, GA where he earned a Doctorate in Comparative Literature and a Masters in Religion from the University of Georgia. Rothacker majored in Philosophy at Manhattanville College in Purchase, NY, and his life has been split between New York (where he was born) and Georgia. His journalism has appeared in periodicals as diverse as Vegetarian Times and International Wristwatch while his fiction, poetry, and essays can be found in the likes of Red River Review, Dark Matter, Dead Flowers, Stone Highway Review, Mayday Magazine, As It Ought to Be, and The Exquisite Corpse. 2015 saw his first published book-length work, The Pit, and No Other Stories, a novella (or "micro-epic" as he calls it) from Black Hill Press. His most recent work is the novel And Wind Will Wash Away (Deeds Publishing, August 2016). He loves sandwiches (a category in which he classifies pizza and tacos) and debating taxonomy almost as much as much as he loves his wife, his dogs, and his cat, Whiskey. www.jordanrothacker.com

BELOVED - DIANE ROOT

It took a while before the villa was sold. It was slowly disintegrating, abandoned for years after her death. Her father had fled from the fierce eyes of the villagers in a vain attempt to escape. He was haunted by his daughter's image. He would have preferred to be slaughtered than live that way, but he lacked the courage to commit suicide. He was, in his own estimation, without a doubt, a spineless man caught within the spider's web of his own illicit, incestuous passion. His despair drowned him, like the tidal waves curling upon the sands. Their ripples glinted, fracturing in tiny sunlit triangles, both beautiful and near lethal, encircling his heart and throat. He contemplated the sea's rolling depths, the crashing foam detonated close to his perch on the rocky beach that curved around a place he could no longer name. Nor did he want to remember.

But the rest he could not forget.

* * *

The once-lush garden had long dried and died beneath a relentless, murderous Mediterranean sun. The patio's flagstones, too, all but crumbled beneath even the gentlest touch.

The new owners, however, knew nothing about its history, and the "realtors," such as they were—a caretaker neighbor and his wife—were careful not to tell them. So it was that they suspected nothing.

Not until they dug up the courtyard did they see first the skull, then the rest of the skeleton.

* * *

In the village, no one knew when she had been condemned to death or what crime she had committed. But rumors flew on the sidewalks and in the cafes, *sotto voce*.

She was young. Many said she was barely 20, if that. Lissome and slender-boned, an oval face as though painted by Modigliani. Her greatest pride resided in her hair, patent leather shining blue-black, which fell straight to her hips, swinging as she walked the streets of the tiny town, which she did endlessly, slowly pacing their cobblestones, rounding beneath her feet, as though counting the beads of a rosary.

* * *

As she passed, the old women leaned toward each other, hunched in shapeless layers of black widowhood. They squatted in front of their fruits and vegetables, their lace and their filigree, their pots and pottery, wizened faces so dark as to be almost featureless, framed in the folds of their shawls. Nothing showed but the glinting coal of wicked eyes. They whispered among themselves in the narrow, bleached-white streets about the vile acts she must have committed. Others observed that she looked exactly like her mother—the mother who had died young in childbirth. A sin, they said, was waiting to happen, if it hadn't already. Their trapezoid, ebony shapes sat on stoops and stairs, squatting on diminutive chairs, facing the street where she passed.

* * *

The backdrop of all these dark voices echoed, embedded in the bleached-as-bone walls, bleak with memories, softened only by the pale pinks, lavenders, deepening blues and purples of the evening, shadows of the graceful archways, cushioning the nameless streets with pastels.

* * *

The day of her execution was unknown to all but her father, who had brought her here from another, similarly sun-scorched place, without warning. Since he had never hidden from her what her fate would be, he told her where it would take place; in the courtyard of the thickly walled house, paved with flagstones and bordered with bright flowers; the house with the foot-long key. By tradition in those parts, couples would marry and live out long lives till death did them part. Not a bad place to die, she thought. But she would die without having been married.

* * *

She had not been imprisoned by her father, although he could have easily done so; she was allowed to roam the few streets of this village.

There were those who were curious to hear her voice, wishing her a good morning or good evening to see if she would respond. She never did.

Her voice, like her life, was her secret, or so she thought.

* * *

The villagers had never seen the Executioner either, but they knew of him. They imagined him masked, perhaps, or with a grim, grey-featured and fractured countenance. Thin-lipped, he would have a cruel bend at its corners. (The edges of the mouth were dead giveaways, her father used to say—they portrayed the real person hidden behind the face.)

* * *

When at last he appeared, there was no mistaking him. In a town populated only by a couple of hundred people, he was the sole stranger. And this was not a place where people would come of their own volition. To come here from elsewhere–the "outside"- was to have a specific purpose. In this case, a deadly one.

He was startlingly handsome-looking, square of face, powerful of body, strong long smooth hands that were deceptively soft. The back and shoulders were strong, the neck massive and muscular. The eyes, unexpected in that chiseled face, were gray-blue, almost transparent. "He's French," said her father, as though this made everything all right—some sort of cultural event.

* * *

The two men stood in the courtyard, taking stock of each other, talking quietly at first. They were apparently pleased with each other, and soon began walking together, to and fro, speaking of death and its throes. Hers, of course. What to expect, how to prepare, what to do "afterwards."

At first hushed, their voices slowly rose with excitement at the prospect. Death, it seemed, was akin to yeast slowly swelling a dough for bread—the so-called staff of life. The tone acquired an unaccustomed near-shrill quality that pierced the quiet of the golden late afternoon, loud enough for her to hear from the aerie of her bedroom overlooking the courtyard, where she stood, stark still in the shadows.

It was then that he opened the case, which he had set on the stone bench. Lined with velvet; its contents glinted and sparkled like so many jewels. There were dirks and daggers, swords and sabers, cutlasses and curved blades carried by the men in Yemen—knives of every description, sharp as the shining sea below.

* * *

The Executioner patiently explained that, in deference to her youth, beauty and obedience, he would see to it that the sword would be as sharp as the slivers of light that darted off the waves. She would suffer little, if at all.

But she remembered what the surgeon had said. "Death takes time," he declared, "and the brain is the last to die."

* * *

It was at last agreed that she would be allowed to live through the next sun-splashed day, and that the sword would catch the last gilded rays of the sun on its lethal downswing. Her deliverance would come just before the lavender shades of dusk.

As befitting her station (she was, after all, a princess), she would, on that last day, sit before an offering table laden with rice, berries, fruit, curries and chutneys, pitchers of wine, because that's what she most loved to eat and drink, which would later given to the guests at her funeral. There would be cool water for her lips and hands. Occasionally, the oldest woman servant, who had brought her into the world, would kneel and splash her feet with water, touch the nape of her neck with numbing herbs, and smooth her forehead with the refreshing pools in her weathered palms.

* * *

She dressed carefully that day. A long white dress foaming with Belgian lace that framed her face and frothed about her ankles, which could have been her wedding dress. She remembered that here, her gown might be considered inappropriate in this island of widows, maybe even blasphemous. In India, white was the color of mourning, and Death was simply a transition to another Life.

She, on the other hand, did not believe that death was anything other than final, but she floated on this foreign wave of hope, robed in an aureole of whiteness.

As was her custom, she wore no shoes, a symbol of humility, and because she wanted to feel the last warmth of stone beneath her feet. The servant bent toward her, shaped, polished and painted each nail until they shone, burnished and almost perfect ovals. So, too, were her hands, blanched and bright with a moon hue.

She fastened her mother's heavy Arabian necklace about her slender neck, all the while thinking to herself that the Executioner would have to remove it, as he would a disgraced knight's armor before he lifted the sword to release the crimson wash of blood—an offering to the setting sun,

* * *

As the table was being set for the last repast, two hours past the greatest heat and two hours before dusk—the servant in her great wisdom and mercy, insisted that food and drink would act as soporifics and contentment, thereby dulling the pain. The young woman, clad in her virginal dress, passed through the gates of her house to walk, very slowly, very straight, down the main cobblestoned main street, past the church, which she did not enter, into the marketplace, which she did enter, walking the circumference of the atrium, silencing the garrulous merchants, one by one, as she passed. Within minutes, the entire town was silenced, the movements hushed.

Later, there would be the swishing of long traditional skirts and petticoats, the shuffling of shoes against the stones as the shrouded townspeople gathered in front of the courtyard's heavy doors, filtering the street with their darkness in broad daylight, waiting for a last cry of anguish.

Then, at last, they would know what her voice sounded like.

* * *

The last meal that she was allowed lasted until well into the afternoon. Lengthening shadows started to turn mauve, lavender and violet—dusk was minutes, maybe seconds away.

The two men, enlivened by the wine, chattered volubly to one another, even jested, as though this was a meal like any other, even a bit more festive.

Of the two, only the Executioner occasionally glanced at her, sometimes smiling, ever so slightly. She, now close to him, gazed and realized that she was in love with him. The only one in her young life. She reached out to touch his right hand—the strong, beautiful long-fingered hand that would kill her. Unmoved, he withdrew without even seeming to acknowledge her.

Her father, since the date of her condemnation, did not speak to her as though his voice might utter a forbidden endearment. He never turned to look at her with his crystal-blue glacial eyes. Ever.

* * *

Outside the hush thickened, smothering the sky and stones. An occasional pebble rolled, displaced by a careless foot.

* * *

The once-laden table stood bare, stripped of the lavish embroidered tablecloth first used at her mother's wedding some 27 years earlier, cleared of wine and food and honey. Now, she thought, we get to the naked truth.

* * *

She stood next to her father, as though she were going down the aisle to bond with a beloved groom. She felt his warmth radiating from the softly-haired, tanned arms, glowing now in the setting sun. He, too, wore tropical white.

A basket, lined with grape leaves, stood in the place of the silver pitcher, was now moved to the center of the courtyard. Near it, a brilliant bouquet of favorite flowers—those whose aroma smelled of the earth in which they grew—zinnias, marigolds, and cockscombs. Cadmium yellows and reds, fiery pinks and oranges and gold.

My last rainbow, she thought.

* * *

Her father, who had abstained from even looking at her all this time, stared at the wooden block on the ground, the last pillow where his daughter would lay her head. Someone, most probably the servant who loved her, had placed real silken pillows in front of the chopping block for her knees.

For the first time, he looked at her, the stillness in his eyes warned her.

"Are you afraid?" he asked.

"Yes," she whispered.

"Good," he answered.

"Why are you doing this?" she asked.

"Because I love you. Too much."

* * *

There were 13 steps between the space where they were standing at the front door of their house that gave onto the patio and the wood block. Slow- motion interminable steps that went somehow at lightning speed.

Before they started down this last aisle of her life, her father handed her a single rose. He explained that he wanted her to see the bloom with which she would be buried while she was still alive. That she was beloved and not left bereft in her grave. That he had done was expected of him.

She held it to her breast so closely, she felt the thorns puncturing her flesh. She was still holding it as she knelt before the beheading block, gradually elongating her proud, swan-like neck as though to ease the Executioner's work.

Her long, heavy, ebony hair had been twisted up, held by her mother's tortoise-shell comb, exposing her fragile nape.

In the quiet of the evening, the last sound was the swish and muffled whistle of the raised sword, and the lightning flash of the downward slash as it caught the last rays of the setting sun, slicing off her head as though it were made of soft butter.

Just before the last second, she craned her neck to take a last look at her father, whom, despite everything, she adored. It was then when she saw the sword.

In her father's hand.

* * *

177

ℭℜ ℬℭ

Diane Root, a dual-national, was born in Paris of an American father, the journalist and writer, Waverley Root, and a French mother. Primarily known as a painter, she is, as she describes herself, "an accidental writer." She never sought to be published but that notwithstanding, she was nonetheless published in the New York Times Magazine ("The Artful Dodger" about lunch with Picasso) and various other venues. View her art: http://matakia.com.

INHERITANCE – KIRSTEN FERGUSON

She stands on the dusty road, heels digging into the dirt, and looks up at the crumbling farmhouse. The once green shutters and painted boards are now bleached and worn, like bones left too long in the sun. The windows are broken, shards of glass grinning back at her. She approaches the house, slowly pushing through the overgrown lawn, before she comes to a stop at the front door. But even as she lifts a hand to the cool doorknob her muscles refuse to grasp the handle.

Turning, she can see the barn where she and her brother used to play. Often they would trap one of the half wild cats stalking the yard and carry them, hissing and scratching, to the loft. They would take turns holding the squirming animals up by their paws and dropping them off the ledge, testing to see if cats really do land on their feet. Once, her brother tossed a kitten too high and it fell to the ground, landing in a heap. She can still remember the sick feeling as she looked down at the still form, neck twisted and paws splayed. "I think it's dead," her brother whispered, as if by not saying it too loud he could make it not true.

Stepping to the side she tries to look in the kitchen window. Through a crack in the glass she can see a light spot on the otherwise yellowed wallpaper. The night her baby sister died her father sat below the clock that once hung there, listening to minute after minute tick away. It had been oddly warm outside, without a hint of wind, as if the farm was holding its breath along with her father. She could clearly recall the empty bottle of scotch in his hand, the glass long forgotten.

Finally, she walks to the front door and turns the key in the resistant lock. Stepping inside the smell hits her first: dust and moldering, nothing like the warm bread she recalled. The blue striped wallpaper is peeling and instinctively she steps over the third board in the floor, knowing it will squeak. Above her, she sees her father at the top of the stairs, hands outstretched, just as he had stood all those years ago. Her eyes travel to the base of the stairs, where her pregnant mother was once sprawled. Her ears echo with the memory of her father screaming, "You didn't see nothing! Nothing!"

At the funeral her family stood around the tiny casket. It was still too warm, but the world had started to breathe again. The wind teased at her mother's hair, her father's jacket. She remembered how they each took turns tossing handfuls of dirt into the small hole, but the wind snatched the dirt from her father's hands.

It became her father's habit to sit under the old clock, watching the hands tick with a whiskey in hand. She used to think that he was still waiting to hear that first cry from Baby Girl. She knows better now.

Starting her car, she listens to the quiet purr of the engine. Finally, she throws the car into gear and drives away. She doesn't look back, because she didn't see nothing. Nothing.

CR   SO

Kirsten Ferguson is a Technical Writer for a small software development company in Idaho. She posts some of her work to a WordPress blog: https://inklingoftruth.wordpress.com/.

"Inheritance" is her first published work of fiction.

HEAVY METAL – AARON RODRIGUEZ

"Hey Adam! You leaving already?" Evan, my closest friend, stumbles out onto the porch of his house. A Metallica playlist blasts for a moment before the door closes behind him. He removes his wolf mask and takes a swig from the beer can in his hand.

"Yeah man, it's getting late." I show him my phone screen, it flashes 12:06 AM. I adjust my skeleton costume. The shadows of tree branches close in on us when my screen goes dark.

"But it's Halloween! I haven't even howled at the moon yet." He points at the moon with his chin.

"I have work in the morning. But it was good to catch up."

"Adam, don't be a ball buster. Here," he puts the beer can in front of my mouth, "just finish this one and call into work tomorrow."

"I'm good, Evan. My Uber should be here any minute anyway." I push the beer can out of my face.

"Wow, Adam. You used to be fun." Evan sneers. "One rough night last summer and you turn into a damn recluse."

"I'm just trying to focus on other things. Don't give me that." I look at the string of mini jack-o-lantern lights decorating the porch.

"Yeah, I'm sure that's it." He sips what's left in his can. "Whatever man."

I check my phone, still 3 minutes away. I crack the bones in my neck. I don't dare think about last summer.

"Looks like your ride's here. Run along now." Evan says and makes a running motion with his fingers.

I shake my head and look at the black car that is almost camouflaged by the dark. If it weren't for the headlights, you wouldn't be able to see it.

"See ya." I say without turning around and walk down the porch. I can feel Evan's eyes burning into my backside. I pick up my pace and open the door of the backseat.

"Welcome." A gruff voice says. I catch a glimpse of his hazel eyes, pale skin, and beard as he turns to greet me over his shoulder. I nod and shut the car door.

"Harlan and 25th." I take off my top hat and toss it on the black leather next to me. A glowing skull sits on the dashboard.

"Aren't you going to put your seatbelt on?" He asks.

"Can you just drive please, man?" I roll my eyes and take off my skeleton gloves.

"Hmm." He snickers and looks at me through the rear view mirror. He begins to drive.

"Can't wait to get home." I say under my breath. My phone vibrates. Evan's face fills my screen. I let it go to voicemail. The driver's long black curls gleam in the phone's light. The phone vibrates again.

"How long have you had your long hair?" I ask him, more to distract myself than an interest to fill the silence.

"What feels like an eternity." He reaches for the radio dial. A silver ring decorates his bony, index finger. My phone vibrates for a third time. Evan's face is inescapable. I press the answer button.

"What's up? No, I have it on silent. It's- no. I already told you, Evan..." I notice the driver's eyes staring at me in the mirror again. I look down. Can't he mind his own damn business?

"Can we please not bring that up? It's one simple rule, Evan. Can you respect that? No! My fault?! You're the one who was driving!" I yell into the phone.

"My idea! Well, it was my idea that saved us! I can't even believe you right now, Evan. You would have kissed your future goodbye if it weren't for me! Oh you're sorry? I'm so done with this conversation." I huff and put my phone down. I expect the phone to light up with his face again but it stays black.

"Anything I can help with?" The driver asks. He makes a right turn.

"Sir, you really need to butt out right now."

"Suit yourself." The only sound is ACDC's Highway to Hell coming out of his radio.

"Fan of the oldies, huh?" I try to ease the tension.

"Oh yeah. I remember when this song was released. Seeing it live was one hell of an experience. No pun intended, of course. It's not like the apps you kids have nowadays. You wanted to feel an artist's essence, you had to do whatever you could to see them in person."

"Hmm." I say, less interested in this conversation.

"If you knew KISS was rolling through for one single show in your state and you had to drive 6 hours to see them. You did it. Anything to get in that crowd. If you had to sell your soul for Zeppelin tickets, you did it."

"I bet." I look out the window and don't recognize the poorly lit backroad he's driving on.

"Hey, do you know where you're going?"

"Of course."

"You sure? Where are we? We should have reached my apartment by now." I open my maps app.

"Just sit back. I'm taking a shortcut. I know exactly where I'm taking you." He turns up the song significantly higher.

"You're not one to relinquish control easily, Adam." He says calmly.

"How do you know my name?" I raise my eyebrows.

"We've met before."

"I'm sorry, who are you?"

"My friends call me 'Old Nick.'"

"I don't know any Nicks. How do you know my name?"

"I'd be less worried about who you think I am and more worried about your consequences." He speeds up. The orange and yellow leaves scatter on the road as we zip by them.

183

"I don't know what you mean." His motor revs as we go even faster.

"Oh, I think you do."

"Hey 'Old Nick' can you slow the hell down, please?" I look around but there's no one in sight and ahead of us is only open road.

"Irony at its finest." He snickers. "Judgment, consequence, punishment. You're getting exactly what you deserve."

"What is this??" I check my door handle but I can't unlock it.

"It's just your time, Adam. I do believe you had a few more years ahead of you but you threw those away last summer after that concert." He says with alarming confidence.

"What are you-I...it wasn't my fault!" I shout.

"Sure it wasn't," the driver says. The speedometer reads 140 mph. Looming darkness ahead of us.

"It was her own fault! She shouldn't have been in the middle of the road like that." I swallow the rising fear in my throat.

"Unfortunately for you, she was somebody that was supposed to be untouchable in our realm. Protected. Fortunately for me, just another name I no longer have to worry about." His voice begins to get deeper. His pale fingers suddenly grow longer around the steering wheel. "Though I must admit, disposing of the body the way you did." His voice gets raspy and low." Even I was impressed."

"Please...please stop the car." My voice quivers and my eyes water.

"Tears? This early?" His hazel eyes in the rear view mirror turn completely black. His shoulders begin to slouch and his spine begins to curve and crunch. "It's just as well, this isn't going to be pleasant for you."

"This can't be real!" I shout and hit the window with my fist.

"Ha!" His guttural voice lingers and fangs protrude from the corners of his lips.

Ahead, I see the large entrance of a tunnel approaching quickly.

"No! Please!" I plead.

"It's much too late for any of that." He smiles back at me, his tongue is suddenly too large for his widening mouth.

I scream. His rough, clawed hand grabs at my skeleton shirt as we enter the tunnel and the thick darkness swallows us. I hope to see a light at the end but all I hear is the echo of Old Nick's rumbling laughter.

C33 &

Aaron Rodriguez is a writer, fashion stylist, and horror movie addict in Denver, Colorado. Whether he's working on pitches at 303 Magazine, drinking coffee around the city, or shopping for anything in black, you can follow what he's up to on Instagram @BlankCanvasFashion

Lucy O'dior is a citizen of the world; she makes her home on the unforgiving sea, which is where we find her—in one of her many ocean liners—powering across the Atlantic Ocean with no discernible heading in mind. The time 7:45 A.M. The trip so far: uneventful. Despite being one of the fifty richest females in the United States, O'dior is discontented. She harbors a dark secret, a childhood pain, and an extensive memory. You, dear reader, are about to discover what can happen when these three things are blended in an isolated container. Join us as we board this vessel, peel back the skin of this one-percenter and discover the horrors in BONED.

The formidable ship did not just push ferocious waves asunder—it pulverized them, cutting the whitecaps like hot butter. While most people fear the sea, or are at least are wary of it, this ship's master—and CEO of the world famous Grand United Industries Liners—finds it calming, at least on most days.

"Fuck it!" she slammed the laptop shut before hurling it through the open window and into the crushing sea below. "No more emails."

Lucy O'dior perched on the edge of her bedstead, she did this with an air of grace that she exhibited even when not being observed. Her thoughts drifted—traveling about the extravagant cabin—eyes darting between immoderate furnishings. Her nose may have turned blind to the stench of high-priced fragrances, but her eyes still recognized that all too familiar stink: success.

Lucy grinned a rare grin—she did not smile much anymore—for her wandering eyes fell stagnant, fixating on a low hanging chandelier. This young lady saw her past lives in each and every one of its gleams and sparkles: an orphaned baby, an abused child, a homeless teen, and an incarcerated young adult. She had come so far since those bygone days, those former realities. The luxurious candelabrum gently swayed, the incandescent twinkles vanished. With a return swing they reappeared. Again faces materialized within the crystal—

yet these were not her likenesses. She recognized the haunting visages flickering in the glass, the cruel catalysts of her past lives': a drunk driver's bewildered stupor, her foster father's evil glint, a landlady's callous glare, and a judge's disapproving scowl. These men and women had caused so much pain and torment in her life. She could clearly recollect it all, and the imagery reflected this fact. As clear as a television set, the crystal displayed the horror all over again.

Lucy is a child. She looks up from the back seat of a car, blood coats the broken windshield, wind whistles through the crack and yawns into the night. Her parents are slumped in their seats; they don't move when a strange man approaches. He stumbles over his feet, blue and red lights flash in the distance. The picture has switched now. Foster father stands at her bedroom door; ogling eyes glinting in the shadows, fingers twitching with imagined pleasures. He rushes for her, arms outreached, but he does not reach her. The channel has changed once more. Lucy is in her twenties now. She watches as three husky men remove her belongings from her apartment. The landlady regards her with a cold, heartless glance from the upper window. Lucy now stands in a courtroom, her voice echoes: "I needed the money." The judge hammers the gavel. "Just because you shoot up, doesn't mean you have the right to distribute heroine. I sentence you to five years in a state penitentiary."

Turning from the harsh memories the light fixture wrought, she caught a glimpse of herself in the cabin mirror. Short red hair, face caked in plush makeup, and body wrapped up in an exquisite dress — the smile returned. None of those past lives mattered, not anymore. That abused, homeless orphan no longer existed. In that child's place, the unblemished glass exhibited a strong and wealthy businesswoman — the CEO of Grand United Industry Liners. She had achieved greatness and overcome the wicked ones shining in the chandelier. The only life that mattered now was her current one.

"Let it go. Those lives are just the ashes from which you arose," she addressed the mirror. "You have more money than God, they can't hurt you any—"

A shrill beeping consumed the room, cutting her sentence short. Lucy silenced her wristwatch. The time eight A.M. blinked pretentiously on the digital timepiece's tiny face, as if it were admonishing the CEO for her reluctance to attend the day's scheduled board meeting. Dragging her patent leather stilettos across the carpet, she meandered to the door. Before exiting she—as she always did—reviewed all of the cabin's extravagant contents, and with that, all she had achieved... and all she had left behind.

* * *

The hallway was alive with radiant color. A golden carpet lay beneath the woman's heels, a ceiling showcasing powerful vessels sailing a sapphire ocean reflected in the surrounding walls' polish. This hallway had taken Lucy years to design, the perfect harmonization of color, art, wealth, and product enhancement. Identical passageways resided in each of her ten cruise liners. Snaking a few times, the corridor finally brought her to the boardroom. Lucy hated the birdcage—as she called it due to its small, metallic interior—and all the accountabilities that came with it: Bradley Moore, Regina Collins, Charlotte Chung, and the worst of the board, Phillip Harris. They were a constant irritant, always droning on about stock market points, business partnerships, and investments. Lucy knew there was no way in hell she could become bankrupt, so the weekly meetings felt like a waste of energy. Letting out a sigh she entered the chamber, eyes refusing to meet the board of directors until absolutely necessary. The doors slammed, the clattering echoed in her ears.

"I appreciate your patience, people. As you know I am extremely busy this time of" Lucy stopped, eyes on her heels and hand reaching for her nose. "What on earth is that awful sme—" The alarm emitted from her watch once more. "Damn thing," she muttered, pawing at the untouchable sound.

Lucy, at last, looked up with a strident squeal. The board members were gathered at a lengthy table, their emaciated figures slumped over its refined surface, ashen faces, frayed and peeling skin, blood-shot eyes, mouths agape—prominently displaying blackened teeth—and, at the epicenter of it all, a small monitor displayed a flickering snowstorm of dots, a crude static emanating from its speakers. Lucy instantly fled back to the doors, mind focusing on her clicker-clacking heels. It was no use. The woman pulled and pulled but the doors would not budge. "Get me the fuck out of here! Hello? Hello?" she screamed—pleading over the static—now relentlessly striking the doors with balled fists, splintering her imitation nails. The exit remained steadfast, appearing to be held shut by a formless force. *Where is everyone?* She wondered.

Exhausted and panting, her soul grew stronger, or desperate. She resolved to face the slouching demons. With intrepid steps she moved nearer and nearer, eyes darting among the corpses, heart pounding beneath her bosom. It was not the odor, nor was it the carcasses' unsightly appearances that disturbed her most, it was not even the stillness—the silence—the lack of life. It was their skeletal-like exterior, comparable to if their souls had been slurped from their bodies, leaving a deflated bag of bones behind. Clutching Phillip—the nearest skeleton—by the collar, she pulled the man from the table—his rigid frame sinking into the chair, a decayed tooth falling from his mouth and plummeting to the floor with a dreadful ding. Fear boiled in her gut and sprayed from her mouth: "My God," the two words dissolved into a whisper.

Phillip's undernourished face resembled an egg on a skillet—gurgling and spiting as additional layers of skin fell away, dancing on the air like October leaves. The last of his sweltering hide was shed, revealing another face. This corpse was no longer that of Phillip Harris, she did, however, recognize its rotten profile. Its nose was missing and its cheekbones had crumbled far beneath its lax husk, nevertheless, she identified the deceased as her late foster father. Her gaze fell back to the other bodies. They too had metamorphosed. Their gaunt appearances were unmistakable: the judge, the landlady... the drunk driver. Even in death those past lives—her tormenters—had found their way to the middle of the Atlantic Ocean.

"Wake up!" she bawled, exhausted from the trauma, collapsing into a seat, head falling onto the tabletop's cool exterior. The monitor nearby was a stark reminder that this was intended to be a conference, not a dead congregation. Wishing on all precious possessions—her ocean liners—that this day was merely a nightmare from which she would soon awake proved fruitless. As the CEO buried her face in her hands, a shiver ran down her spine, for a swift draft brushed by, causing her hair to flutter. Lucy's muscles tightened. She jumped away from the seat, knocking it to the ground. The resounding clang merged with the television's heavy static, producing a dramatic amalgamation, akin to the tunes played at climaxes of Saturday morning serials. Escorted by this unwelcome hymn, she turned back to her faux father's corpse, eyes falling upon an empty seat. Thenceforth a hand, freezing to the touch, crawled its way up the woman's back on nimble fingers before implanting itself firmly atop her shoulder. Lucy's vision blurred with terror, "My *darlin'*, come show *daddy* some love!" She sped away, the hand clasping—tearing a strap from her dress.

The corpse shuffled forward, strap dangling from its fingertips, a toothless smirk beaming from a dislocated jaw, fiery, blood-sodden eyes scorching Lucy's soul and boiling her rapidly beating heart. Wilting from the approaching terror, half-repressed memories returned to the CEO with great clarity, comparable to if she were a little girl all over again. The table jolted, the other bodies began to animate—hands clawing at empty air, mouths snarling as if at an electric current's behest.

"Did ya think you could get away from us that easy?" Foster father asked, in a low voice—the kind of voice that causes souls to shudder.

"All I want is to be left alone, just go away!"

"Guilty!" the judge wailed, rising from the table and hammering her fist upon its surface. "Guilty!"

Returning to the entrance, Lucy again yanked, heaved, and hit as hard as she could in a vain attempt to open the immovable doors. Finally, she turned to face the horrors, back sliding down the cold metal until she lay on the ground in a hopeless heap, acquiescing herself to her apparent fate, observing the harbingers of her past lives—foster father's twitching hands, landlady's cruel glare, judge's shrill scream, and the inebriated driver's unsteady gait. Lucy did not fight it anymore—just watched their subdued ascent, tears falling from her eyes—ready for the last of her lives to come to a macabre culmination.

The phantoms stopped, inches from her sunken figure. Reaching into their pockets, each one pulled out a tiny scrap of paper and dropped it at the CEO's affluent footwear. Lucy awaited their wrath but that wrath did not come... they did nothing—just lingering in place. Scrambling to the pile of papers, she lifted the nearest shred, and then another and another. They were all identical: Complimentary tickets to a two-week getaway on Grand United Industries Liner...

Ten. The air fell still. The monitor's static dispersed, a somber news anchor appeared onscreen in its place.

"I have the unfortunate responsibility of bringing our viewers some distressing news. We are just being told that the coast guard discovered the remnants of the missing cruise liner this morning at approximately eight A.M. It appears that the tenth Grand United Industries Liner sank due to an explosion onboard which damaged the hull. Over 200 people are confirmed dead while 50 more remain missing. Grand United Industries Liners had ten luxury ships in service, the principle owner, Lucy O'dior, resides on the eleventh. Stay with channel six news for more, after this—"

The screen cut back to static before repeating the message.

"Did ya *really* think it was that easy, did ya think you could leave your *daddy, darlin'*?" foster father asked again.

Lucy looked up, into the corpse's crimson eyes. "Yes..."

"Guilty! Guilty!" the judge squawked.

Lucy, no longer afraid, got upright. "Bet your fucking *ass* I'm *guilty*! Those complimentary tickets I mailed each of you were meant to take you on a luxury cruise to hell!"

The drunkard stumbled forward, "I didn't mean to kill your parents, but you meant to kill us, and all the people aboard with us."

"I would have sacrificed the lives of thousands to furnish your sunken graves. I would have done anything to get away from you fuckers—to punish you all for what you did to me and mine!"

"But, darlin', darlin'... darlin', you can't get away from *us*." Her adoptive father smiled, lunging forward, clutching at her slender arms with an icy grip, and wrestling her to the ground. "We will *always* be with you."

She felt like that child again. Lucy kicked and punched, heel penetrating putrid flesh, fist cracking brittle bone—coagulated blood oozing from now open wounds. The corpse did not abate, its unyielding hands as swift as ever. It reached for anything it could seize, but she intercepted its fingers and tore each digit from its hand. The extremities dropped, Lucy rose, driving a heel into its skull, over and over until nothing remained above its shoulders save powdered bone and brain.

"Guilty! Guilty! Guilty!" Beep. Beep. The judge's voice morphed into that penetrating alarm. Lucy lifted her wristwatch—the time: eight

A.M. *How is this possible? The time my cruise liner sank, the time I left my cabi—*

She lowered her arm to see that chandelier once more, sparkling in all its brilliance—the faces from her past leering at her from within its garish shimmers. The CEO was back in her cabin, limp from the visions exhibited in its luster.

"My darlin', Lucy."

That smooth voice again, this time from the mirror—foster father smirked from the other side of the glass with more substance than any dream's phantom, he appeared as alive and as wicked as the day Lucy first came into his care.

"Leave me alone!" she screeched. She—as she always did—reviewed all of the cabin's extravagant contents, all she had achieved and all that she had never left behind. Every single extravagant item bared their faces, from bureau's sleek surface to glitzy makeup case, their presence loomed large. Her past lives were recapitulated over and over again. The stink of success no longer hung on the air.

* * *

Bradley Moore, Regina Collins, Charlotte Chung, and Phillip Harris waited impatiently with sweat on their brows and laptops open in the boardroom.

"Where is she?" Charlotte finally asked.

"You know how she is," Phillip replied.

"Yeah, so just think how she will be when she reads that email. Nobody takes kindly to being investigated, especially when that investigation includes murder and, least of all, insurance fraud."

"Hell of an email to wake up." Bradley piped up. "Looks like we will need to dock at the next po—"

"Hold it, People," Regina's voice was heard for the first time. "It looks like the email has been opened—she's seen it already. I think somebody needs to go find her. She can't be taking it well."

* * *

Phillip pushed open the cabin door to see a once opulent chamber in ruins. The room's chandelier had been torn from the ceiling, the bed had been overturned, and mirror had been shattered into a spider's web of cracks. Lucy O'dior sat amidst broken glass and tattered clothing. "Where are my parents? We were on the way to the boat show, but there was a crash. Where are they?" she mumbled.

"Pleading insanity isn't going to cut it. We are in deep shit here. I am not taking the fall for this."

She looked up through a haze of smeared markup. Their gaze met.

"No, I don't want to stay with him, he looks at me funny."

Phillip saw something different in her eyes.

"Lucy, we are in *big* trouble here. They think you sunk that ship. They want us to reroute."

"No, don't take my home away, I can pay next month... just one more month."

Phillip kneeled beside her, his arm reluctantly draped over her shoulder, as tears built in her eyes.

"Don't send me away, judge. I don't want to go to prison."

Lucy O'dior is a one-percenter; she owns fine fragrances and luxury clothing. She eats premium food from deluxe silverware. Unfortunately for O'dior, she also consumed poison from a cold dish labeled revenge. This citizen of the world makes her home on the ocean in attempt to escape her past lives—to be alone. But, try as she might, she is never alone. She is accompanied on that merciless sea by the four unforgiving souls whose earthly forms now reside far beneath its cobalt surface, in a rusty relic identified only as Grand United Industries Liner Ten. Or, as O'dior knows it: G.U.I.L.T.

CR ഔ

Dean Moses is the author of A Stalled Ox, *entertainment contributor for the* Spring Creek Sun, *wordsmith extraordinaire, and hungry vegan.*

GOING BLUE – JEFFREY WOLF

Cast

Morgan

Mindy

Blue Fairy

Setting:

A bedroom, late at night/early in the morning.

(At rise MORGAN and MINDY are in bed. MINDY is sleeping. MORGAN is awake and keeps lifting his covers to look underneath.)

MORGAN:

Honey?

MINDY:

(Barely stirring:)

Nhmm.

MORGAN:

Honey, wake up.

MINDY:

Sleeping.

MORGAN:

No – I – need your help.

MINDY:

With what? Can't it wait until morning?

MORGAN:

I – um – I'm not going down.

MINDY:

Huh?

MORGAN:

I'm still – erect.

MINDY:

Seriously?

MORGAN:

Yeah. It's –

MINDY:

You woke me up for that?

MORGAN:

It's been a long time.

MINDY:

You're insatiable. It's been like – four hours.

MORGAN:

No – it's –

MINDY:

I got you off twice. I guess I can just lay here if you need to go again.

MORGAN:

I know – it's not –

MINDY:

I already brushed my teeth so I'm not –

MORGAN:

Mindy, I don't think that's the problem.

MINDY:

What do you mean?

MORGAN:

I don't think I actually need to –

MINDY:

Fuck?

MORGAN:

Well, yes.

MINDY:

You're still so cute, Morgan. It's three a.m. and I can still make you blush. I guess I can brush my teeth again.

MORGAN:

No – wait –

MINDY:

You want me to get the whipped cream? I don't want that much sugar this late –

MORGAN:

No – I think I'm actually – empty.

MINDY:

Huh?

MORGAN:

I'm all – shriveled up – at that part.

MINDY:

Really? *(She reaches under the covers.)* Wow – you are. Then why are you hard? Wow – you're really hard. You didn't take one of those blue pills, did you?

MORGAN:

No. You know I don't need –

MINDY:

Believe me, I know. I can walk into a room in sweats and you're on fire.

MORGAN:

You're pretty.

MINDY:

Thank you, sweetheart.

Did Evan secretly drug you?

MORGAN:

No. I don't think so. You know I don't like to put any foreign things in my body.

MINDY:

No, just into my body.

MORGAN:

Can we stay focused?

MINDY:

Who can focus at this time of night?

MORGAN:

Mindy, please?

MINDY:

How long have you been like this?

MORGAN:

I think like six hours.

MINDY:

No wonder you were ready to go right when you got home tonight.

MORGAN:

I thought it might make it go away. And there's something else.

MINDY:

What?

MORGAN:

It's a different color.

MINDY:

Say that again.

MORGAN:

And I think it's – glowing.

MINDY:

Seriously? *(MINDY puts her head under the covers.)* Wow! That's amazing! It's like a bug zapper. Or a lightsaber. You're like a Jedi master.

MORGAN:

It's really freaking me out.

MINDY:

(Under the covers:)

No wonder you handed me the blindfold just after you threw me on the bed.

MORGAN:

I didn't want to scare you.

MINDY:

(Under the covers:)

It doesn't feel any different.

MORGAN:

Wh – what are you –

MINDY:

(Under the covers:)

I wanted to see if it tasted different.

MORGAN:

Oh. You surprised me. So – does it?

MINDY:

(Under the covers:)

No. *(A beat.)* It's hypnotic.

MORGAN:

Honey –

MINDY:

(Under the covers:)

I feel like I could stare at this for days.

MORGAN:

Mindy – can you come back out?

MINDY:

(Under the covers:)

What? *(MINDY comes out from under the covers.)* Oh sure. That's so incredible.

MORGAN:

Yet terrifying.

MINDY:

It'll be OK, Morgan. Maybe we can take you on tour.

———

MORGAN:

Tour? Like a circus show?

MINDY:

I'm just teasing, babe. Does it hurt?

MORGAN:

It doesn't really feel any different at all. I just want it to go back to normal.

MINDY:

Is your pee blue, too?

MORGAN:

Not that I've noticed.

MINDY:

You really don't know how this happened?

MORGAN:

I feel like I would have lead with that. It is starting to get a little uncomfortable. I'm a little lightheaded.

MINDY:

I'll get you some water.

MORGAN:

Don't take the blankets.

MINDY:

But I'm cold.

MORGAN:

I don't want to –

MINDY:

What? Expose it to the air?

                    MORGAN:

It's embarrassing.

                    MINDY:

Use a pillow.

                    MORGAN:

Fine.

                    MINDY:

Here's your water.

                    MORGAN:

Thank you.

                    MINDY:

Did that help at all?

                    MORGAN:

A little. It still feels – weird.

                    MINDY:

Kind of like when I had my clit pierced.

                    MORGAN:

Your what?

                    MINDY:

I was a teenager. It was so distracting that I took it out in under a week.

                    MORGAN:

Did it hurt?

                    MINDY:

You have no idea. The only thing that made it worth it was the non-stop orgasms.

MORGAN:

That would –

MINDY:

I could be walking down some stairs and boom. So intense. But now I have you, so I don't need that.

MORGAN:

I – uh – try to please.

MINDY:

You succeed. *(A beat. MINDY looks under the covers again.)* I can't believe it's blue.

MORGAN:

(Looking under the covers:)

It looks like I fell into some paint.

MINDY:

Neon paint.

MORGAN:

Glow-in-the-dark neon paint.

MINDY:

And nothing strange happened to you today?

MORGAN:

There was one thing.

MINDY:

A bucket of blue paint?

MORGAN:

I – uh – think I met a leprechaun.

MINDY:

A what?

MORGAN:

I couldn't really understand him. He talked so fast. But he looked the part.

MINDY:

Was it just some guy in a costume?

MORGAN:

He was only about a foot tall and had the bowler hat.

MINDY:

A beard too?

MORGAN:

Yeah. And nice vest.

MINDY:

Are you sure you didn't take any pills? Eat some mushrooms?

MORGAN:

No – this really happened. He charged into my office and started yelling at me. He had this incredibly squeaky voice and talked really fast. It was like gibberish. I couldn't figure out what he wanted and so he shook his fist at me and left.

MINDY:

Why didn't you mention this earlier?

MORGAN:

We were – busy.

MINDY:

You were ravishing me as I lay blindfolded while you tried to get rid of your unending erection.

MORGAN:

And then you were tired.

MINDY:

Wouldn't you be? You think he did this to you?

MORGAN:

Maybe?

MINDY:

Wouldn't it be green instead of blue?

MORGAN:

That's where you're stuck?

MINDY:

I'm just saying.

(The glow under the covers gets brighter.)

MORGAN:

Oh! Oh!

MINDY:

What's going on?

MORGAN:

I think – something's coming!

MINDY:

You?

MORGAN:

Apparently.

(A BLUE FAIRY crawls out from under the sheets.)

MINDY:

Holy shit!

BLUE FAIRY:

Thank you for harboring me in this time of need.

MORGAN:

Harboring you?

BLUE FAIRY:

The leprechauns hunt fairies like myself for food, so I needed a place to hide.

MINDY:

You look like a blueberry with wings.

MORGAN:

Don't be rude, Mindy.

MINDY:

Maybe a plum?

MORGAN:

So you hid in my –

MINDY:

Dick.

BLUE FAIRY:

I needed a warm and lovely cocoon. Thank you again for your hospitality.

MORGAN:

You're welcome?

MINDY:

Did you leave anything behind?

MORGAN:

I hope not.

MINDY:

So what now?

BLUE FAIRY:

I leave you. But not before delivering a blessing upon you both.

MINDY:

Thanks?

BLUE FAIRY:

You are welcome. Thank you again. Farewell!

(BLUE FAIRY exits.)

MORGAN:

That was so weird.

MINDY:

I'm still trying to figure out if this is an acid trip.

MORGAN:

That would make more sense.

MINDY:

What blessing do you think she meant?

MORGAN:

I have no idea.

MINDY:

I – do you think I'm pregnant?

MORGAN:

Really? We've tried so hard –

MINDY:

Maybe, honey. Maybe it finally happened.

MORGAN:

Then that truly is a blessing.

(They embrace.)

MINDY:

I wonder if the baby will be blue.

(Blackout.)

ଔ ଓ

Jeffrey Wolf (Playwright): In addition to authoring the short play, The Scientific Study of Human Comprehension; he recently received a staged reading of Shakespeare's Curse by One Night Stand Theatre at The Vintage Theatre in March 2016. Shakespeare's Curse also enjoyed a workshop with playwright Matthew Lopez at the Denver Center for the Performing Arts' Colorado New Play Summit in February 2015. Jeffrey is also the writer of the children's play, The Worst Play in the History of Ever, being produced by the Center for the Arts in Homer, New York, part of the Chameleon Theatre Circle's 14th Annual New Play Festival in Minnesota in 2013 and the 2013 Ronald M. Ruble New Play Festival at Caryl Crane Youth Theatre in Ohio; Memories of Lost Time, (winner of 2012 Firehouse Theatre Project's annual new play festival and part of The Edge Theatre's "On Your Feet" series); the award-winning Slipping into Anarchy (performed in Colorado, New York, England, Los Angeles, Ohio, Rhode Island, and chosen for production in Romania); Starters (Denver Repertory Theatre Company 2005 production); and No Ideas Today (2012 North Park Playwright Festival in San Diego). (jeffreywolfplays.com)

THE CURSE OF ATTRACTION - STEPHANIE ESCOBAR

The light-hearted sound of the mandolin and the fiddle played loudly through the wooden walls of Tanairy's horse-drawn caravan. She sits at the edge of the bed lacing up her boots; quickly reaching for her patched multicolor skirt and releasing it as she stands up. The jingles the tambourine makes as its being played sends vibrations through her body.

She rushes to peek through the window to observe Romani folks happily dancing. Delirya, her best friend, waves as she runs towards her. Tanairy smiles and makes her way to the door, quickly picking up a hip scarf from the bed.

Delirya opens the door to the caravan.

"Tanairy come quickly, the dance has begun," she says through a huge smile.

They both rush out making their way through the crowd, joined by fellow friends.

They reach the dance circle that surrounds Aemiliamus as he dances the flamenco with multiple women. Tanairy's eyes immediately fix on the handsome Aemiliamus' every move, and she bites her bottom lip.

"He's so handsome, sadly he will never look your way, Tanairy," a rough voice creeps up behind her.

Tanairy and Delirya turn around to face the woman who dared to say such a thing.

"What makes you so sure of it?" she answers.

The old Haitian woman laughs as she looks at Tanairy. "Child, please, Aemiliamus is a man and you my dear, you're not woman enough."

Tanairy lifts her chin up and raises an eyebrow while grabbing her skirt.

208

"You watch, old woman, I'll show you," she says as she signals her friends to join in the flamenco.

Tanairy's heartbeat begins to race as she joins Aemiliamus in the dance.

"Ole!" the townsfolk shout as they clap their hands to the rhythm of the music.

Her friends join in and dismiss the other women dancing around him by moving their skirts aggressively around them. Aemiliamus' intense brown eyes meet Tanairy as he slowly circles her giving her a good look from head to toe, while caressing his black beard. His earrings hide under that long curly hair covered by a brown bandana.

Delirya looks at Tanairy dancing with Aemiliamus and smirks back at the old woman.

"You see woman, you were wrong," she says folding her arms across the chest.

The old woman laughs mischievously.

"I'm never wrong, child" she answers, not losing sight of Tanairy.

"Who are you? I never seen you in our camp before," Delirya asks intrigued as she studies the old woman.

"Patience, You will find out very soon my dear Delirya," she says softly sending a cold shiver down Delirya's spine.

The old woman turns around holding herself up with a black cane with a skull head; the coins clinking on her belt as she walks away.

Delirya watches as the old woman disappears in the crowd.

* * *

The night has fallen and the music has stopped playing, Aemiliamus approaches his caravan. Tanairy runs after him holding on to her skirt.

"Aemiliamus!" she shouts for his attention.

He turns around and smiles.

"Tanairy, you should head back to your home, is late, my dear," he says caressing her chin.

The single touch of his hand makes her weak in the knees; they exchange strong glances when suddenly another woman wraps her hands around his strong arm.

"Come on my love, it is time," she says softly in his ear.

Aemiliamus quickly lets go of Tanairy and turns around to be guided by the woman.

Tanairy eyes get filled with rage as she stands there watching Aemiliamus walk away with another woman.

Delirya walks up behind her.

"Tsk, tsk you should let it go Tanairy, he is not the kind of man to be tied up to one woman," she says.

They watch Aemiliamus devour the other woman's neck as they head inside his home.

"I will not let this go! Aemiliamus will be mine even if I have to sell my soul to Legba himself!" Tanairy says, walking away furiously.

Delirya catches up to her.

"Where are you going?" she asks, worried.

"I'm going to see Rasheeda."

Tanairy walks faster avoiding eye contact with Delirya.

"Have you gone mad? Have you not heard the stories? Rasheeda sold her soul to Legba to have the power to see the future."

Delirya stands in front of Tanairy preventing her passage.

"Move aside Delirya, I shall find out if selling her soul was worth it," she argues, pushing her friend aside.

Tanairy stands outside of Rasheeda's caravan and takes a moment to think it over.

"Tanairy are you sure you want to do this?" Delirya asks staring at Rasheeda's black caravan with a red bulb hanging outside the door.

"It is said she is blind and underneath her bandana she has a third eye that allows her to see the future." Delirya feels a chill as she says it aloud.

"Nonsense, that's just a bedtime story," Tanairy says as she pushes her curly hair back.

"Bedtime story or not, we shouldn't be here Tanairy."

A crow lands on top of Rasheeda's home, cawing as it stares at them. Delirya takes a step back, grabbing Tanairy's arm.

"Let's head back, we are far enough from camp," she says fearfully.

"You head back, or stay here. I'm going inside," she says as she pulls her arm away from Delirya and runs up the steps to Rasheeda's place.

"Tanairy!" Delirya shouts but is useless as Tanairy is already inside.

There are only many candles providing light as she closes the door behind her. She stands still, too fearful to take another step.

"Rasheeda?" she calls out.

"Come in Tanairy, I been waiting for you," a rough voice says from the table behind the beaded curtain.

Tanairy slowly walks through the curtain; petrified when she lays eyes on a mature woman with blind eyes sitting in front of a crystal ball and a black bandana covering her forehead.

"Come child, do not be afraid of a blind woman," the woman says as she caresses the crystal ball with her burgundy pointed nails. She wears a big onyx ring on her index finger and tattoos of the planets decorate her fingers.

"You know why I'm here?" Tanairy, intrigued, asks as she comes closer to the table.

"Aemiliamus is the reason of your visit," she says grabbing her tarot cards from the table.

Tanairy, eager to find out more pulls out a chair from the table and sits in front of Rasheeda.

"Tell me more woman! Will he ever be mine? I want to know will he ever look my way." she rambles on.

"Silence child, remember there's more time than life," she says calmly.

Tanairy frustrated jumps from her chair slamming her hands on the table.

"You will tell me what I seek!"

She grabs her leather pouch and pulls out a couple of silver coins and throws them on the table.

"Is it money you desire? Here! Take it! Now speak."

Rasheeda smirks as she hands over the cards to Tanairy to shuffle.

Tanairy shuffles the cards and hands them over to Rasheeda.

The blind woman slowly spreads the cards on the table. "Pick a card, child," she says, staring at Tanairy.

Tanairy carefully stares at the cards, tries to find the right one, and finally she picks a card.

Rasheeda turns it over.

"The High Priestess... mmm?" Rasheeda stops to evaluate the card.

"What? What's wrong?" Tanairy asks, concerned.

"The Priestess represents a love that has become an addiction; she often craves what she cannot have," Rasheeda adds. "Draw another card."

Tanairy quickly picks another card.

Rasheeda uncovers the card. "Reversed Empress; the loss of personal power through placing too much emphasis on another person," she says.

"What are you trying to say? Aemiliamus won't be mine?" Tanairy begins to get flustered.

Rasheeda ignores the question.

"Pick your final card my dear," she says.

Tanairy, harried, reaches out to pick her final card. Suddenly she feels Rasheeda's hand gripping her arm.

"Don't be too hasty child. Look into my eyes. Believe," Rasheeda says, slowly releasing Tanairy's arm.

Tanairy pulls her arm back. She looks deeply into Rasheeda's vacant eyes and carefully reaches for the card.

Rasheeda turns it over.

"Death," she says.

Tanairy jumps from her chair and takes a step back.

"You lie! You're nothing but a scam artist," she shouts angrily.

Rasheeda, unbothered, collects her cards.

"The universe has spoken child," she says.

"You lie! Aemiliamus is mine, I'll show you and everyone else in this miserable camp," Tanairy says as she makes her way to the exit furiously.

"Wait! There is one other thing you can do child that will guarantee you the love of the man you desire."

Tanairy immediately freezes at the door and quickly turns around.

"I won't give you another dime!" she answers aggressively.

"Come now, my dear. Your money is not valid here. Rasheeda wants only to help." The blind woman releases a slow cackle as she moves her fingers around the crystal ball.

Tanairy raises an eyebrow intrigued. "I'm listening," she says as she stands at the door.

"Come, come." Rasheeda signals her to come closer.

Tanairy sits again.

Rasheeda removes her bandana, uncovering a real third eye on her forehead.

Tanairy is horrified as she sees the blue eye staring right at her.

"I see in your future that Aemiliamus will be yours forever and you will become the greatest woman he ever loved," Rasheeda says.

Tanairy, speechless, sits there petrified as she remembers what Delirya said about Rasheeda. The clack sound of a small bottle hitting the table brings her back to reality.

"You must drink this love potion with a drop of your own blood tonight, and I guarantee you that your precious Aemiliamus will love you by sunrise," Rasheeda says.

Tanairy looks up at her empty white eyes and grabs the bottle.

"If I do this... Are you sure Aemiliamus will be mine?" she asks with uncertainty.

"If you don't trust in Rasheeda, then why waste my time?"

The blind woman begins to retract the bottle, but Tanairy pulls it away.

"I'll do it! I'll do anything that guarantees the love of Aemiliamus," Tanairy reassures her.

Rasheeda smiles.

"Remember, a drop of your own blood," Rasheeda repeats slowly.

Tanairy listens carefully as she hides the bottle in her chest and she runs out with a smile from ear to ear.

Later, Tanairy stares back at her reflection on a mirror hanging inside her home, smiling joyfully. She reaches for the love potion inside her shirt, looks the bottle over, and then opens it.

"Remember a drop of your own blood." Rasheeda's voice plays in the back of her mind.

Tanairy picks up a knife from a nearby table, and without hesitation, slashes her hand. She holds the potion bottle steady and drips a single drop of her blood into its open mouth. After wrapping her bleeding hand in an old rag, Tanairy swallows the concoction to the last drop.

"Aemiliamus... The things I do for you," she whispers as she winces in disgust from the taste.

In bed that night, she fights herself to stay awake, but her eyes refuse.

* * *

Tanairy wakes up to the sun's rays cutting through her window. Her her bed sheets, covered in blood, startle her. She quickly jumps out of bed and runs to the mirror.

Tanairy lets out a bloodcurdling scream when she sees her reflection. Half of her face has rotted in the night. Her skin peeling away from the bone. Blood rolls down her chin, pooling along the seam where flesh meets exposed skull. She reaches with trembling hands for her face. Crying in agony, she peels the rotten skin from her lips, leaving nothing but her bared and glistening teeth.

A dark form appears behind her in the mirror. She turns with a start, but no one is behind her. Tanairy looks back at the mirror, and the dark form becomes clear. The old Haitian woman from the dance stares back at her in the mirror.

"My name is Atibon Legba, my dear, Tanairy," she growls. "I come to take you with me. Your soul now belongs to me."

Legba cackles.

Tanairy falls to her knees, weeping.

Outside, Delirya is hanging laundry to dry. She watches as a black butterfly lands and perches on one of her sheets. Goosebumps course through her body.

"Tanairy?" she asks, dropping the basket of clothes.

She turns and runs to Tanairy's home. Inside, she finds her friend's lifeless body on the floor.

Distant echoes of Atibon Legba's and Rasheeda's cackles drown and mix with Delirya's blood-curdling scream, and are heard throughout the camp.

Elsewhere, Aemiliamus quietly sings a love song to himself, picking flowers for his dear Tanairy.

ↈ　ↈ

Stephanie D. Escobar is an aspiring writer. She loves to spend time watching the latest movies and reading books. If she is not writing, she is spending time with her biggest fans: her mother and her loving pet, Onyx. You can follow her on Instagram at @OnyxandMe.

THE RING – DIANE ROOT

In this country of myth and mystery, both brutal and beautiful, death is celebrated. The Day of the Dead fiesta lasts from dawn to dawn. Death is literally gobbled up. Sidewalk vendors display macabre wares, the most popular of which are candied skulls, adorned in gaudy frostings.

Entire families make their way, joyous and jaunty, to the cemetery, toting striped serapes, an abundance of tacos and tortillas, pulled pork and hot peppers, bottles and flasks full of tequila and mescal, guitars, small drums and flutes. Once there, they spread out their picnic baskets on the broadly banded rainbow blankets at the grave site, where they eat, drink, sing and dance throughout the night. At the break of day, they rise wearily to trudge back, replete with food and drink, filled with song, hearts and souls swollen with stories oft-repeated and embellished with each retelling–ancestral memories to which they cling—ever-present lifelines. The line between the two, they like to say, is thread-thin, either one or both poised to strike at any moment.

Quetzalcoatl, the plumed snake god, lives forever.

* * *

He had left the remote *finca* where they lived, a few days earlier, bound for Taxco, to find a jeweler who would accomplish his "mission," as he called it. The town was famous for its silver, gems and artisans who worked both silver and gold.

He was fond of side streets, those alleys less travelled and usually totally ignored by tourists. There, he knew, he would find the best craftsmen at the best prices.

It didn't take long. A narrow, shadowy shop seemed to beckon.

Its owner, obviously of Indian descent, was rotund, cherubic, and short of stature, at once both respectful and solicitous. He flashed a brilliant smile, broad-toothed and porcelain white, accented by a single gold incisor. After the customary opening banter, the husband unwraps his wife's wedding ring nestled in a small square of velvet, followed by a ring-sizing chart. He points to the smallest circle, manifestly destined for a pinky finger.

"But senor, your wife must be tiny! This would fit a child! Are you sure?" He stares at the golden circle laid on the counter before him. There was no getting around it; she must have had tiny hands.

"Absolutely," he said. "The ring no longer fits her. She lost a lot of weight after our marriage."

This explanation clearly delighted the shopkeeper, who winked and broke into an "I gotcha" expression of enlightenment, obviously enjoying what he perceived to be the sexual innuendos of the conversation. He gave his 6'4" customer who towered over him a top-to-bottom once-over, even though he stood ever so slightly bent in a shop not meant to contain a client of this man's height. *Un hombre muy poderoso y, por supuesto, muy potente,* without a doubt.

"*Si, señor, ahora entiendo. Pasado mañana a las doce—que le parece?*

"That'll be fine. Day after tomorrow. Noon."

* * *

He liked her to sit in her favorite chair, next to the floor-to-ceiling window, that gave onto the garden, where she sat today, their 10th anniversary. Despite her French origins, she preferred English gardens—stylishly unkempt, with a slightly devil-may-care attitude, but nevertheless planted with a secret order not immediately obvious to the eye. So unlike the English themselves, she mused—unless, of course, you counted the eccentrics.

The French favored those formal gardens, clipped and stiff, precise layouts, unnatural—so unlike her countrymen, unless you considered the academics who still instilled draconian principles of logic. Odd, she thought, that their gardens were so diametrically contrary to the character of the people who planted them. Perhaps they represented an acceptable release from culturally stringent constraints.

* * *

Summer was his favorite time, when the sunlight stroked her face, so finely wrought, so beautiful, he thought. Still now.

He never let her put the wedding dress in storage, only allowing it to be packed in a carved chest sculpted by her grandfather, upstairs in the attic. (In those days, it was called a hope chest.) Every anniversary, he would gently unpack it and insist that she wear it on this special day as she did now, facing him. Hope, he thought, springs eternal.

He loved the Alençon lace veil that framed her face, which he had bought on a trip to Europe and brought back to her when he proposed. It seemed to accentuate the dark pools of her eyes, almost cavernous, shadowed by the pronounced brow. Now bleached by the slanting sun of the late afternoon, the gown gleamed satin, matching her.

"Do you remember our wedding day?" he began. "You came to me, virginal, more beautiful than ever. You never lost that luminous beauty. It will remain with me forever in my mind's eye, in my dreams."

He leans toward the bouquet of white roses on the table—white is the color of mourning in India, he thought—adjusting a stem, changing the vase's position just a tad, so as to see her without a bloom blocking his view of her face. The glasses of champagne glowed gold, splintered sunlight in the glass, as they always did at what was a holy hour for him, a sacred space, a shrine in time, an altar in his soul. Later, he thought, I will light candles for her. She always loves them.

The champagne—Don Perignon (nothing but the best would do)— stokes his memories of their lives together. Most of them were deliriously happy, considering the years spent in each other's company. They rarely argued, both of them being of even and forgiving temperaments. And then, of course, there was the fact that they were deeply in love with each other, a gold-patina love burnished bronze with every passing year.

* * *

It was only when their baby son died at 18 months that things changed. The depth of her distress caused her to distance herself. Not just from him, but from everything. She became as remote as the place where they lived in the hinterlands of Mexico. That is, until his best friend came to visit them. He listened to the story of the son's death, went to the child's grave with her, bearing flowers. Held her hand. Brushed away her tears. Spoke softly.

218

"Only later did I realize that he had stolen your wounded heart. He gave you a kindness that I no longer knew how to give.

"I couldn't bear going to the cemetery, remember? Not even with you. I blamed myself for the child's death—incompatible blood—a child. born on Christmas Eve, defective, without even a fontanelle. No amount of medical ministrations could save him. In my guilt, my heart had turned to something darkly nebulous, a storm cloud within. Yours had turned to stone. I no longer knew what grief I was suffering—they both melded—the child or you. Probably both. I couldn't really love the child, imperfect, a living reproach during his brief life—worse yet, once he had died. I grieved because of your loss—but I knew I loved you above all. I still do."

He remembers their laughter that night, their handsome faces illuminated by the candlelight. No reason why a lethal libation can't come with tiny bubbles, he thought.

Both died in their drug-induced sleep, soundlessly and peaceful in their beds.

* * *

The summer breeze wafted through the French doors, blowing ripples of lace across her face. Again, he leans forward, rearranges it, so as to see her in her entirety once again, then sips the champagne. He moves her glass closer to her, gently closes her hand around the crystal stem.

"We loved to go to the Caribbean. You delighted in the turquoise and emerald waters, and I delighted in seeing your shining magnificent body, tanned and golden, rising out of the waves, my very own Venus. My Botticelli. Your hair, so thick. Ropes of gold cascading over your body, sometimes covering a breast, curling over your rounded belly, draped over a nonchalant shoulder. (Those tresses are thinning now, slightly russet with age, but no matter, I shall brush it as I always have.) We should go to that island again.

"When your mother died, we spread her ashes there. Yes, we should go there again. Pay our respects to be carried by the azure ocean to her resting place.

"Once the urn was emptied, you tossed that enormous bouquet of scarlet roses into the sea, one by one. You had to order them specially, since there were none on the island. The town's florist said that she would get them for you. It would take a couple of days, she explained. She was true to her word and announced, not without some pride, that they had to be flown in from southern France by plane. You asked from where. 'From Grasse,' she responded. 'Good,' you said. 'Where they grow acres of flowers and make perfumes. Not far from Nice, where my mother was born.'"

Carried by an invisible tide, the roses set sail toward an anchored boat offshore. The crewmen shouted each to each, summoning those below decks, mystified by the sudden tidal wave of cadmium flowers on a cerulean sea.

* * *

"You always kept her perfumes after she died—vintage bottles that you couldn't part with. There was that angular gold one—your favorite- once filled with an attar of roses. You could still smell it years later, even though the perfume was long gone."

* * *

When she left, no one questioned the circumstances. Not the neighbors, not the police. Her grief, everyone said, had driven her to distraction, to looking for a calm somewhere. She would be back, they predicted. Just give her space and time.

Eventually. she was listed as a "missing person" as indeed she was. Above all, to him–her husband, her lover, her partner. She was his missing heart. Stolen by his best friend, his buddy, his surrogate brother. He, too, disappeared, probably to whence he came, but no one knew just exactly where that "whence" was. There again, nobody asked or seemed to care.

He, of course, never told anyone. He knew exactly where they were, but he waited. When he thought it would be the right time, he went to get her, hidden in the distant forest. "Asleep, awaiting her prince's kiss," he thought.

And then, suddenly, she was back. Not that anyone knew.

* * *

As always, every time on this special day, he served the dinner. This year, avocados, precisely at the creamy ripeness she liked, followed by a curry, one of her favorite dishes, redolent with spices. Strawberries and raspberries nestled in a custard cream for dessert. In the future, he would make paella, bouillabaisse, or whatever came to mind—those dishes they learned to love during their travels together.

* * *

He had inherited gold-patterned china from his parents, delicately decorated with vines and floral designs, which he saved for only these "special" occasions. This was certainly one of them.

By now, the afternoon had begun to deepen into a lavender evening. The fading light still glinted off the facets of the crystal, the gold of the plates, the cutlery. the stemware, the table settings.

* * *

But something was still missing—a finishing touch without which the tableau before him would be incomplete. He stepped out into the sun-streaked garden; the late afternoon breeze wafted wisps of perfume rising from the flower beds, enveloping him. Wrapped in its cloak, he stands still, then bends to pick two intensely blue bachelor's buttons and one white zinnia, a favorite of hers, ever so slightly tinged with a spring green, near odorless, but redolent of the earth from whence she came.

Once back inside and before he sits back down at their banquet table, he tenderly places the zinnia in her hair, the bachelor's buttons in each of the now- empty orbits of her eyes, mimicking the brilliant hue of her living gaze.

* * *

"This year," he told her, "I have a very special gift for you."

Still bereft, just as he was on the very first day, he held out the resized wedding ring in his palm for her to "see." Since her long fingers were now stripped of flesh, as was her body, he placed it very carefully on the fourth digit of her left hand.

It was a perfect fit, gleaming gold in the setting sunlight, against her bare bleached bones swathed in ivory satin, now tinged with the encroaching twilight.

"With this ring, I thee wed," he said.

CQ   ♋

Diane Root, a dual-national, was born in Paris of an American father, the journalist and writer, Waverley Root, and a French mother. Primarily known as a painter, she is, as she describes herself, "an accidental writer." She never sought to be published but that notwithstanding, she was nonetheless published in the New York Times Magazine ("The Artful Dodger" about lunch with Picasso) and various other venues. View her art: http://matakia.com.

FINLEYMANIA – NATE RAGOLIA

The ceiling comprises sixty-four square tiles. Each tile has two-hundred and fifty-four dimples, except for the eight tiles that are occupied by light fixtures and that venting cowl that looks like a metal flower. Where the ceiling meets the walls, on the three sides I can see, there is a bead of wood, painted calming blue, that accents the room like a fancy cake. I don't know if the walls are decorated–unable to move my head–but my memory of hospitals leads me to believe there would be a television on one wall flanked by inexpensive, mass-produced landscape paintings. Hopefully, if there are paintings, they are tasteful and well-composed, and none of that hideous Theodore Finley shit.

Finley had died a few years earlier, drugs and pills, after his wife filed for divorce. He was famous among his audience, a well-branded man, with calendars and classes and all the selling out an artist can accommodate. Was the real him reflected in his paintings? Did that mean that one of his paintings, perhaps on my hospital room wall right now, was a portal by which his essence viewed my own?

I tap the call button for a nurse. She said that this could happen as a side-effect of the medication. She called it Finleymania. She said the early signs were a sudden awareness and interest in the painter, followed by the belief that each individual image contained its own universe, and eventually escalating to a sense that contact with the man himself is happening. These manifestations were colloquially called "Teddysits," a term that sounds almost cute until the nurse explains that the associated fugue state usually results in death.

But this is all normal.

It's all part of the procedure.

I'll be whole soon. I'll be able to move again. Like the accident never happened. Like I was never pulverized against the rocks.

It's all part of the procedure.

She's coming down the hall now, and I can hear her footfalls on the linoleum floor. She's carrying another dose of Osinum, in a thin needle that she'll jab into my meaty belly and all these thoughts about the painter will slip away, buried deep beneath everything else I want to do when I finally get out of here.

There's a knock knock at the door. A courtesy knock. The nurse knows I'm in here. Where else would I be? I'm not going to make a break for it. Nurse B_____ nudges the door open. Light splashes across the ceiling from the hallway. Its hinges creak like a whisper. B_____'s shoes squeak on the floor and she clomps back a step in a nervous stumble.

"Sorry, Mr. R_____," she says. "I hate that noise."

I do my best approximation of nodding.

"You rang?" she says, in a comedically not-deep Lurch voice.

"Pntr!" I grumble.

She understands right away. She steps over me, and my nostrils fill with the delicate scent of vanilla. Why is it that the infirm are always closest to physical temptation? B_____'s scrubs billow out over me, and the aura of her breasts is so intense that I think for a moment that I feel them resting on my doughy chest. She adjusts my pillow and folds down the blanket. Then out comes the needle.

"Remember what I said," she says. "The instant you start thinking about those paintings you call me. No close calls."

She holds the needle over me.

"Now, this'll sting, but in a second you won't think about any of it again."

The needle slips in, and I think it might go right through me. It could, really. Nothing to stop it. I feel the liquid Osinum surge through me like electricity darting from neuron to neuron. And then in a quick flash I can't even remember what painting I was thinking about.

Picasso?

Matisse?

Renoir?

224

B_____ sets the needle aside on a cart outside my vision and touches the mass of my forehead. Her nails are nice. Clean, manicured. Her hands look soft, but strong. She'd probably give good hand.

"Okay, Mr. R_____, that's it," she says, stepping away toward the door. "Everything looks good. Your vitals are sharp. You're lucky to have walked away from an accident like that one. Sorry, I shouldn't have said *walked*. It's an expression, though, you understand. You are lucky though. The ocean doesn't usually forgive people so easily. Of course, modern medicine makes a lot possible, and in time you'll be right as rain. The Osinum will take about twenty minutes to cycle in, and you should start to feel some real results this time, since it's dose number six."

I want to mumble something about her making my recovery all the better, but I can't find the words. Nurse B_____ smiles, pats the side of my hospital bed, and disappears from sight, leaving only the creak of the door, and the latch as evidence of her complete departure.

Hours must pass because the dim tan curtains visible from the corner of my right eye are now just black darkness. I close my eyes and inhale deeply.

Some light peers in through my eyelids. It's the reason I realize I'm no longer asleep. I blink my eyes open and right there on the ceiling is some distant island alcove, a hidden bay, with a ship approaching, all under the white, creamy glow of the moon. It's one of those motel paintings... one of those images from a calendar.

Panic overcomes me as I stare transfixed into the light. It's happening again, and it has never been like this. I begin to wonder how Finley brings the light to life. So nuanced, so energetic. And yet so still. I feel as though I'm falling up, toward the painting. This isn't right.

I mash the call button and hear the chime. Now, I just have to wait for those footfalls, and that scent of vanilla. Meanwhile, there's a figure on the ship in the painting that I shouldn't be seeing, and it's moving toward the bow, waving tiny arms that perfectly reflect the milky moonlight.

The figure dives off the front of the ship, splashes into the water and then emerges on the shore, in the foreground, arms up, still waving.

At me. And then with superhuman speed, the figure strides up the beach, toward me, until it reaches the canvas surface of the painting.

"I'm Theodore Finley, and I'd like to talk to you today about secrets of my creativity," the figure says.

It leans in close, and while it has no discernible characteristics like a nose, mouth, or eyes, the figure is wearing one of those over ear microphones that self-help gurus and convention speakers wear.

"The biggest secret is that there are no secrets," the figure continues. "There's only light. Once you start seeing the world for all its light, and nothing else, you really understand how to make art."

I begin to appreciate the boring composition of Finley's images, instead seeing the virtue of the light in them. His voice is soothing, and his high-octane self-assurance is infectious. I wonder if I'm a painter, too, and if not, why not. I keep mashing the call button. My heart races, nearly leaping around inside of me. Nurse B_____ will arrive soon. She has to.

"The only thing is," the figure says. "The only thing is that you have to give yourself over to the light. Once you let go, the light will paint itself for you."

Then the figure extends its hand to me.

"Come with me," it says.

Even if I could reach out to it, I wouldn't, but then somehow my hand is fluttering up toward the figure's. My heart's racing gives way to pain and I can't scream, so I gurgle something that sounds hideous to my ears, but quickly washes away beneath the figure's persistence.

"Come with me," it says again.

I can't retract my hand, and it's almost touching the figure's hand, and I feel like my brain is liquefying, and...

Footsteps.

Clap clap clap.

The blade of light cuts across my ceiling.

"Oh no!" Nurse B_____ screams.

She runs up to the headboard of my bed and hits the emergency button. I hear a faint alarm sounding, but it's cloaked in the figure's soothing tones.

"Come with me."

More footsteps, running now.

Clapclapclap clapclapclapclap.

"I don't know what's gone wrong," Nurse B_____ says. "I just administered the sixth dose three hours ago. He shouldn't be convulsing like this. Is that the best way to describe it? Convulsing? It's like a lava lamp. Undulating?"

"I think *convulsing* remains accurate, Nurse. *Undulating* lacks the requisite medical implication. The protocols changed last week," someone says. "We sent a memo. For a man of Mr. R_____'s height and weight, it's now seven doses of Osinum."

As if the figure weren't there at all, the Doctor leans over me, smelling of aftershave and rye bread. She shines a penlight in my eyes, and looks me up and down.

"Mr. R_____, if you can understand me please blink three times," the Doctor says.

I blink three times.

"You're in the throes of an episode of Finleymania brought on by your Osinum dose, but we're here and we're going to help you. If you understand blink twice."

I blink twice.

"Good," the Doctor says. "Now, whatever you do, do not take the hand of any figure you might be seeing. That could result in a very bad thing."

Could? A very bad thing? I have no way to tell the Doctor that I can't control my hand and that the figure nearly has hold of it.

I blink frantically.

The Doctor seems to understand.

"It's happening," she says. "Nurse B_____, prep the crash cart. And bring me a seventh Osinum dose."

Nurse B_____'s footsteps are speedy but deliberate. I hear wheels rolling. I see a shadow flicker out over the ceiling as she leaves, and then flicker again as she returns. My outstretched hand begins to tingle. My head swims with light and white noise. The figure leans ever closer.

"Come with me."

And then it takes my hand. Suddenly everything goes white, bright, but cool. The only thing I hear is something like the ocean that day when the boat turned, and the undertow, the rocks...

* * *

Then darkness. Noise. A jolt. Red light, pulsing across my eyes. I grunt, maybe aloud, maybe just inside my head. My heart speeds and slows. I breathe.

"That was closer than I'd've liked," the Doctor says. "Nurse B_____ please administer the Osinum."

Vanilla. Breasts. The nurse over me. The needle.

"Mr. R_____, this last dose of Osinum will do the trick. Your skeleton will regrow over the next twelve hours, and parts of that might be painful, but it's only temporary. We'll be monitoring you closely, and Nurse B_____ will employ some sedatives to prevent any additional relapses of Finleymania."

I try to say 'thank you,' but without a skull, jaw, or palate, it comes out as "Thrrrk." I try again. There's something around my tongue now. It must be starting already. I try again.

"Thnkoo," I hear myself say.

If I could move, I'd clap triumphantly.

"Good, Mr. R_____," the Doctor says. "You'll be a chatterbox in no time. You know, just ten years ago, someone in your condition would have gone straight to the morgue."

"Ysssss," I utter.

"It's really quite amazing," the Doctor says. "Modern medicine."

CB ‏ ‎ SO

Nate Ragolia is the author of There You Feel Free; a novella. Creator of the Illiterate Badger and Lark & Robin web comics, and occasional chatterer on music, film, &c. He also edits Boned.

OLD POTATO – MIKEY SIVAK

I.
How many lie hidden buried,
Potato Gods all starch and earth-skin,
humongous and horrible in vegetable
inanimateness, beside centuries old
foundations of American fieldstones,
and strange archaic mortars, built
by hands and joints of animal flesh
that had been quick in youth but slowly grew
arthritic, gnarled as root matter only uglier,
in corporeal spoilage?

II.
Have our generations lived and died above
potato matrons, brown skinned earth
queens, silent mothers griping generations
of replicate daughters knowing-nothing, but
if something, then nothing save the freezing
and flexing of a lightless dirt-world; have
our American centuries of toil, self-enslavement,
the produce and industry of man-minds in
tissular automata passed meaningless
as the extra-dimensional?

III.
When we found the American religion, shall we
bury our dead in potato patches so that
when man rises he might carry a potato up with him,
to feast upon its dense white flesh, swallow raw
the stoic meaninglessness of its existence,
or place him in a field of dead writers, farmers,
messianic bastards, and tuber shaped infants,

---

which had rotted in life and in death became
somehow sterile with mummified flesh, brown
as the earth, stretched across snow white bones?

ೞ ೞ

Mykl Sivak is a writer and artist unfortunately based in New Haven, Connecticut. His writing and art have appeared in a number of international indie zines, journals, and anthologies. He used to work as an animation artist for a global mass media corporation but he doesn't do that anymore. Mykl is an atheist, a nihilist, and an anarchist, which means he doesn't believe in anything. It is his opinion that you shouldn't either. http://mykls.tumblr.com/

THE MOST INTERESTED MAN IN THE WORLD – NATE RAGOLIA

[#1]

A gray bearded man, dressed in a fitted suit sits in the booth seat of a two-top drinking a beer in a green bottle speaks directly to the camera

MOST INTERESTED MAN:

Oh, I don't normally drink beer... [beat] But enough about me. Tell me about you.

HARD CUT

MOST INTERESTED MAN:

Blue, really? What shade of blue would you say is your favorite?

HARD CUT

MOST INTERESTED MAN:

And you say that you work as chick sexor? What IS that like?

HARD CUT

MOST INTERESTED MAN:

Stephanie? What's the origin of that name? Will you spell it?

HARD CUT – Camera pulls back to show a woman sitting across him at the table

STEPHANIE:

[Looking at a text on her phone] Oh, gosh, that was the babysitter. I really have to go.

STEPHANIE gets up hurriedly and leaves, walking past the camera that still frames THE MOST INTERESTED MAN

MOST INTERESTED MAN:

[calling to Stephanie who is already gone] Babies? What are their names and ages!?

MOST INTERESTING MAN TURNS TO HIS RIGHT – CAMERA PANS – TO SPEAK TO AN ELDERLY GENTLEMAN AT THE BOOTH SEAT/TWO TOP NEXT TO HIM

MOST INTERESTED MAN:

That meal looks delicious. What are the ingredients in that dish?

CAMERA PULLS BACK SLOWLY and SLOW FADES TO BLACK

VOICE OVER:

He's a better listener than Gene Hackman in THE CONVERSATION

When his grandchildren want to talk to him at family functions he turns his hearing aid up. He's the MOST INTERESTED MAN IN THE WORLD.

[#2]

A gray bearded man, dressed in a fitted suit sits in the booth seat of a two-top drinking a beer in a green bottle speaks directly to the camera

MOST INTERESTED MAN:

A fourth floor walk up? How did you get your furniture in there?

HARD CUT

MOST INTERESTED MAN:

Pullies?

HARD CUT

MOST INTERESTED MAN:

Ramps like they used to construct the ancient pyramids?

HARD CUT

MOST INTERESTED MAN:

A burly team of men with a truck? How much did you pay?

HARD CUT – Camera pulls back to show a Man in a bear suit sitting across him at the table.

MAN IN BEAR SUIT:

Roars loudly and angrily... non-language

MAN IN BEAR SUIT flips the table and stomps off past the camera, claws flailing – shot still frames THE MOST INTERESTED MAN

MOST INTERESTED MAN:

[calling to MAN IN BEAR SUIT who is already gone] What language is that? Dutch?

MOST INTERESTING MAN TURNS TO HIS RIGHT – CAMERA PANS – TO SPEAK TO AN ELDERLY GENTLEMAN AT THE BOOTH SEAT/TWO TOP NEXT TO HIM

MOST INTERESTED MAN:

Are you reading a newspaper? Do you read the newspaper every day?

CAMERA PULLS BACK SLOWLY and SLOW FADES TO BLACK

VOICE OVER:

He loves hearing about your day more than your own mother.

When people quote movies at parties he asks them to act out their favorite scenes. He's the MOST INTERESTED MAN IN THE WORLD.

[#3]

A gray bearded man, dressed in a fitted suit sits in the booth seat of a two-top drinking a beer in a green bottle speaks directly to the camera

MOST INTERESTED MAN:

Did you purchase that beautiful shirt from a department store? Macys? Sears? JC Penneys? Boscovs? Dillards?

HARD CUT

MOST INTERESTED MAN:

A shrimp allergy? Would you say you swell to this big [motions with hands]? This Big? THIS BIG?

HARD CUT

MOST INTERESTED MAN:

Oh, your mother sounds lovely. What is her favorite flower? Chrysanthemums?

HARD CUT – Camera pulls back to show a HEALTH CLASS SKELETON wearing a hawaiian shirt sitting across him at the table. THE RESTAURANT IS COBWEBBED AND CLEARLY ABANDONED LONG AGO

SKELETON:

Creaking noise and then its head falls off

Shot still frames THE MOST INTERESTED MAN

MOST INTERESTED MAN:

[still speaking to SKELETON] You look so slender. Do you have a personal trainer?

MOST INTERESTING MAN CONTINUES SPEAKING THE SKELETON QUIETLY AS CAMERA PULLS BACK SLOWLY and SLOW FADES TO BLACK

VOICE OVER:

He's done four-hour interviews with each animatronic robot in Epcot's HALL OF PRESIDENTS.

When Jehovah's Witnesses come to his door invites them inside for tea. He's the MOST INTERESTED MAN IN THE WORLD.

 G&   ଉଚ

Nate Ragolia is the author of There You Feel Free; a novella. Creator of the Illiterate Badger and Lark & Robin web comics, and occasional chatterer on music, film, &c. He also edits Boned.

SCARECROW – DIANE ROOT

It was a peaceful country, she thought, with rolling verdant hills and freshly plowed fields in spring, exuding the wonderful aroma of dark earth, pristine towns and prim steeples, winding dirt roads dotted with plain white clapboard houses. Then there was the promise of the glorious spring, after the blue-white silence of winter that sparkled in the sunlight like diamonds The sun-drenched summer, sliding in just after the rains, heralded and harbored the seasonal harvests: cornucopias by the bushel spewed beans and beets, radishes and rutabagas, corn and cauliflowers, spinach and salad greens, at the very least.

Then again there was the village green, a one-room schoolhouse, country fairs and 4-H clubs. The sole diner manned by a jovial woman named Mabel, whose pies were prized by all, and who almost invariably won all of the baking contests, despite fierce competition from the local women. The women, whether through their poverty or their thrift, clothed themselves in the patterned cotton of flour sacks, occasionally adorned by a bit of lace here, a little tatting there. Without apologies.

Thick groves of maples turned gold and tangerine and red and russet come fall, framed by the blue-green black of the spruce and pines. Blanched birches held up the sky, cupped and captured between their graceful branches.

"We can spend our lifetimes together in peace," she said to her blinded mother, whose husband had gouged out her eyes. With a knife. She would never again look at another man ever again, he thought to himself. Never.

She describes the seasons, the landscape to those glass eyes.

"Yes," she told her, "This is perfect."

* * *

They had only married a year before, she a "city girl" as he called her, he a "country bumpkin": as he called himself. He had just bought the farm in the wilds of Vermont at the end of a winding, five-mile dirt road. Five-thousand dollars, he said, a song for 730 acres, a house, a barn and a stable.

He forgot to tell her that the house was all but falling down under the weight of peeling paint, and that it came with an appendage: namely an outhouse attached to the woodshed, frequented by porcupines bent on demolishing what was left of the house's underpinnings.

* * *

She had fallen in love with his squared-off jaw, the sunlit blond of his hair, the startling green eyes, the muscular, tight frame. The powerful shoulders and the heavy, large-boned hands. Hands that were used to work.

Soon she would regret loving them.

* * *

He was a hard worker. She admired his curved body when he planted an acre of vegetables. She followed the arc of his arms when he swung a scythe to fell the hay. She marveled at the curtain of sweat that streamed off his forehead and onto his face during the heat of the day.

Trouble was, he drank as hard as he worked. Since she was beautiful, he conjured imaginary lovers to justify his rages.

* * *

It was not long before she too wore flour-sack dresses with long sleeves and down to her ankles which she hand-sewed herself. By then her body sported the bruises, purple, blue, green and yellow depending upon how old they were from his nearly daily drunken beatings. Her face was marked with the bruises he inflicted, the eyes darkened. She no longer went into town. She could no longer hide the beatings, short of wearing a mask. Besides, he would hide the keys to the car. For her, there was no escape. Especially after he had broken her legs. Walking five miles on a dirt road was no longer an option. It took months for them to heal. Crooked.

It was then that she remembered her mother's advice: "Never marry a man you haven't seen drunk."

Too late.

* * *

Now she reveled in the footed bathtub long ago emptied of the acid and filled with the farm's dark loam. The rose geraniums and purple petunias grew joyously seemingly wanting to outdo themselves in generosity. They spilled over the sides of the tub, Next year, she thought, I'll plant morning glories.

* * *

She had waited until he stumbled outside in his usual stupor to relieve himself in the bathtub that he had refused to install, just to spite her. She hobbled after him and then pushed him as hard as she could. He fell in, cracked his skull, his penis still in his hand, and died. She didn't touch him. She poured the acid over him that she had managed to acquire on the Internet without his knowledge. A door, not yet installed, made the perfect cover.

The disintegration lasted over the waning months of the summer, into the fall. The stench, only slightly muffled by the wooden cover of the door, slowly diminished.

She didn't mind. It was perfume to her.

* * *

Now that she could go into town, some of them asked her about the whereabouts of her handsome husband. "I don't know," she answered. "He left on foot to shoot a deer—it was the season, don't cha know? He never came back," Rumors flew, of course—divorce, "the other woman" in town, or anything else that occurred to them. But Vermonters aren't big on asking pointed questions. Even answers are oblique. They believed in privacy like they believed in privies. The authorities combed the forested areas of the farm. They found nothing.

By this time, the bathtub was blooming.

* * *

Her daughter was born after he died, the result of an encounter that smacked of a wrestling match and a rape. Like many of the country women in these parts, she managed to deliver the child by herself. It was, strangely, an easy birth, almost painless. Not to mention that she was young and strong, despite her warped legs.

Five, six years passed like water on the acre of vegetables that she planted every year despite the infirmity she endured. Around about then she erected the scarecrow. The skeleton dressed in her husband's faded, patched and tattered clothes, were highly effective. Crows screeched and circled, soon vanishing; deer disappeared in a flash.

The children loved the skeletal scarecrow. They played around it. Ring-around the-rosy, hide-and-seek They made up scary stories at noon.

"Here," they said, "it's like Halloween every day." The adults, only slightly more suspicious, more used to straw and burlap, take on the kids' interpretation. They recognize the tattered overalls that her husband wore. When asked—and few did—she would say that it was a way of remembering him. No one questioned her anymore. It was far safer. Dry is the drink of the day in these parts.

* * *

She loved to sit on the porch on one of the two squeaking rocking chairs during the early evening as the sun set and the shades of twilight crept across the sky.

Tonight, as she would on all warm nights, she leans over to set the second rocking chair in motion. She looks at the deepening blooms in the bathtub.

She leans over to put the empty rocking chair in motion. She listens to the breeze flapping her husband's tattered work clothes on his scarecrow, the creak of the rocking chairs and the rattling of his distant bones.

No matter, It was music to her ears.

Yes, she tells herself, this is perfect.

ʘ ⁊

Diane Root, a dual-national, was born in Paris of an American father, the journalist and writer, Waverley Root, and a French mother. Primarily known as a painter, she is, as she describes herself, "an accidental writer." She never sought to be published but that notwithstanding, she was nonetheless published in the New York Times Magazine ("The Artful Dodger" about lunch with Picasso) and various other venues. View her art: http://matakia.com.

MISS BONEY – MIMI HAYES

It must have been a bustling city, some 100 years ago. There were strange frames of buildings, now toppling over into the deserted streets. Abandoned cars littered the roads; windows shattered and items strewn across the sidewalks. A street sign dangled from a crooked post, "*Welcome to Denver, Colorado: The Mile High City.*" The trees lining the buildings must have been beautiful in the fall; their golden leaves gently landing on the heads of passerby's on their morning commute. But that was all gone now.

At the intersection of Josephine and 2nd Avenue was a crumbled building. A billboard with several letters missing and discolored from the sunlight read, "*Sa-nt Thomas High S-ho-l.*" The entrance door had been ripped off of the building and laid lifeless on the lawn. Inside desks were toppled over and textbooks disseminated on the tile floors. The classrooms were boarded up with thick plywood and nails that had rusted and stuck out at odd angles.

In one classroom sat the skeleton of a woman. She was sitting in a chair attached to a desk, stuck upright as if waiting for something. Or someone. Her posture suggested that it pained her to sit up this straight for the bones in her shoulders and arms looked heavy. Shreds of clothing hung from her bones like slabs of uncooked bacon. A pencil skirt, blouse perhaps. The skirt seemed to be caught in the frame of the desk. Her legs were crossed politely. What once were heel wedges were now worn down and dangled from the bones that used to be feet. Her jewelry must have been fashionable in her time; it contained elements of shiny things and reflected the sun as it crossed the windows. But there was no wedding ring. Nobody had "put a ring" on this boney broad.

The hot wind picked up as the skeletal woman sat in her desk, resolute. Engraved into the desk was a riddle. It looked as though the words had been etched into the wooden table; the dark pencil marking created grooves in the surface.

Beware the Jabberwock, my son!

The jaws that bite, the claws that catch

Beware the Jubjub bird, and shun the frumious Bandersnatch

Suddenly the winds shifted. A silver pod emerged from the sky and careened to the hot Earth with a thud on the corner of 2nd and Josephine. The dust settled. The Boney Lady did not stir.

Two aliens surfaced from the smoking ship. They were green. Obviously. They muttered to themselves in disarray as they dusted off their gangly green limbs. The language they spoke resembled odd clicks and slurs.

"Blark bloop bee bloop bingo?" The taller one, named Blarp said.

"*You're* the one who insisted on not stopping for gas on Planet 12," The shorter one, Dingo said. "Idiot."

"It wasn't my fault," Blarp said. "The fucking generator broke down."

"Practice proper English, won't you? We don't want to scare off any survivors."

Blarp dusted off his vest and craned his neck around. "*Mile High City*. Well I hope they were high when the shit hit the fan –"

"Don't be such a jerk, Blarp." Dingo said and unearthed a large trunk with wheels out of the back of the pod. "We have a job to do. Let's just go inside this school already, at least that's what I think it is."

Blarp and Dingo walked toward the school. Dingo eyed the door on the lawn with suspicion. *Looters*, Dingo thought. Earth had fallen 100 years ago. Their alien race had been investigating The Fall for the past 10, slowly uncovering more clues. But they'd hit a standstill. They needed teams to be on the ground to collect data and bring back samples. Dingo joined the exploration crew during his summer break at the local university as an adjunct professor. His course was *Appreciation for Human Poetry 101*. The problem was, fewer and fewer students were enrolling in his class each semester. The university was now threatening to shut down his beloved poetry department. He would never admit it to Blarp, but he was looking for something; a purpose, an answer, anything. Blarp was only looking for a paycheck.

They walked cautiously through the deserted halls, crawling over broken desks and books with their pages flapping as the wind came through the gaping entrance.

"All these rooms are boarded up," Blarp yelled from behind a turned over and gum-covered desk. "This is a waste of time. We should just go back to that abandoned Whiskey Bar back in Alamosa. I liked that place –"

Dingo tuned out Blarp's shrill nonsense and walked further down the hall. A particular room caught his eye. Light reflected off of one of the nails and drew him closer. He inched his face to the boards to peek through the spaces of wood and cobweb.

"We should get paid overtime for this shit, you know. It's just pointless –"

"Shut up!" Dingo interrupted. There was a shadow of a figure on the other side. "Hey, there's someone in here. Get over here and help me!" Dingo shouted and began pulling at the boards. "*There's someone in here!* HELLO?!"

Blarp rushed over and the two of them pulled madly at the wood. They created a hole just large enough for one to fit through and squished themselves inside. It was the skeletal woman. Dead, but very much alive with expression.

"Fancy meeting *you* here," said Blarp with a devilish smile. "It's like she was waiting for us. Would you like some coffee, my love?" Blarp walked across the room to a broken coffee pot and raised it up to the air.

Dingo eyed her closely. She was unlike other specimens they'd encountered on their journey so far. He flipped over an overturned stool and sat before her. Blarp looked to the bag beside her and opened it.

"What is all this?" He began to pull out tight wads of crumpled up paper; the markings hardly legible. Also in the bag were books, paperclips, and what looked like an old sack lunch.

"I can't make it out, Dingo," he said. "This can't be English. Oh man, lady! What did you eat? This smells awful." Blarp made the mistake of picking up the deteriorating lunch sack. "Check this out, '*Worldwide*

School Catastrophe: End Is Near?'" he read from a coffee stained newspaper headline in the front pocket of the bag.

"The schools collapsed," Dingo took the article clipping from Blarp and poured over it in his stool. "Teacher walk-outs, school shootings. Once the schools went, everything else followed –"

"What do we do with all this crap?" Blarp interrupted as he began emptying the contents of bins onto the floor.

"Put it all in the ship," Dingo called over from the stool as he eyed the article closer. "And go get the camera."

As Blarp hauled the heavy bag back to the pod, Dingo pulled his stool closer to the desk to get a better look at the woman. A pencil was hanging loosely in her hands. It was snapped clean in half.

"What's your story...what have you seen..." Dingo moved closer, whispering to the Boney Lady as if asking her a secret. He looked into her eye sockets, straight through to the inside of her nonexistent brain. Her eyes were fixed down at the desk. Dingo shifted out of the stool to read the engraving.

Beware the Jabberwock, my son!

The jaws that bite, the claws that catch

Beware the Jubjub bird, and shun the frumious Bandersnatch

"Beware the Jabberwock –" he whispered. *"Beware...that's Alice Through the Looking Glass.* Lewis...C.S. Lewis –" He looked back into her eyes.

" –It's going to take them years to make this out," Blarp said as he stumbled back into the room. "All I can decipher is *Period 2, U.S. History* –what are you doing?"

"Shh! She was about to say something to me –" Dingo was now inches from her skull, holding his breath.

"Knock it off, Dingo. All this Earth sun is getting to your brain tubes,"

Dingo continued to eye the woman. She was sad, but strong. It was possible she once held power in her world. But that power was dried up, possibly along with her patience and the Denver tourism. Her fists were clenched, accounting for the snapped pencil. By the stature of her body she looked broken. Not by an accident of any kind, but by years of wear and tear. This looked impossible as her bone structure itself suggested she couldn't have been a day over 25. She must have been beautiful, Dingo thought. Well, for a human anyway.

It was hard for Dingo to tell, but he could have sworn he saw a glimpse of a tear roll down her cheek as he turned away. He did a double-take but the tear was nowhere to be found.

"Get the pictures already," Blarp interrupted, snapping Dingo back to his senses. "Let's just get our samples and go. I don't want to wake the dead."

Dingo aimed the shiny, black camera square at the Boney Lady and clicked down on the shutter. The flash filled the unkempt room and then vanished in an instant. Dingo stood motionless.

"Come on, let's get out of here." Blarp said and finished rummaging through the remains of a drawer by the window. "I want to get back to Base for the Blingo Buffet." They turned to leave out the boarded up door. Dingo lingered for a few moments, looking at the writings on the desk and back to the woman.

"It feels wrong," Dingo said, packing his tools and camera back into the ship for departure. "She used to be somebody."

"Well she's nobody now," Blarp said closing the pod door loudly behind them.

"Don't worry, Miss Boney," Dingo whispered, clicking down his seatbelt in the cockpit and eyeing the crumbling school beside them. *"You are somebody to me."*

* * *

Upon Blarp and Dingo's return, the photographs and bone samples were handed over to Headquarters. Their job was over. The deal was done. But Dingo felt uneasy. He asked to be informed about Miss Boney when the results were in. He wanted to know. He had to know.

After months of analysis the research team identified *The Woman in the Chair*. Unlike *The Man on the Bike* and *The Dog in the Wagon*, her story seemed to be monumental clues that could uncover the truth of The Fall.

"Here's your girl," A lab technician smiled handing Dingo a lab report. Dingo held tight to his coffee cup. He wasn't sure if he'd be relieved or disappointed to learn about who she was.

Name: Elizabeth Miller

Age: 24, Single

Gender: Female

Height: 5 ft 4 in

Hair: Blonde

Eyes: Blue

Cause of Death: Dehydration

Profession: High School Teacher

The Records Team was able to track down her picture in a school yearbook that was stashed in her bag and cross-referenced it with her DNA. Her name was actually Ms. Miller, but Dingo continued to call her Ms. Boney. She wasn't married but was a beautiful as Dingo hoped she would be. Her hair glimmered from the pages of the yearbook and her eyes held strong and sturdy like she was on a mission of some kind. It was hard for him to contemplate how she'd ended up in that boarded up classroom.

Her files revealed that she taught at St. Thomas High for five years and was an avid member of the afterschool Tutoring Program. She attended school events regularly and always had her grades in on time. A crumpled up lesson plan revealed that she was passionate about teaching History. She'd created simulations about the stock market crash of the 1920's and tracked down touching firsthand accounts of the Vietnam War. A stained napkin with pen markings on it revealed that she was even more passionate about helping her students. *Bring Johnny stress ball Monday. Tell Kimberly that I'm sorry about her grandma.*

The newspaper article found in her bag described a worldwide educational collapse. Ms. Boney's school was hit hard by budget cuts and overcrowding. She had too many students and not enough textbooks. School test scores were dropping every year as kids were forced to take lengthy tests that decided the fate of their schools.

Soon tensions rose and schools from Denver to Paris began shutting down. Teachers walked out by the masses and school shootings began in large cities as teachers were blamed for their failing students. Riots caused the shutdown of the banks and then the government. The Fall of Earth was a result of the Fall of the Human Mind.

"How did she die?" Dingo asked the technician.

"Poor girl died of dehydration," he said. "Found some videotapes in the wreckage. The janitor was boarding up all the classrooms and she was in her room grading papers. I guess she was listening to music or something. Whatever it was, she was so intensely into her work that she didn't notice when she was sealed inside. The janitor must not have heard her. She yells for a bit, paces, here and there, but it's like she knows it's over... and just goes back to grading the papers. Poor broad must have died a few days later sitting in that chair."

"No one came looking for her?"

"Humans thought teachers caused the collapse. They blamed them for almost everything. She probably would have had it worse if she had escaped."

Dingo was stunned. Miss Boney must have dedicated her young life to her students; grading their hard-to-read hand written assignments late into the evening, sacrificing her own health to lesson plan the best lessons for them each day and calling parents daily to try to help them be successful. Her life outside of teaching was minimal. There were no letters from friends or dates in her calendar for social gatherings outside of school. Instead, her planner was filled with extensive To-Do lists with items like: *Organize special education plans, make copies for tomorrow, email administrator about observation, plan new assessments, seating charts so that Jarred doesn't bug anyone and make sure Judith can sit in front.*

Unfortunately, none of this seemed to matter during The Fall. Even Miss Boney's undying dedication could not save her or her students from the ravage of the planet.

Ms. Boney's death was not celebrated or mourned. It wasn't long after she was boarded up in her own classroom that the rest of the world fell to pieces around her. After several days of crying out for help she gave up. She reached for her bag and slowly etched the words from her favorite poem into the desk. She traced the words over and over until her pencil snapped in half and she felt her last breath escape her lips.

Dingo sat looking at the yearbook picture of Ms. Boney. *"Beware the Jabberwock, my son,"* he repeated to himself. He wondered why she'd chosen those words. It was a nonsense poem, of course, Dingo had studied it many times before and come to minimal conclusions.

But maybe the Jabberwocky wasn't a real monster, but the monster that education could become if left unchecked. The Fall of Earth was due to the crippling of the educational system. It could have all been avoided. Miss Boney could have lived. If only humans had figured out that education was the key to their survival.

He sipped his black coffee and sighed heavily into the mug. He pulled from his jacket pocket the Polaroid picture he'd taken from the desert and placed it next to her shining and hopeful face. She was warning him, she was warning everyone.

"You are somebody to me, Ms. Boney," he said. "You will always be somebody to me."

⊗ ⊗

Mimi Hayes is a Denver-based high school teacher, comedian, and occasional buffoon. When she is not covered in ungraded papers and pizza sauce, you can find her telling jokes to strangers and 14 year olds about her brain bleed. She is currently writing a memoir titled "Break Ups and Brain Hemorrhages: How You Can Make It Through Anything" which she hopes her mom will read.

GHOST'S GHOST – JENNIFER MOORE

Say it out loud—

in the machine of bones there's a ghost,
a continually cooling breath

headed elsewhere.
A mouse

builds a burrow
with the bones of a crow,

and in her building
makes a case for rearrangement—

after it expires, repurpose the body.
In every honeycombed structure,

find the ghost's ghost.
Say it out loud:

unsettle the argument,
unmake the bed;

drive past the house
full of history that never happened

then build it, room by room—
door and jamb, bones and all

from memory.

ભ્ર   80

Jennifer Moore is the author of The Veronica Maneuver *(University of Akron Press). Poems have appeared in* B   O   D   Y *Literature,* The Volta, TYPO, Transom, *and elsewhere. A native of the Seattle area, Jennifer is an assistant professor at Ohio Northern University and lives in Bowling Green, Ohio. More work is available at jenmoorepoet.com.*

TRICKS AND TREATS – AARON RODRIGUEZ

"Okay, Serena, what good is hiding inside a closet going to do?" Bailey, my younger sister, says over the phone as I smile at the tv screen in my living room. A frantic Jamie Lee Curtis crouches inside a closet as Michael Meyers finds her in *Halloween*. I reach out to my coffee table for a skull sugar cookie.

"She's playing *Laurie Strode*, it's not like she's not going to make it." I say between bites and push my witch hat back to get it out of my eyes.

"True, they need her for Halloween 27. I don't know how you takes these movies seriously."

"We should do this more often." I say.

"What? Watch the same movie at different locations?"

"No! I mean take the time to talk more. I know you're busy with studying interior design and nursing school on my end equals no social life but we should try anyway."

"I should be free next weekend." Bailey says.

As Michael Meyers breaks through the closet door on screen, my doorbell rings.

"Hang on, I think I have some trick or treaters." I reach for a plastic cauldron half-full of candy corn and licorice.

"This late? You kept your Jack-O-Lantern on, didn't you?" I can almost hear her pursing her lips.

"Excuse me for being festive." I roll my eyes. "Happy Hallow-" To my surprise, there is no one there when I open my front door. I look down the walkway and either side of the porch. No one in sight. The Jack-O-Lantern sits on the first step, most of the candle inside it has melted. Across from us I can see my neighbor Evan dressed as a wolf on his patio, flirting with a girl in a cat costume. He holds his door open when a guy in a skeleton costume and a top hat walks up. I close the door.

"False alarm." I say and slump onto the couch.

"What do you mean?" Bailey yawns. Jamie Lee Curtis whimpers on screen.

"No one there. Probably a prankster. Although there's a party next door that looks like it'll run late."

"You should have just gone to that. Instead of handing out candy by yourself." Bailey huffs.

"I wasn't alone, Jen was here earlier but she had to give her brother a ride. She made these delicious skull cookies. Besides, I've spoken to my neighbor maybe twice. I barely know the guy."

The doorbell rings again. I look back at the door.

"Someone just rang again." I take a second to look at my living room window.

"Do you think it could be some stinker from the party?"

"Maybe. Hang on." I walk over and look through the peephole. No one. I lock the security chain and open the door. All I can hear is a faint breeze and some laughing coming from the party.

"There's no one there, Bailey." I close the door.

"That's odd. I'm sure it's someone who's messing around."

"Let's hope so." My blacks boots clack on the wooden floor as I walk back to the the kitchen and look out the window above the sink.

"It's too dark to see out in the back." I tell Bailey. I try the knob of the kitchen door. I gasp when I notice it's unlocked.

"What?! Did you see something?" Bailey tries to hide the bit of panic in her voice.

"My kitchen door was unlocked but I don't remember if I locked it to begin with. Shoot. I'll call you back."

"Don't forget, Serena! Otherwise I'll think something bad happened. That Megan girl that disappeared last summer after that metal concert. Her body still hasn't been found."

"Thanks for the reminder." I sigh and click END. I slowly open the kitchen door. An orange envelope sits on the square of pavement in front of me. It's too dark to see anything else. I pick it up as fast as I can and pull out a white square that says "BOO!" in sharpie.

"This isn't funny!" I yell into the darkness and turn on the flashlight on my phone and I gasp when I see a tall man in black, wearing a skull mask.

He lunges toward me from the darkness.

I scream and rush back inside.

I swing the kitchen door closed and try to lock it with my shaking hand but he shoves it open. I push over a chair behind me before reaching for a knife from a wooden cutlery block and run out of the kitchen as fast as I can. I reach my front door and can hear the running footsteps coming behind me. I'm unlocking the security chain when I see him coming at me, a butcher knife in his hand.

I scream and I bolt for the stairs as his knife dives at me, and I feel a fiery sting when the edge slices into my forearm.

"Stop, please!" I yell as I'm running up. He's right behind me and he grunts as he grabs my black dress and pulls me back before I can reach the second floor. I land on his body, and stab violently with my knife. The blade punctures his hand. As he reels, I kick him in the chest, and he lets me go for the quickest of seconds. I run back upstairs, and don't dare look behind me. I shove through my bedroom door, slamming it, and locking it. The blood running down my arm paints the wall as I turn on the light switch.

I look for ways to escape. I see the window, but it's too late. I hear footsteps outside my door. I throw myself into the deepest corner of my closet. I adjust blankets in front of me and crouch as much as I can.

I dial 911.

"911, what's is your emergency?" The operator says.

The door bursts open. I'm afraid to utter a word. *If I risk saying something out loud, would it matter if it got me killed?* The closet door opens. *Why is this happening to me? I don't want to die like this.*

My body shakes. My eyes water.

"Serena, what good is hiding inside a closet going to do?" A familiar female's voice says.

The blankets in front of me topple down. I look up and gasp at the sight of a girl in a black spandex jumpsuit and a black mask that only covers her eyes standing before me. She taps an orange envelope against her leg and takes off her mask.

It's Bailey.

"...What's going on?" I say between gasps.

"Happy Halloween, big sister." She smiles.

"What is this?" I wipe the tears from my eyes and clutch my legs tight, still seated in the closet.

"It was a prank," she replies. "I sent my friend Eric before me to drop the envelope on your back door. He rang your doorbell."

"...A prank? Your friend Eric?" I stand slowly.

"Yes, the guy with a matching mask," Her eyes look concerned. "He's about this tall."

Bailey holds her hand up above her head to show Eric's height.

"You do know the difference between me and a boy, right?" she prods.

"The one here... he... He wasn't wearing a mask like yours..." I shake my head, climb to my feet–still shaking–and step out of the closet.

"Serena, you're bleeding!"

I look down and watch the blood drip off my arm and onto the carpet beneath me. There's a damp, crimson pool where I huddled in the closet. I feel a little woozy.

Suddenly, there are footsteps running up the stairs and I raise the knife in my hands.

As another figure steps into the doorway I hold the knife out like a defensive scorpion.

"Serena!" Bailey yells. "It's only Eric!"

A young man, out of breath, stands in the doorway rubbing his head. He is wearing a similar getup to Bailey and a matching mask.

"Eric, she's bleeding, the plan was to scare her not get her killed. I mean what were you think–"

"Bailey, I didn't do this." He takes off his mask and his widened eyes are filled with alarm. "I dropped off the orange envelope in the back like you told me but someone hit me. I couldn't see who it was but they came from behind me and all I felt was someone hit me on the head before I blacked out. When I came to I saw the kitchen door was open and everything was trashed."

"It wasn't him, Bailey." I say.

"What are you talking about, Serena?"

"It wasn't him," I whisper, dialing 911 again. "This monster was taller, was built differently, and he had a skull mask."

"911, what is your emergency?" A male operator says.

"Hello, I have to report an intruder. A man broke in and tried to kill me. I'm afraid he might still be nearby." I say into the phone. I clutch the knife close to me.

"If it wasn't you, Eric..." Bailey trails off.

"4345 Cedar Street," I tell the operator. "Please hurry."

I put the phone down and walk into the hallway.

I gaze at the stairs before I place a foot the first step. The doorbell rings and I jump. Bailey and Eric come out of the bedroom.

"That's the police, I'm sure," Bailey says. She walks ahead of me and opens the door.

"Bailey, be careful," I plead as she looks into the peephole.

"Yes, it's them. Thank God!" She opens the door and lets two policemen in. As she begins to explain what happened, I slowly walk into the kitchen and scan the scene that the kitchen has turned into. I can't help but feel as if someone is staring at me. I look out the kitchen window. My heart races, and I jump back.

The skull mask is out there, looking right at me.

255

"Officers, in here!" I yell. I turn around to look for a new weapon with which to arm myself. The policemen rush in with Bailey and Eric following cautiously behind them. By the time I turn back to the window again the mask is gone, and the only thing visible is darkness.

ଔ ଓ

Aaron Rodriguez is a writer, fashion stylist, and horror movie addict in Denver, Colorado. Whether he's working on pitches at 303 Magazine, drinking coffee around the city, or shopping for anything in black, you can follow what he's up to on Instagram @BlankCanvasFashion

MY FRIEND SKELLY - RACE GARBER

My parents wouldn't let me get a dog. They said I wouldn't take care of it. They wanted to know if I'd feed it, walk it, not tape wings to its back and throw it off the roof to see if it would fly. I tried to tell them that I'd fed my two hamsters and three goldfish I used to have; that they hadn't needed to be walked, but I had given them a wheel and a spacious bowl.

So if those were the three things a dog needed, I'd managed two out of three already. And that was was still like a C, and I shouldn't be punished for being average.

Besides, it wasn't my fault. The hamsters hadn't really tried that hard. That was the problem there. And the goldfish...I think the flippers threw off the wings. I knew how to fix the problem, if my parents hadn't stopped buying me goldfish.

But my parents weren't very reasonable. I told my dad that it wasn't fair, that he had a dog when he was a kid. But all he said was that he had, that it was buried in my grandparents' backyard, and that if I had a dog, he didn't think I'd dig the hole for that either.

He was wrong. I loved digging holes. Besides, my grandparents' house was boring and I really wanted a dog.

My dad had named that dog "Sparky," which I thought was a stupid name. I didn't have a better one, not right away. But when I was duct-taping the bones together, it came to me.

Skelly was a really good dog. He wasn't good at fetch or sitting or anything. He was pretty much always playing dead. A lot of people made fun of me or screamed when they saw him.

But he was a good dog. I didn't have to take him out all the time when he had to go to the bathroom. It was easy to hide him from my parents (who still wouldn't get me a dog!) because he didn't need to eat. And he was so good about flying lessons. He didn't need a soft landing like those lame hamsters, or water to breath like the fish. He never once whined or spasmed or started to decompose when I had to tape a limb back on.

The thing about life, though, is the best moments of life are just that...moments. And Skelly was probably too perfect for this world. He was a loveable dog. He got along with children, even when they screamed or wouldn't pet him. He never bit anyone. And he never barked or growled at other dogs.

Unfortunately, other dogs were not as nice to Skelly. Maybe it was because he was too friendly, that he wouldn't stand up for himself. Maybe it was because he was made of bones. I guess I'll never know.

What I do know is, the first time I took Skelly to the dog park was also the last time I saw him all together.

I remember I almost cried when it happened. I felt my eyes tearing up.

But then I realized that nothing lasts forever. Skelly was a good dog. Skelly never demanded anything from me. I think what Skelly wanted most was to make others happy. So when I saw how happy Skelly had made all those other dogs, I knew this was what he would have wanted.

I kicked a stone most of the way home, clutching a string I'd used for a leash, still dragging a collarbone. It was the only thing left I had of Skelly.

Every place I looked, it reminded me of some great memory I had with Skelly. So I just kind of drooped my head, trying not to see anything but the ground.

My parents were really excited when I got home, but I was still sad. I couldn't tell them why, couldn't tell them about Skelly, on account of them saying I couldn't have a dog. I knew they'd be sore at me if they find out I went behind their backs.

But then I heard it. My mom walked into the living room, some metal rattled, and I heard a high-pitched yip. When the puppy rounded the corner, I was really happy again. I felt guilty, what with losing Skelly that same day, but I think Skelly would have been happy for me.

My parents said that I had been so well-behaved that week, that I hadn't been bothering them, or trying to light stuff on fire, or stealing my dad's coats and hats to put them on sticks outside the windows of people's houses at night so they thought someone was stalking them. They said they realized I had grown up, that I was being responsible and ready for a dog.

To be honest, I was a little disappointed at first because it was a puppy. It seemed like a puppy would be more work. He bounced around a lot and my mom made me clean up when I got him too excited and he peed on the floor. But then I realized a puppy was a lot lighter than a normal dog, so I probably could use smaller wings. I went straight up to my room to get the tape.

CR &O

Under a variety of job titles and post-nominals, Race has written public speeches, court decisions, and formal pleas for (varying degrees of) justice. His work has been widely distributed, most often under the names of or on behalf of his previous employers. Breaking that trend, he is happy to have been published in f(r)iction, Tethered by Letters Quarterly, and on this humerus website.

BONE MALLOW – ANTOINE VALOT

I liked it because of the crunch, but also because it becomes spongy when you chew it. Chalky at first, but then chewy too. Like marshmallows used to feel.

Rog and Del found the stash in an old train car. Hundreds of old peeps, dead mortals, stuffed in there. From the time before, obviously.

Rog is old. He remembers a lot about the time before, when things were so complicated. Del forgot, like me, because we jack-up a lot. But Rog is weird, he almost never jacks. He talks a lot, he's sad a lot. But he remembers a lot of things.

We were out playing train-up with guns and lazes, blowing buildings up, and looking for ammo in the city ruins. But mostly playing train-up, no teams. Rog had norside, Del was wesside, I had the park. I was winning good, I had found Rog from behind and pumped a dozen rounds in his back, and I was cutting his arms off with laze when Del got me. She popped me right in the head, blew my brains out. I didn't even see it coming.

By the time I fixed it was night. I saw my old braincase on the grass in front of me, so that's how I knew how she got me. I called for Rog and Del but they'd gone back. So I went back too. I wanted to jack-up because I was mad. Del just pops me all the time, right in the head. What's the fun in that?

But when I got there Rog had hauled back that big train car, with the stash of old mortal bones. Del was ripping him up, putting the old dead bones inside him in place of his nano ones. They were laughing like mad. Del was making a mess of it, crushing the bones sometimes while she put them in, and they didn't fix, so once Rog's skin was closed up, and he lifted his arm, the end of it was just flopping down. I said "Hey Rog your hand's a limp dick!" and we all started laughing real hard. Del grabbed Rog's other arm and squeezed, and we head the dead bone inside crack and crush, and then he had both arms flopping and Del was calling him "double dicky."

I'm the one who had the idea to chew on some of the bones. I'm the one who always likes to eat things. I started with a long one, and it splintered a lot and cut my cheeks a little, so the chalkiness soaked up my nanoblood and that's when I found out it was chewy too.

I haven't tasted anything since the time before, when I was a kid, and of course I couldn't taste the flavor of the bone. But the feel of it in my mouth, it brought something back. I remembered something from before. I remembered marshmallows. Back when I lived in a house, and we had clothes, and we had pain and lots of things were dangerous. I had my mom, who was an old mortal, she was complicated. She was nice to me, gave me marshmallows. They tasted fantastic. Sugar. Sugar was like buzzing.

The feel of the chewy bones made my mouth wet. I remembered shoes. I had shoes with color spots under them, on the soles. One was red and the other was another color. It was so I could tell which one went on which foot, but I never could tell which color meant what anyway. I remembered the backyard, with the short little brick wall. I used to walk on it, with my arms out. There was a sand pit too. I remembered my mom patting the sand off my pants.

I had feelings then, before. Sometimes I was afraid. Tall people, angry at me. My mom didn't get angry though. I would put my hand in her hand and stand next to her. I remember her hand was very warm.

I kept chewing and chewing and there was more water in my mouth, it was spilling out my lips, and my nose, and my eyes. I couldn't swallow because my throat was stuck so I spit out the wet bones, and wiped my face with my hands.

Then I got tired and I wanted to jack-up, and Del too. Rog didn't want to, he asked us to cut off his limp dick arms before we jacked, so I lazed them off for him, and Del ripped out some old bone ribs she'd put in him. He had to stop breathing for a while, so he was out. We finished cleaning up his insides, and we left him opened up, to fix, while we jacked-up.

I was very hyper, so it was good to jack-up. I pushed the dial to the top, and buzzed hard. I must have been out for days. When I came back there was no more bones in the train car. Rog and Del had crushed them, for fun. I tried to remember again, but I couldn't. I could just remember that I had remembered some of before, but not the feelings. I put on a powersuit and crushed the train car. Then I jacked-up for a minute, and we went off to play train-up.

* * *

This story was inspired by People of Sand and Slag by Paolo Bacigalupi.

ജ ഝ

Antoine Valot does software, performing arts, and fiction. He crafts experiences that empower and delight.

ANKLEBONE CONNECTED TO THE... HEART? – JON-BARRETT INGELS

I wanted to run that morning. Maybe I needed to run. I was getting soft after the breakup, softer than I had been, which may have contributed to the breakup. The depressive binge-drinking and accessibility to snacks at my buddy's place, where I crashed, made it easy to let myself go. There was no way I would be able to win my ex back with my muffin top, and no way I would attract another girl to make my ex jealous looking the way I did. I needed to get back to running.

It was an activity I loathed growing up, an activity required for every sport I attempted, and ultimately an activity that led to the demise of my poor attempt at a high school athletic career. I attributed my distaste for running to two things; my severe case of asthma, and my more severe case of laziness. Once, in high school, I attempted to run more than a mile. Only once. It took me four years to try again, running alongside my lean, muscular college roommate. Again, it wasn't for me. My chest got tight, my face beet-red, my shoes came untied, my legs cramped. It was football practice all over again. I had to stop halfway on our joint exercise and walk back to the dorm to have my own joint exercise. Pot jokes! I know...

I was twenty-five the first time I ran more than one mile. I was living in Redondo Beach, right near the water. My drinking and smoking buddy (funny how asthma stopped me from running but didn't prevent me from smoking) wanted to get in shape. His thirty-year-old body wasn't keeping up with his twenty-one-year-old lifestyle. We tried running along the beach. Astonishingly, I out lasted my partner. He made it maybe three quarters of a mile before the hands went to the knees, chest heaving. I kept on running, and kept on running after that. I eventually, and painstakingly got to a regular five-mile run with three years of effort. I was living in West Hollywood and had plotted out a route that I would consistently run at least three times a week.

My practice continued for a couple of years, putting me in the best shape of my life. It was around that time I met my ex. Things were good, or they were ok, for a while. Thirty hit, and then I became a dad, and moved, and lost my job, and things slowed down. It doesn't matter if you step away from a routine for a couple years or a couple weeks, it is ten-times more difficult to get back into it. I tried. When we moved to Grenada Hills, I struggled up and down hills, having to walk a lot of the route with hands overhead just to get three miles logged. When we moved to Atwater, I'd force myself onto the treadmill after I saw the way she would look at me, or heard her joke about my gut, or watched her close her eyes every time we'd have sex. The struggle was real, as they say, but I finally established a new routine of running at dawn along the LA River, logging about four miles. And then it ended. We ended, dramatically, and I moved out. She wasn't satisfied. I wasn't satisfied with myself.

My friend on the Westside had a room available. He and I would drink, and eat out, and watch *Man Vs Food,* and eat more, and drink, and drink. I added twenty pounds to my already heavy frame. I discovered this as I watched the cute nurse move the slider on the scale way past the number I was familiar with. I got a new job that came with really, really great medical insurance, along with cute nurses adding a 2 to the beginning of my weight. This new number associated with my body messed with my head. The squish around my midsection messed with my head. The constant fatigue I experienced trying to keep up with my three-year-old messed with my head. I started running again. I started moving past my comfort zone and pushing through my lungs urging me to quit.

Remember that new insurance I was just talking about? It was great! Acupuncture, massage therapy, cheap prescriptions, cheap doctors visits. I took advantage of it all. Full physical, heart and lung monitoring, blood work, urine, everything for one low price. My doctor asked if there was anything I was concerned about. I talked about my asthma, my fear of skin cancer, and I brought up the old injury to my foot.

Here we go.

I broke my foot four years prior to that visit. I was in a comedy group, a hip-hop comedy group with the dude who just offered me the spare room. He and another dude would rap-sing stupid, hilarious, vulgar songs while girls paraded the stage in lingerie. I was a back-up dancer (we were called Man Slices.) We would perform the most ridiculous choreographed routines, eventually running through the audience, rousing the crowd. We'd tear off our jackets in the most unsexy version of *Chip and Dale, Magic Mike, Thunder From Down Under* you can imagine. It's not lost on me that my pale puffiness was all part of the parody, but that pale puffiness procured potential partners (alliteration points.) That show got me laid. Digress, digress. One fateful finale had my sweaty, soft self leaping off the stage into the audience. In mid air, as if in slow motion, I could see that where I was about to land some girl had left a purse while she groped for me and my fellow Slices. I course corrected before landing, rolling my ankle painfully, and continued to hobble through the crowd, trying not to let the pain hinder my performance.

I went home and iced it, and thought nothing of. I eventually got to a doctor who said there was a small fracture in my metatarsal. He said there was nothing I could do except to wear secure shoes while working my waiter job. End of story.

Cut to:

Four years later, my crazy-great insurance plan at my disposal. My doctor sent me to a podiatrist, a fast-talking, self-proclaimed genius who designed his own orthotic shoe insert, which he immediately prescribed for me. He showed me how my foot hung limp, explaining that my epic stage jump may have torn all of the ligaments in my foot and ankle, and ordered an MRI for me all without taking a breath. Insurance is great!

"Can I run?" I enquired.

"Just keep doing what you're doing until we get the MRI results. Maybe wrap your leg in an Ace bandage to keep it stable." Great.

I wrapped, I ran, I worked eight-hour shifts on my feet at a restaurant. A week later I went for my MRI; forty-five minutes lying still as magnetic rays bounced off my foot and ankle, or whatever it is that happens during an MRI. That afternoon I picked my daughter up from school and chased her around the park jumping off the equipment, trying to be Superdad. The increase in my running regimen had increased my energy. Still, it was exhausting being with a three-year-old. That night I went to a project meeting with some friends. At one moment of deep thought, I crossed my leg, ankle to the opposite knee, and felt a slight tenderness right above the anklebone. Odd.

Next morning I went for a run. I needed to run. I was almost back to my five miles; it was becoming routine again. My friends ran the LA Marathon a couple years prior and I started to think maybe I could give it a go with a little more practice. My lungs were clear, my legs weren't tight, I found the perfect music mix to energize my footfall, my kick. My gut hadn't shrunk yet so I needed to keep the pattern going, keep my momentum, get rid of the softness. I got one mile into my route (I knew it was one mile, I had mapped out the course in my car, finding the landmarks representing my miles. I was concerned about the distance, not the time or the speed, but the distance traveled. It was how my brain made sense of the exercise.) *Crack! Pop!* The kind of *pop* you are not supposed to hear from your body. Sharp pain in my ankle radiating through my leg down to my toes and up through my thigh, into my gut, tightening the internal organs about to expel what little water I had drank before leaving the apartment, up through my esophagus. My eyes pushed out tears, my lungs forced out a scream. My body wasn't my own; it belonged to the pain. I was one mile away from home. I was wet with sweat and tears and saliva and morning dew. I didn't have my phone. I didn't have ID. I didn't know whether to flag down some SUV taking kids to school and ask for a ride, or to knock on some stranger's door, or just lay down in the middle of the sidewalk, heaving and crying until someone stopped to ask if I needed help. My ego rejected all options save for hobbling back for a mile until I got home. Any amount of pressure on the foot would constrict my spine and tug on all receptors in my brain. It was the longest walk I had ever taken.

I popped two leftover Vicodin I was saving for some sad night of binge watching *Adult Swim.* I iced the affected area, as per my nurse practitioner mother's instructions. I wrapped tightly in an Ace bandage and experienced some relief; from a 15 to a 9 on the 10 point pain scale. I had a week until my MRI results came in. I took a couple days off work. I elevated the injury. I visited my acupuncturist twice. I was going to be ok. Right? Hehe.

My motor-mouth podiatrist showed me the MRI results; tears in the calcaneo-fibular ligament and torn anterior talo-fibular ligament, none of which had ever healed properly in the last four years.

"Cool. Ok. And what about what happened last week while running?"

"More stress on the ligaments trying to heal. You should wear a walking boot for two weeks and see if anything improves."

"Ok, cool. And what about this tender slightly raised part of my ankle?"

"More than likely related to continued stress on ligament. Wear the boot and we'll go from there. And here's a prescription for Vicodin"

"Cool!"

I wore my boot fitted with a Reebok Pump device enveloping my leg with a cushion of air like a blood pressure cuff. I had a legit excuse to eat opiates. Things were looking up.

Two weeks passed and I returned to see if there were any improvements. Doc held up my foot and it flopped back down.

"Hm. Ok. Well, we can try physical therapy for a bit. Surgery would be our last option."

"Cool. What about this tender lump above my ankle bone?"

It was the same spot I had pointed out before. It was raised now. I iced it regularly to keep down swelling and my acupuncturist treated it for pain using needles and electrodes. Doc looked at it as if seeing it for the first time.

"Does this hurt?" He touched it.

Alarms went off in my brain, forcing a strong exhalation, and squeezing out tears.

"Whoa! Let's get a quick x-ray."

"Yeah, let's."

My fibula was shattered in what he called a "spiral fracture," where a piece of the small bone was about to puncture my skin from the inside out. That understandably was the pain and discomfort I had been feeling since my fateful run. Apparently, my acrobatics off the stage severed some ligaments. Without being able to heal, I had been walking and running incorrectly, putting weight and pressure on the fibula, the small bone not designed to carry weight, but rather to stabilize the leg muscles. So every time I ran, every time I worked those eight-hour shifts, every time I walked anywhere I was putting weight, all of my extra, depressed, post-breakup weight on that poor little bone.

Emergency surgery was scheduled. I was to have the bone reset with a plate on top and five screws bored into the fibula to hold it in place.

Guess who came to my rescue? Well, my mom, the nurse practitioner came down to be with me before and after the surgery, but also my ex! I was going to be out of commission for six weeks, not able to walk. I was given a scooter to push myself around on. She offered for me to stay with her and my daughter while I recovered. She cared about me and wanted to care for me. She wanted to help me. Clearly she wanted me back, right? I was going to be the injured bird she resuscitated back to health, a twisted sort of reverse Stockholm Syndrome.

The night before the surgery I imagined the flesh on my ankle being split apart with a scalpel, blood vessels cauterized as they pulled the incision, exposing whatever is underneath the skin; muscle, tendons, my destroyed ligaments. I pictured my surgeon putting the bone pieces back together like you would a broken broom handle, finding the right grooves of bone fragment to match together. I wondered what sound the drill would make, high pitched like a dentist's, or buzzing like my Mikita? Would that scent of burning come, like when you drill into hard wood, or would the bone splinter around the screw? I felt everything I was imagining in my gut, in my flesh, in the tension I created in my fists. I didn't sleep.

I was prepped early the next morning at the hospital. My belongings were logged and placed in a bag as if I was going to jail. They gave me something like Xanax to calm down. I watched the pre-op room fill with nervous patients and their family. What were they here for? Something as benign as a fractured leg, or something more serious? Maybe an organ removed. I thought about my step dad's triple bypass and imagined my own sternum being cracked and split open, allowing my most vitals to be exposed to the air for the first time ever. My surgeon came in, same amphetamined podiatrist who put me there, quickly went over everything that would happen, marked the correct leg, and signed it. I didn't even think about the possibility of the incorrect leg being incised; something else to add to my trepidation. He had twenty other surgeries scheduled that day, TWENTY. I was an item on the assembly line to be processed in and then out, ready for the next. My mother came in, held my hand, and said she'd be waiting for me. Was this goodbye? It felt like a goodbye. Complications could happen. Anesthesia could cause the brain or heart to stop functioning. Should I say something to her, prepare for the worst? She was gone.

They wheeled me into the operating room. I tried desperately to memorize the path we took to get there for some reason. The Xanax had me calm, but I couldn't help but think about all the worst possible outcomes. What if I woke up in the operating room and everyone was gone, like *28 Days Later?* They laid me on a horizontal cross, needles placed into my hands and arms. I thought about the death penalty, lethal injection, a needle in your arm and then nothing. The masked faces were gentle in their precision, eyes smiling at me. I counted back, 10, 9, 8, 7, oblivion.

* * *

"Oooh, I need your love, babe. Guess you know it's true." A voice sang out. "Hope you need my love, babe, just like I need you." I opened my eyes. "Hold me, love me, hold me, love me." The voice was my own, all cracked and off key, but filled with passion. "I ain't got nothing but love, babe, eight days a week." The nurses were laughing in the recovery room. I couldn't tell if the song was playing on the radio or if it was my head from my anesthesia dream. Time didn't exist, I barely existed until I looked down and saw my heavily bandaged leg elevated in front of me.

One of the nurses came over. "You've been singing for a while. Quite funny. Are you in any pain?" I wasn't in anything. I just was.

I sang some more because, why not? I loved the pharmaceutical cloud I was engulfed in. As moments passed, the pain increased along with my awareness of my surroundings. It wasn't even 11 yet. It had only been an hour or so. It could have been a lifetime. The next rotation, the nurse gave me some strong pain pills. I sunk into the bed waiting until I was released.

My mother wheeled me out to the car, allowing me to thank everyone with a handshake. We stopped to pick up my meds, my shower boot, and my scooter. She dropped me off at my ex's place and left to shop for groceries. I was her baby boy again, needing his mom. I let her dote on me because I needed it, but she kind of did as well. My ex helped me in and onto her couch. She smiled as she gently touched my shoulder and my face. It was the beginning of my six-week stay with her and I planned to win her back before it was done. She smelled the same, her skin glistened the same. She smiled at me as I lay on the couch asking if there was anything she could do to make me more comfortable.

"A hand job?" I thought. You know, to relieve stress. It was too soon, though. There was work I needed to do to insert myself back into the situation. I asked for water to take my pain pill. I didn't need it yet but I wanted to let her help. That, and it would feel real good!

My well-imagined plan was that she would get used to having me around, that it would spark whatever memory of joy she had of us together, watching shows together, making jokes together, sleeping together. What I ended up being was that clichéd character from 90s sitcoms who was sick, with a bell they kept ringing, doing nothing but annoying all the other characters. I could see the contempt grow as she brought meals to me, did my laundry, sighing aggressively every time I made some sort of flirty joke.

She worked a lot, which was one of the factors of our demise, at least in my head, but she seemed to be working even more while I was there recovering. I got extra quality time with my daughter. We'd watch whatever kid's show she was into until eventually she would climb on me, or run around the apartment and make me look for her. All my mobility was limited to hopping. Hopping from couch to bathroom, from couch to kitchen, hopping to search for wherever my daughter was hiding. I fell three times and may have thrown out some choice words that might have been inappropriate for her. I fell once hopping onto one of her toys left on the floor, and I fell twice trying to take a shower, hanging the injured leg in a vacuum-sealed boot over the tub.

Most of my time was spent alone in the apartment, foreign in its familiarity. It was my stuff in someone else's space. Furniture we had bought together, or that I had donated to them, clothes I had bought for my ex, toys for my daughter, my kitchen appliances. Yet none of it was mine. It wasn't my home and that hurt more than the screws holding my leg together. I was tempted to nose through my ex's room, find out secrets, or find something to give me some sort of hope for us; a letter I had written her, a picture of us. I thought about going through her underwear drawer just to feel some sort of intimate connection. I know! Creepy! My snooping had gotten me in trouble in the past, finding out thing I didn't want to know and at the same time breaking her trust, another factor of our demise.

I watched movies, and fixed her door handles, and we all ate dinner as a family fairly regularly for the first time in a long while. We would watch our shows together, her and I, just like we used to. She would even cuddle up with me on occasion, being careful of the leg of course, but we never came back, back to what we were, or what I imagined we were.

Three weeks into my recuperation, I was up late one night. I couldn't sleep. I saw a light flicker from her bedroom and heard the tapping keys of her computer. I lifted myself off the couch and hopped over to her door. She was propped up in bed writing a message to someone. A broad smile reflected in the computer light.

"Can't sleep either?" I inquired from the doorway.

"My god! You scared me!" She shut her computer.

"You working?"

"What? No, I was sending a message." She responded quickly.

"To who?" I meant to ask why so late, or really anything to keep the conversation going, but I didn't. I knew it was none of my business.

"No one!" So quick, so dismissive.

I should have gone back to the couch. I didn't. I hobbled over and flopped onto her bed.

"What are you doing? I am going to sleep now." She said as she rolled over.

"I just wanted to lay here with you, next to you." It was all I wanted from the moment I came over, post-surgery. I wanted her to want me, to take me back, to forgive me, and let me forgive her. I wanted to lay there, and touch her face, and watch her respond to my touch. I wanted her and I needed her to want me. We had slept together a couple times after the breakup but it had never felt right. It was rushed, a brief moment away from our daughter, or it felt like I had to prove something, like I was being tested. I reached over and touched her and felt her recoil.

"Go back to bed. I am going to sleep and you are not sleeping here." There was a playfulness to her stern voice, or maybe I created that in my head. I lay next to her, wanting so much more, and out of the nothingness between us I asked, "Who were you messaging?"

I left the next day, opting to finish the last couple of weeks of my recovery at my apartment, my friend's apartment. It felt more like home to me than my ex's. I bought her a necklace. A thank you, and an apology. She would wear it every time we saw each other after that.

* * *

I just started running again, four years later. I'm at two miles. Every time I run I half-imagine the moment when the screws rip from my fibula, piercing the thin skin around my ankle from the inside, and leaving me in a wet heap in the middle of the track, but I keep doing it. Trying to lose my softness. My leg aches when the rain comes, I guess the drought in California helps limit my aches. My heart aches less and less.

CR   ಐ

Jon-Barrett Ingels takes a long time to complete things (ask him about his ten plus year old novel, or his plays, or screen plays, or TV shows.) That is why he is excited about this short essay. Accomplishment! Encouraging him to finish the laundry list of other projects. When JB isn't writing, or thinking about writing, or tasting wine, or playing with his daughter, he hosts and produces The How The Why podcast for 1888. He is also a contributor for Flaunt Magazine. Everything he does is so that his daughter will always think he is cool. Weird, but cool.

He's also the author of How to Succeed by Failing, a novella.

SEASONS – BRIAN DICKSON

Fall

Four hawks circle quakes
of bones, wild marrow through pre-
dawn precincts, scrawled.

Winter

On cool paths for cool
folks, no camping, X marks ap-
ertures, slivers of bones.

Spring

Gentle, this bone on
a wire, strapped to a high-
light reel on a loop.

Summer

Bones all around time.
Explain that–prefer apoca-
lingo down our spines.

໐ຂ ຂຠ

Brian Dickson keeps this line from Charles Simic with him at all times: "A vision for your life is a work of art." Life as a messy art form where wayward brushstrokes reveal happy accidents...and not-so-happy accidents. This vision has led him to creativity, infusing it into cooking, gardening, writing, letterpress printing, worm farming, riding a bike, relationships, and teaching. He has published in journals around the states including two chapbooks, In a Heart's Rut (High5 Press), Maybe This is How Tides Work (Finishing Line Press), and one book All Points Radiant (WordTech Editions).

Brian lives in Denver with his partner, Sarah, among joy everyday.

THE ERECTION – MATH TRAFTON

It had taken Castor at least ten minutes to pull the heavy thing out of the bog. He'd edged it up along the steep muddy slope of the pool with particularly cautious deliberation, partially out of concern of damaging his net and partially out of curiosity.

He wasn't quite sure what to make of the thing. It was dense—it held its weight. Once he'd finally extracted it from its tenuous hold in his net's fine weave, he set it down in the grass beside him. He collapsed and caught his breath, looking at it. It was long, less than a meter in length, and mostly cylindrical from what he could tell. And when he wiped away some of the spongy black muck, he found that the thing was mostly white and maybe twenty centimeters thick. Its ivory tone was immediately suggestive of the several animal skeleton fragments he'd occasionally pull up, all perfectly preserved by the bog's creeping hold.

But he'd never seen any bone like this. This thing was absolutely foreign.

For a moment, he thought could use a bone like this in his project. He hadn't properly started the project yet, but he dreamt of erecting a statue of himself or somebody just like him, ideally life-size. He had only considered using moorwood, but maybe there was room for this thing. He thought about how it might fit. It was smooth enough, and at least one of its ends bulged and rounded like a mushroom cap, as though meant to interlock with another piece. But if it were a bone, it was far too large to fit within any animal he'd ever known, even any prehistoric beast that would have lived in this area.

He wondered if instead this was a natural formation, like an old branch whose imperfections had eroded away through the initial stages of petrification. It could have been a stone of some sort, yet once the slime was rubbed away, it felt too light.

Castor let the thing sit while he adjusted the length of his net's rod. He carefully dipped the net back into the same pool, no wider in circumference than his own cabin. Though it was silly, he hoped to find another similar thing that might help explain this one beside him. Maybe another symmetrical piece to help him erect his project.

At its maximum length, the rod could reach the bottom of the pool. Generally speaking, he tried to avoid the bottoms because slugfish never dwelt that low, and he'd only end up pulling up tangled hunks decayed plantlife. He prodded the soft bottom, feeling the black pool's deadening pull on the weight of the net. For a moment, he thought he felt the gentle impact of something hard, but after a careful scoop back toward the surface, he found he'd netted only a mass of roots that had rotted off some plant.

Fatigued and quite hungry, he dismissed the catch, though just before he threw it back into the pool, his eye caught a faint glimmer in the mass. What looked to be a disappointingly unsuccessful day suddenly held a faint promise. He pulled in the net for a closer look, and after a moment of sifting through the root's twisting contours, he withdrew a mucksnail—then another. He excitedly emptied the net's contents onto the mossy ground, right next to where the thing lay. Squishing through the blackened roots, Castor squeezed out one mucksnail after another until he'd collected at least a dozen. It had been several months since he'd found a mucksnail, though at the sight, the savor quickly rushed back to him.

It would be dark soon, so Castor decided to pack up. The thing aside, the day had been a successful enough with the mucksnails. He collapsed his net and stowed each of the mucksnails into his leather satchel. He stood and looked fondly upon the thing, a sudden charm of sorts, which seemed to have grown there in the grass. He wondered if he should leave it where it lay, and maybe he'd come back to try to find it again tomorrow. Or he could dump it back to the bottom of the pool. If, in the infinitude of the marsh, he could ever locate this pool again, let alone the thing at its bottom, then that would be a true testament of his luck. He paused a moment, considered the challenge, and looked around at the barren trees and mountainscapes in a rough attempt to memorize his surroundings.

But ultimately, for no particular reason, he decided to kneel and pick up the thing to take it with him. It was heavier than he remembered, and he had to hoist it up and balance it over his shoulder to stand with it. He quickly got used to the weight, though, and after several paces, it started to feel somehow natural on him. It wasn't right, he thought, to use it in his project. At least not yet.

Using the setting sun as a guide, Castor navigated his route back to the trail, and it wasn't much more than an hour before he was well on his way home. He speculated about the thing along his walk. Perhaps it was some prehistoric weapon. As it rested on his shoulder, he steadied the base with both hands, and he imagined what kind of brute it would take to swing such a massive club. He wondered how many skulls a weapon like this would have cracked through.

Lost in thought as he was, he somehow managed to spot a small patch of gray mushrooms just off the trail. He had walked this trail at least twice daily throughout the season, and his watchful eyes had somehow never spotted these treasures here—in the dimming light no less. He paused and lowered the thing to rest it against a tree. After he filled a satchel pocket with a handful of the spongy mushrooms, he lifted the thing back up to his shoulder and continued onward.

He decided that if he was to fully enjoy the day's harvest, he ought to stop by Paola's house. His sister didn't approve of how he spent his days foraging for edible plants and small fish in the bog pools; she said he'd grown odd out of the company of other people. However odd he'd become, though, she always welcomed him home, and she'd let him cook whatever his searches would yield with whatever spices she had handy.

Castor reached Paola's home just as the sun had set. The house, the only structure in sight, was the same one the two of them had grown up in. Castor knew every detail of the entire plot of land—he would skip school and spend his days hiding below the towering yellow grasses where he could catch and take care of creatures.

He approached the house and set the thing down on the edge of the porch before opening the door and walking in. He made enough noise taking off his boots so as to announce his arrival.

"Mills?" Paola yelled from the other room.

"No, it's Castor," he yelled back, removing his satchel.

Paola walked in and greeted her brother with a gentle hug. "Mills ran over to town," she said. "He had a deal."

Castor asked what kind of deal, but Paola didn't respond. Instead she poked a finger into the satchel to spread it open a bit. "Good day?" she asked. "How many slugfish did you get?"

"Look at this." He pulled out a mucksnail to show her. The snail's head, a small pink mass about the size of his pinky tip, had emerged from the iridescent crescent shell. Castor would come by to borrow a tool or to cook a small meal for himself, and as often as not, Paola would try to talk him into a visit to the city where he might meet somebody kind so he wouldn't have to spend his days alone. When he produced treats like mucksnails to share, however, she tended to take less pity on his ways.

Paola took a snail in her hand and held it up to the light. "Lucky day," she said with a smile, and she gave it back.

"It's yours," he said. "I got at least a dozen. I only want a couple."

She tilted her head and looked at him inquisitively. Mucksnails were one of the few creatures that could survive within the bog pools, which made them unique as edibles go. And rare. Their shells, made of some a strange compound that resisted the decomposing acids, were positively poisonous. However, the meat was very edible. Not only was it very rich in all the minerals the creature used to produce its shell, but it was also mildly hallucinogenic.

Castor and Paola had gone to the kitchen and started to heat the stove. Paola asked Castor about his project. "Are you still working on it?" she asked.

"What project?" Castor asked.

"That thing you're erecting. The statue. Of you."

Castor vaguely remembered he'd told her about the idea. To create a likeness of himself, to whittle sticks together and wedge them, sinew by sinew, and create something of himself. He was looking for an answer when suddenly Mills came through the front door. "What's this thing on the porch?" he yelled.

Paola looked at Castor, shrugged, then walked into the front room. "What do you mean?" she asked.

"That thing. It's like a long—thing," Castor heard him say. "I don't know how to describe it."

Paola poked her head back into the kitchen. "Is that thing yours," she asked.

Mills followed behind her and walked into the kitchen and made friendly eye contact with Castor. He nodded. "Oh, hi, Castor. Is that thing yours?"

"Yeah."

"What is it?" Mills asked. Castor could hear the front door open and shut in the other room, as Paola presumably went out to have a look for herself.

"I don't know," Castor replied. "I don't know what it is."

"It looks like some kind of bone," Mills said.

Paola came back into the house and walked straight into the kitchen. "What is that?" she asked. "Is it yours?"

Castor shrugged.

Mills left the room and let brother and sister speculate about the thing. Castor didn't have much to say, but Paola did. She left the house at least three times while Castor minded the snail and mushrooms on the pan, as well as some rice and a few greens in a separate pot. Paola at first agreed that the thing was the bone of some prehistoric beast, especially the way that one end had a knob. On closer look, she became certain that it was some rare mineral. Or perhaps some alien device, she chuckled.

Once the meal was ready, all three of them sat down to eat around the table. They ate comfortably, slowly. Mills mentioned his unsuccessful efforts to sell a small corner of the great property to a potentially interested buyer in the city, a topic Paola was hesitant to elaborate on. They talked about Wilma and Yolk, the two chickens out back who increasingly thought they belonged inside. Inevitably, the conversation came back to the thing, though.

After dinner, Paola had Castor and Mills bring the thing in and set it on the cleared table. In the light, it somehow looked smaller. Paola, perhaps particularly inspired by the snail, determined that they would fill a bucket and use some rags to wipe the thing clean. Within a few minutes, it looked relatively fresh.

"I know what this is," Paola said. "It's a relic."

"Why?" Castor asked.

"What do you mean a relic," Mills asked.

"This is part of an ancient monument," she said. She pointed to the striations and said that it must be some refined mineral like marble. But look how smooth it is, she said. It was polished, and look how preserved it is. This isn't from any recent civilization, though.

Castor looked closely and wondered at the history. He could almost feel the thing pulse under his light, unconscious stroke.

"It's perfectly shaped," she continued, "except for this end. Here is where it broke off from something." On one end, she pointed to a jagged break, which would have been impossible to note before the thing was cleaned. "You've got to inquire into this."

"Why?" Castor asked.

"She's right," Mills added. "Don't you want to know what this is or where it comes from?"

"It came from the bog," Castor said.

"But it has a history," Paola chided. "It has an identity, and we deserve to know what that is—don't you agree?"

"Why?" Castor asked.

"You've got to start thinking about what ahead," she said. "You can't keep doing this forever!"

"Why?"

"Stop repeating yourself," Paola said. "You always do this."

"And who knows—it might be worth something," Mills added.

"Are you going to write somebody to inquire?" Paola asked.

Castor was silent.

On the walk home, Castor stumbled a little. His pace was quick and deliberate. He didn't want to sell the thing, whatever it was. He wasn't even convinced it was some historical artifact. It might just be a sunken bone fragment of a creature our minds couldn't even fathom and may not be able to fathom. He balanced the thing in the groove just inside the round of his shoulder, holding it tight around the base, near the jagged break Paola identified.

Half an hour later, he was home, and in the light of his small cabin he felt his senses restored, though the edges of his vision were somewhat dulled with fatigue. He gently placed the thing on the edge of his mattress, where, within minutes, he himself retired into a quick and ultimately dreamless sleep.

Three days passed in peaceful solitude. Castor saw nobody else on the trails, which was not particularly remarkable. Remarkable was, however, the fact that each day's harvest was uncommonly bountiful. Not only had his own garden seen a heightened bloom, but also had he managed to confidently net some of the largest slugfish and tiny bog mule sliders that he'd ever seen. He even managed to catch between his fingers a dragonfly that had casually landed on his bent knee one afternoon.

He had somehow harvested enough meat to last him weeks, but he had also found corresponding success in finding a suitable tar mix to help mash with the clay near his house to repair some leaks in his cabin. He'd even been lucky enough to stumble upon a newly felled moorwood, close enough to his cabin that he was able to transport home enough to whittle for this project to erect that life-size statue of somebody.

He more or less attributed this unprecedented success to the thing, which he nonchalantly carried with him wherever he went. He would carry it through along his journeys, and when he needed a rest, he would lay it flat on the ground and sit on it as though it were an oblong stool.

On the fourth day, it rained harder than it had all month, and Castor decided to stay in. He lit a small fire in his cabin. He had just picked up his only pen with the intention of writing in his journal, which he hadn't even picked up—let alone written in—in months, when there was a knock at the door.

Castor realized he was sprawled along the thing, which was positioned comfortably on his mattress. He first put the journal away on the shelf, then he covered the thing with his blanket. He stood, adjusted himself, and opened the door to find a tall man, well dressed, soaked from the rain.

"May I come in," the man asked.

Castor stood aside.

"I'm sorry to barge," the man added. "My name is Quincy." The man extended a powerful hand outward, which Castor took with mild interest.

"You're not from here," Castor added.

No, Quincy said. He was from the city, and he had gotten a letter from somebody named Paola, and he immediately set out to this address. "I had trouble finding the place," he said with some degree of congratulations. "But here I am. This is charming. Do you rent the land here?"

"My sister contacted you?" Castor asked.

"She mentioned that you may have a particularly interesting artifact. She wrote to me, yes. In great detail. It struck our interest, indeed." Quincy explained that he was an archaeologist, which is just a fancy word for somebody who studies ancient remains to try to better understand a culture. Castor thought better than to interrupt his guest to tell him he already knew quite well what an archaeologist was. "May I have a look?" Quincy asked.

Quincy smiled down at Castor, who felt a little compelled to humor this man who had travelled so far for a mere look. With any luck, this city specialist could confirm that there's nothing special about this found fragment of nonsense, and everybody could move forward. Aside from all this, now, more than ever, Castor wanted to start his project. He'd collected more than enough moorwood to start erecting his dream and figure out what's ahead.

So Castor led Quincy over to his mattress where they both sat comfortably. Castor uncovered the thing. "I'm Castor," he said.

Quincy nodded a couple of times, then he looked up to Castor. "This is really something, isn't it? Where did you find it?"

Castor hesitated a moment, then he stood and walked over to the stove and nervously rubbed his hands over the small flame. "I don't have much to offer, but would you like something to drink—or maybe a bite of fish? I have lots of fish."

"All right," Quincy said. "That would be nice."

Castor withdrew some of his smoked slugfish from a storage container buried just slightly beneath the dirt floor. He set two small fillets on a grate above the stove, then hovered above the mattress. "I found it at the bottom of one of the shallower pools in the bog over north."

"What on earth were you doing in a bog pool, Castor?" Quincy asked.

"I—"

"Never mind. This is tremendous, isn't it?" he asked. "Look at the ridge here, and the fine cutting to etch this curve." Quincy's eyes never left the thing. "This isn't from this century—not even from this millennium in all likelihood."

"Why?" Castor asked.

"Yet it's preserved so perfectly. If you truly found this here, this would change everything about what we know about history. Do you realize that?"

"Why?"

"We actually have little knowledge of the ancient cultures that used to live in this continent before us. We have traces of the barbarians who ransacked the land and burned the ruins before them, but because of their blatant disregard of cultural artifacts, we know virtually nothing of the civilizations who ruled before them."

Castor smelled the fish cooking, and he asked his guest how he liked his fish cooked.

"We have never found any such relics this far north before. We of course assume that the bog was once a rich lake land, nothing like it is now—but we hadn't known any ancient civilizations to sprawl so far in this direction," Quincy said, his fingers and his eyes all the while attending the thing. "And I'm not picky about my fish. However you like yours."

Castor grabbed a few stump rounds he kept in a bucket, and he placed a fish on each, serving one to his guest. "It's not much," Castor said.

Quincy took the small fillet between his fingers and dipped it whole into his mouth. His eyes widened with what appeared to be pleasure, and his lips formed a pursed smile as he chewed. "This is fantastic, Castor," he said.

Castor looked down at the thing and smiled. He tore off a small chunk of his slugfish and took a bite, chewing thoroughly threw all of the small, tender bones.

"Listen," Quincy said, his mouth obviously full. "You're going to be famous."

"Why?"

Quincy withdrew a magnifying glass from his breast pocket and held it tentatively toward the thing. "May I?" he asked.

A little unsure of what was being asked, Castor replied, "Of course, absolutely."

Quincy knelt his head in only a few centimeters from the thing, following its contours from top to bottom in a slow even pace. Castor's eyes followed the movements, wondering what could be seen in a magnifying glass that couldn't be seen with the naked eye.

"Clearly," Quincy said after what seemed like several minutes of close analysis, "You have something remarkable here. There is no doubt in my mind that this is the element of some grand statue. The unrefined part here, near the end, is where it must have broken off from something larger. I can't imagine what this may be—perhaps the sword or cudgel of some ancient warrior."

Castor bit off a little more of his fish.

"We are making history, Castor. We are," Quincy said. "You have stumbled upon something of great importance. If what I suspect is true, then the rest of this ancient relic is down there in the bog, buried for thousands of years. If we are lucky, it will all be as perfectly preserved as this." Quincy took a pause. For the first time since it was revealed to him, he took his eyes off the thing, and he stood to look out the window. "Who knows, this thing may be small—but it may be part of a larger monument, a standing statue. Do you think you could take me to where you found this?"

Castor looked up into Quincy's beaming eyes. "I suppose I could try."

And so it was set. They arranged for Quincy to return the next day with a small team, presumably students of his who were as eager as he was to uncover something of supposed historical significance.

"You're going to be famous," Quincy said to Castor the next day as they deviated from the trail in the direction of Castor's original find. Castor's boots had no trouble in the black sludge, though Quincy and his three young students had a harder time. Whereas they would necessarily test the firmness of each step before committing, Castor, who had little regard for the purity of his own boots, trod on. More than once he had to stop so the others could catch up to him.

Castor wore his satchel and carried the thing upon his shoulder, as he'd grown accustomed to, and Quincy and his crew likewise carried strange instruments and devices—and one also carried a what appeared to be a wide variety of foods to accommodate their trek.

After twenty or thirty minutes of pressing through the bog, Quincy managed to catch up to Castor, and he again reminded him of the fame to come. But Castor showed little interest. He only held the thing tighter in his grip.

"Do you think we'll find the precise spot?" Quincy asked. "There must be a thousand of these pools out here, and they each look identical."

Castor paused and looked back to Quincy, following his gaze around the landscape. He looked back to Quincy's hopeful expression.

"This means a lot to you," Castor said. So many questions threatened to push through him, but he contained them all, each left unsaid.

"Without you, I'm pretty sure I couldn't even find my way back to the trail at this point," Quincy said. "But luckily I have you."

Something in this startled Castor, and he looked deeper in Quincy's expression. "We'll find it," he said.

It didn't take long. Castor first recognized the pool by its shape, mostly round, but pointed at one end toward the middle peak of a scant mountain range off slightly in the distance. Castor wanted to point out the pool, but he took a survey of the area to assure himself first. Immediately, he noticed the black root he'd pulled up days before, the one that had been full of mucksnails. "This is it," he said.

Quincy paused and caught his breath, then looked closely into Castor with apparent disbelief. He squinted his eyes and asked if he was sure. "That's uncanny. Splendidly uncanny."

Immediately Quincy unloaded his gear onto the hard ground beside the pool and let out a large sigh. Though he had been keeping pace with Castor, it had clearly been a bit of a struggle. Shortly after departing from the trail, Quincy resigned any attempt to keep his clothes clean, which afforded him a more significant pace, but he was clearly not accustomed to the nimble footwork and the wide arches of the step. Nor did he seem accustomed to carrying any amount of weight for any length of time. Castor had offered once to carry something, but Quincy immediately declined the offer, either ashamed or possessive. Nevertheless, Castor'd gone considerably slower, but they still managed to lose the students along the way—yet Quincy didn't seem especially bothered.

Quincy, clearly delighted, put an arm around Castor. Castor eased the thing to his side, a light burden lifted from his shoulder, and he allowed himself to drift with gravity slightly toward Quincy.

"How can you be sure this is the pool?" Quincy asked. "They are all the exact same."

"This one is different," Castor said.

"You," Quincy said, "are different."

Quincy opened his pack and took out several devices Castor didn't recognize. He opened a tripod, then extended a telescoping rod and fit it into the tripod. He placed a counter balance on the short end and dipped the long end into the pool with seemingly no difficulty.

Castor wanted to offer help, but he thought better of it. Instead, he stayed back and watched in wonder. He admired Quincy's dedication, but he mostly admired Quincy's dexterity. What grace Quincy lacked in treading through the bog was compensated for in operating these obtuse devices.

After the little while, the strange device was apparently all set up and at least partially operational. Quincy sat on the ground beside it, beside Castor, and he leaned back with a wide smile.

"Should we go find the others?" Castor asked

"I warned them to keep up," Quincy said. "Anyway, they'll find us eventually." Quincy's eyes caught hold of the thing again, and he looked up to Castor, as though asking for permission. Castor's smiled meekly. "If you could only imagine the possibilities," Quincy said.

Quincy reached over and, his arms beneath the thing, tried to lift it toward him, which was no small effort on his part. Castor helped leverage it and then let it rest in Quincy's lap.

Only a few minutes later, the three students stumbled upon Castor and Quincy. Castor, somewhat startled by their sudden intrusion, stood up quickly, the thing protectively fallen from his grip. Quincy seemed to simultaneously chide them and congratulate them as he pointed out the pool and describe its features in terms Castor didn't properly understand.

Quincy and his three students set to work in a way that simply didn't seem natural to Castor. The more they plunged their sophisticated instruments into the pool to gauge one thing or another, the more Castor started to step back. He took the thing in his arms and found another small pool three or four meters away. He settled comfortably, his back to Quincy and his students, then took out his own net and swirled it about the pool. He passed the greater part of an hour or two, one hand controlling the net, the other comfortably resting upon the thing.

By lunch time, Castor had pulled up three or four slugfish, and he was just ready to offer to share the bounty when he turned to find Quincy feverishly bounding between the several devices set up around the pool. Before Castor could speak, Quincy caught his eye and yelled, "We found it!"

"We found it," Castor uttered back.

And it began. The point was marked on the maps, and it suddenly became a known place. Quincy came and held Castor by the shoulders, looked him in the eye, and congratulated the two of them, but Castor began to wonder if Quincy thought he was looking in a mirror at that moment. In the coming days, Castor almost felt as though he had nothing to do with the discovery. At first machines rolled in and worked only through the shorter daylight hours, but once they had lights, the machines worked tirelessly through day and night, unaware of the sun's position around the planet.

Castor went to visit what had now been called The Site, and the first day or two seemed promising. At first, Quincy would immediately step away from whatever he was doing, and he'd congratulate Castor. The first two times, Quincy announced to all the crew there—every time a new set of workers—that this was the one and only Castor.

Quincy would look to the thing, and he would speculate that this was an arm, with the little knot at the end somehow forming a very crude fist. He would speculate that instead this was a weapon, or perhaps some alien limb. He didn't even ask for permission anymore before reaching for it, stroking it as though divining some of its ancient powers.

After a week or so, Quincy seemed far more interested in the thing itself than in its bearer. When he said that "we've done it," it became increasingly clear to whom he was referring. There, in the late hours of the night, the lights shining heavy on the pool, somebody yelled that they had it, whatever it was. The devices—which had been lowered on lines to scour the bottom, to dig, to grapple, and to perform whatever ungodly feats their creators had them do—had finally done it. Castor, out of curiosity, stayed through the night to watch them lower dozens of cables into the pool. A diver wearing a thick, protective layer, went to oversee the operation. Several calculated hours later, they raised from the pool what appeared to be, through the blackened muck, an enormous head. There was a round of cheers, and the cables held the head stable, connected to whatever else lay below.

The head and its shoulders was nearly beyond the size of the pool itself—and there was talk of excavation to extract the full body of this ancient relic. It could take days or weeks in order to do it properly, to minimize potential damage. Quincy spread open some papers on a desk that had recently been installed nearby, probably to consider different possibilities. It would tear up the area, but it was the price of history. It was late, and Castor headed home, the shrunken thing on his shoulder.

He didn't go back to The Site.

Paola came by Castor's cabin a few days later. "I read the news," she said. "Something happened. Where have you been? You haven't come by in weeks."

"Do you want to come in?" Castor asked.

"There's no room in there for two people," she said. "Come out here."

"Quincy was in here," he said.

She asked who Quincy was, and he began to tell her about the letter she sent. Defensively, and possibly unconsciously, he edged the thing away, under a low-hanging shelf.

"You ought to be out there at the site," she said.

"You mean at The Site," he replied. "And there is no place for me there."

"Mills has been trying to sell larger and larger plots of the land, you know." She turned away. "We can't keep earning our life on this land. Not like we used to."

"Why?" Castor asked.

"This isn't about our land," she said.

"Why?" Castor asked.

"Castor! Stop repeating yourself. Your mind is fried from eating this toxic shit you pull out of the pools. You can't think straight. Listen to what I'm saying to you!"

"Why?"

"You found that thing, and you're entitled to some recognition for it." And, upset for one reason or another, Paola left.

Castor smoked the remainder of his fish that afternoon and later through the night, and he resolved to withdraw with the changing season. Let Quincy and his friends find what they would out there in the bog. Castor lay there on his mattress, filled with himself and the thing. Yet, he wondered about The Site. It wasn't his history, to be sure. He wasn't here a thousand years ago. Whose history would this be, and why would it matter?

In the morning, for the first time in what seemed to be months, he resumed work on his project. He gathered all of the moorwood he had dumped around the backside of his cabin, and he began to whittle them into parts that would fit within the structure. The thing by his side, he finally felt the confidence to transform a misshapen branch into a puzzle piece that would fit within the whole.

As the days grew shorter, his work grew more focused. He worked on—and he worked harder—because he knew what was ahead of him. He created a heel, and he knew what was ahead: an ankle. He created a calf, and he knew what was ahead: a knee. Every step created the demand for a new step. Every new piece worked into what was already there, and it created a new need of what was to come.

Two or three days later, Quincy came to the cabin, and with only a little hesitation, Castor let him in.

"Castor—do you have any fish on the stove?" Quincy asked.

"Not yet," he said. "But I'll set some. Why?"

"We resurrected the thing—I mean, the statue. The ancient beast we've been searching for all along."

"Oh?" Castor smiled for Quincy. For days, he'd secretly hoped that the statue or whatever it was would be pulled from the hole and removed, taken to the city, and essentially disappeared. Gone forever. It was strange to see Quincy here again.

"We have you to thank, you know," Quincy said. "This is going to revolutionize our understanding of our history. You know that. Everything of the past will change."

Castor could see Quincy's wavering eyes.

"You and—" Quincy looked back to Castor. "We really have something."

"We?"

"Where is the thing?" Quincy asked.

Castor's throat grew cold. "It's in the back. It's fine."

"May I look at it? May I have another look?" Quincy looked a little desperate, but Castor thought this could be the necessary farewell sequence.

"Yes," Castor said. "I was working on a project out there. Do you want to see? I'm erecting my own statue of sorts."

Castor took Quincy behind the cabin, right where the thing lay beside Castor's project. Quincy took a momentary glance at the erection and asked what it was. Castor shrunk a little, and told him it was a statue—or at least it would be when he finished. He'd been growing it with sticks he'd collected from the area, though admittedly, in its presently incomplete state, it looked more like a haphazard palisade than a statue of himself.

"That's lovely," Quincy said. "You ought to see the marble one we pulled up, though. It must be at least thirteen hundred years old—and, fully erect, over dozen meters tall. It seems to be a warrior god of sorts." And he proceeded to the thing, lying there so peacefully. Without a word, he wedged the knotted end into the ground and hoisted the jagged end up toward him. Squinting his eyes, he reexamined the edge. "This is it," he added.

"What?"

"This is the missing piece."

Castor stood still a moment. There was nothing *missing* about this. Still, again, he asked, "What?"

"I'm not sure how to say this," said Quincy, "but the statue we pulled from The Site was remarkably intact. The builders were especially adept at connecting the limbs and elements of the warrior's armor so that its structural integrity was maximized."

"What?" asked Castor.

"Except for one element."

"What?"

"There was one protruding element we found that wasn't otherwise structurally bound to the main statue."

"What?"

"You drop the statue sideways, everything else will remain intact," Quincy said. "It's all grounded together. Everything is tightly bound—sword to shield. Arm to arm. Even leg to leg. Except for one piece."

"What?" Castor asked.

"Except for your thing."

"What?"

"There's no other way to put it." Quincy paused and looked deeply into the thing. "The phallus."

"What?"

Quincy began to explain the nuances of the ancient cultures and their primacy of virility, but Castor heard only one thing, that one utterance yet to come: "We need the thing."

"No."

Quincy took his eyes off the thing and stepped toward Castor. "Think of it as borrowing."

"No."

"History will be incomplete without it."

"No."

"But think of the statue in a museum where millions of people will be able to see it and touch it and understand it as part of a foreign, ancient culture."

"No."

"But what is this statue without its thing?"

"No."

"Think of a man without his thing."

"No."

"Think of science."

"No."

"Listen to me, Castor. The thing looks very tough and sturdy, but it's really not. It may be heavy, but it's very fragile. And it's only getting worse," Quincy said. "Now that it's exposed to air, it's poisoned. I've suspected this, but I've confirmed it with the other materials we've brought up. It needs to be treated. Or before long it will split and splinter and shatter."

"No."

"It needs to be taken care of. Don't you want it to be taken care of?"

"No."

And Quincy took a step back, accidentally snapping off a piece of Castor's project. He glanced down at the thing, the phallus. "Look, Castor."

"No." Castor drew closer to the thing.

"This land isn't your land," Quincy said. "And that bog isn't your bog."

"No." Castor lurched over the thing.

"And that thing isn't your thing. It belongs to us."

In one motion, Castor heaved the narrower end of the thing into his hands and swung it around in an unsavory arc toward Quincy. He wondered what kind of brute it would take to swing such a club. Before Quincy could react, the thing had collided with his forehead in a quick and savage clap. And that seemed to be it. The impact split the bones—Quincy's, the thing's and Castor's. Precariously aligned, Quincy stumbled backward toward Castor's project and smashed into the erection. Skull fractured, his body was impaled by a thousand sticks pointed outward.

Castor looked over the body, his thing split, splintered, shattered. He did not know what was ahead.

ଓ ଛ

Math Trafton is an assistant professor of English at the University of Alaska Southeast. He earned his Ph.D. in Comparative Literature from the University of Colorado, and his main interests are in ghost literature and the love letter. He lives in Sitka, AK with his family.

AUTUMN RAIN – SIMON EDGETT

November dies slowly.
Cold wind and crisp leaves
cover the browning grass.
Naked tree skeletons branch out
from the ground,
stretch and scratch
at the sky.
Honesty contradicts itself;
what else can it do?
I am cold. My heart
doesn't beat fast enough
to warm all the way
to my feet and my fingers.

Trees eat themselves.
They lose their leaves,
allowing them to fall to the ground,
to deteriorate into the ground,
to nourish the trees' roots,
to grow new leaves next year.

we bury our dead.

The woods, which surround my house,
smell of this rich compost:
dying, decaying, feeding.
All this brought on by life,
the cold,
and tiny bacteria,
hoveling through fallen leaves,
dead before they hit the ground.

❦

Simon Edgett (@simonedgett) is a fraud. He lives in Connecticut where he pretends to be an administrator for a public school system. He spends the rest of his time running the blue-blazed trails of Connecticut's woodlands, chasing his four-year-old son, and occasionally writing poetry.

A CRÈCHE OF BONES – MIKEY SIVAK

For Nate R.

> *and she gave birth to her firstborn, a son.*
> *She wrapped him in cloths and placed him in a manger,*
> *because there was no guest room available for them.*

> –Luke 2:7

I.

In December's wood the bone child bides,
perpetual, never-waking, half-buried
in the litter of some seasons before.

Vapory eventide, some night snow,
leaf and coffeecup, styrofoam slumber
and grocery cart, old-twisted, mysteriously
abandoned this deep in the little cut, that
separates the project from I-95.

Wreath of rat snake, which each winter
freezes, only in spring to reawaken its reptile heart
like a yearly raising of Lazarus, quiesces coiled
beneath *sternum and costae* like a crèche of bones.

Little dead boy, tiny non-Christ,
gone most forgotten, who by now
might be just some kid, but instead
was discarded to the dirt in the woods
behind the brown ghetto where
no one goes, save the little lost boys.

None ever found him there.

Small skull like theirs washed by time,
hollowed of anything that made him whoever
he was and might eventually become.

II.

Strange Nativity in an urban junk wild.
Madonna a field mouse.
Joseph a crow.
Melichior, Casper, and Balthazer,
whitetail, opossum, and skunk.

And down the berm where the street runoff
stream trickles most frozen, crayfish winter
in old soup cans like shepherds of the fields
and in the rainbow puddles sewer minnows
are the sheep.

Vapor of the dirt pile the breath of the god-child.
Some stupid streetlamp the nativity star.

Last season's bittersweet, a galaxy of berries
red erupting from school-bus yellow husks
like skulls from hairless babes' scalps or souls
from dead children, the sons of god or kings of men,
crowning from the million vulvas of their child
mothers, raped as if by god.

In the tenement windows the Christmas lights pulse.
Old boy in the gutter prays for quiet death.
The men round the trash fire, Communion of Saints.

Feral cat and wild pit-bull, lean and searching, prowl
the places for anything to eat like the Beggars of Nazareth.
Their own bones visible through stretched fatless skin
like the ribs of a child swaddled in a mâché of old leaves.

And in the dirt gully, "round yon child,"
Gloria in excelsis Deo, little lamb of God,
the frost, the rat, the dusk lark and her vespers:
O Come O Come Emmanuel. Joyful and Triumphant.

III.

Holy Mother at the pharmacy checkout:
welfare formula and pampers
her frankincense and myrrh,

womb vacant as the quiet crib waiting
like men for god or a manger for another
failed child Christ, never to be neither
god nor man, hungry son of New Dirty
Bethlehem in America's East.

Gone baby, fatherless dead child, lost covenant,
broken promise, sin without redemption,
death without hell, empty bosom, useless milk.

And no one asks:

What parent took the child from his bassinet,
tossed him down to the floor of the woods,

and why did Our Father dump his children
into the slum of this world?

ଔ ଓ

Mikey Sivak is a writer and visual artist from New Haven,
Connecticut. http://mykls.tumblr.com/

THE SKELETON'S SKEDADDLE – DIANE ROOT

I twitter
I tweet
I'm light on my feet.
I'm white and I'm sleek.
I trick and I treat
I slink and I sneak
I meet and I greet
I groan and I creak,
But I'm always at my peak.
When in pique
I prattle and I rattle
I titter and I tattle.
I rock and I roll down by your creek
I'm slim and I'm trim,
Sometimes I'm even prim.
(Give me a bonnet with a few lilies on it.)
I'm the boniest, bonniest model you will ever seek.
I galivant with ghosts
I hobnob with goblins
I bob and I weave
I lob, I lurch and I leave
You to memories at last past
I dance and I prance
I swing and I sling
Caution to the winds
I'm hell on wheels
While the bell peals
Don't care how to you it feels.
I clink and I clank.
I once boogied and more than often drank.
I live in someplace often dark and often dank
Where I once sang, I then sank
Now bleached and blank
(Down here, no one pulls rank.)
I slip and I slink

I write in invisible ink.
I wink and all is gone in a proverbial blink
The way of all things, I think.
I'm serious and I'm mysterious:
I'm nothing if not downright deleterious
A hazard to your health and your earth-bound wealth.
I slide in silent slippery stealth,
Heedless, needless of your cries
In protest
Against your demise.
I may have a waddle in my skedaddle
But right here
I'm all the rave
In my grave
Beneath the grass and the stone
Betwixt the groan and the moan
Of the bereft and fleshless bone
Never fear, whether I am far or whether I'm near
I will be close to the place
In this race called strife and life
Where you and I
Will one day be together far too soon
Perhaps under the sun
Perhaps beneath the moon.
(Friends and foes, don't share a tear
The New Year is almost here.)

ᎡᏍ Ꭴ

Diane Root, a dual-national, was born in Paris of an American father, the journalist and writer, Waverley Root, and a French mother. Primarily known as a painter, she is, as she describes herself, "an accidental writer." She never sought to be published but that notwithstanding, she was nonetheless published in the New York Times Magazine ("The Artful Dodger" about lunch with Picasso) and various other venues. View her art: http://matakia.com.

BONED: A Collection of Skeletal Writings is a project started by Nate Ragolia in 2016. Each Tuesday, a new story, poem, play, or essay posts. The common theme is that all content features either bones, or a skeleton, in some capacity.

Read each week at bonedstories.wordpress.com,

Or follow BONED on Medium.com.

ABOUT THE PUBLISHING TEAM

TJ Stambaugh received several commendations for his bravery as a battalion commander in the Meme Wars. After the war, TJ retired to Catonsville, MD, where he paints, enjoys movies you have to read, and is Art Director for Spaceboy Books LLC.

Antoine Valot, Graphics Bot is a 2015 Nexus™ series Replicant from the Tyrell Corporation, communications/design model. He enjoys designing book covers, nitpicking about words, functioning within his operating margins, and making the most of the two years he has left to live.

Learn more about Spaceboy Books at readspaceboy.com

This book features the font Skullphabet by Noah Scalin (Skull-A-Day). Learn more about Skull-A-Day at skulladay.blogspot.com